BETWEEN MONSTERS, GODDESSES AND CYBORGS

142 European medieval folklore

BETWEEN
MONSTERS
GODDESSES
AND
CYBORGS

FEMINIST CONFRONTATIONS WITH
SCIENCE, MEDICINE AND CYBERSPACE

Edited by
Nina Lykke & Rosi Braidotti

ZED BOOKS
London & New Jersey

Between Monsters, Goddesses and Cyborgs: Feminist Confrontations with Science, Medicine and Cyberspace was first published in 1996 by Zed Books Ltd, 7 Cynthia Street, London N1 9JF, UK, and 165 First Avenue, Atlantic Highlands, New Jersey 07716, USA.

Copyright © Nina Lykke and Rosi Braidotti, 1996

Permission to reproduce the following illustrative material is gratefully acknowledged: Figure 3.1, reproduced by permission, *The Global Brain Awakens: Our Next Evolutionary Leap*, © 1995 Peter Russell and Global Brain TM, Inc; Figure 3.2 and Plates 3.1 and 3.2, reproduced by permission, *The Mind of the Dolphin: A Nonhuman Intelligence*; © 1967 by John C. Lilly, MD; Plate 4.1, Oroboros, Illustration Séville 92, reproduced by permission Michèle Dehoky for *Sciences et Avenir*, Paris; Plate 4.2, The Big Bang, Illustration in *Back to Creation*, CERN Publications, 1991, reproduced by permission, CERN; Plates 11.1 a and b, 11.2 a and b, and Plate 11.3 reproduced by permission, the Department of Geriatrics, Utrecht University Hospital, the Netherlands.

Typeset in Monotype Bembo by Lucy Morton, London SE12
Printed and bound in the United Kingdom
by Redwood Books Ltd, Kennet House, Kennet Way,
Trowbridge, Wilts, BA14 8RN

A catalogue record for this book is available from the British Library
US CIP data is available from the Library of Congress

ISBN 1 85649 381 4 (Hb)
ISBN 1 85649 382 2 (Pb)

CONTENTS

ACKNOWLEDGEMENTS

The idea for this volume grew out of the international feminist research
network, Gender–Nature–Culture, and the feminism and science cluster
of the Network of Interdisciplinary Women's Studies in Europe
(NOI♀SE). I want to thank both networks for their inspiration and for
fruitful debate. I am especially grateful to Mette Bryld and Randi
Markussen, my co-coordinators of the Gender–Nature–Culture
network; to Pat Spallone, Ineke van Wingerden, Gloria Wekker and
Bettina Leysen, members of the NOI♀SE science cluster; and to my
co-editor Rosi Braidotti, who is also the coordinator of NOI♀SE.

In addition, I wish to express my gratitude to the Danish Research
Council for the Humanities, which funded the Gender–Nature–Culture
network and made the networking activities that led to this book
economically possible. Finally, I want to thank Anna Fredenslund, for
her linguistic revisions of the manuscript.

Nina Lykke

INTRODUCTION

Nina Lykke

This book emerges from the expanding field of feminist science and technology studies. The growth of the area reflects the fact that science, medicine and technology are central to contemporary feminist concerns and that the topic is controversial. If we trace the genealogical roots of contemporary feminist science and technology studies, it is obvious that feminist confrontations with science, medicine and technology have called forth strong commitment, mixed feelings and heated feminist debate from the very beginning of second-wave feminism around 1970.

Certainly, feminist science and technology studies did not emerge as a visible research area until the end of the 1970s, somewhat later than feminist research within the humanities and social sciences. This 'delayed' emergence was, however, in no way tantamount to feminist neglect of the political significance of the area in the 1970s. On the contrary, science and technology questions have been woven into second-wave feminism from the very beginning.

A technological takeover of both work and childbearing was, for example, included as an important path to women's liberation in an early second-wave feminist manifesto, *The Dialectic of Sex*, written by one of the initiators of the New York Redstockings, Shulamith Firestone (Firestone 1970). The book, which quickly became an international bestseller, produced heated debate, especially as a consequence of its plea for the elimination of female childbearing through reproductive technologies. The same was the case with another feminist world-bestseller, Marge Piercy's utopian novel *Woman on the Edge of Time*

(Piercy 1976). The novel gained much popularity for its representation of a non-sexist, non-racist and non-classist high-tech utopia. But it generated discussion among feminists as well. As in Firestone's vision of a liberated future, the utopia of Piercy's novel had eliminated female pregnancy and childbirth in favour of babies conceived and born in 'brooders'. Furthermore, the novel speculated on a technologically mediated transformation of another aspect of biological motherhood, lactation. In the utopia of the novel, lactation had become a bodily option for both women and men. Through science and technology, the biological capacities of women and men had been equalized in order definitively to prevent the (re-)emergence of gender inequality.

Viewpoints which held that science/technology had potentials for liberation were, however, far from being the only ones voiced by early second-wave feminism. Indeed, not even 'technophilic' feminists such as Firestone and Piercy embraced science and technology uncritically. Their visions of a liberated future in high-tech societies were contrasted with images of the present-day state of affairs, characterized by science and technology as mediators of oppression, marginalization and exclusion. Other feminists made critical perspectives the primary focus. For example, an important feminist attack on the sexism, racism, etc. of the biomedical sciences and the health care system of the USA was launched by the Boston Women's Health Book Collective in *Our Bodies, Ourselves* (Boston Women 1971). The book became a major source of inspiration for the women's movement in the USA as well as in many other Western countries.

The science/technology-as-liberating-potential arguments were also opposed by science/technology-as-threat arguments, which not only criticized present conditions but also simply rejected modern science and technology as inextricably bound to logics of domination, violence and destruction. Another feminist novel of the 1970s, Sally Miller Gearhart's *Wanderground* (Gearhart 1979), is a famous example of this trend. The novel contrasts a utopian women's community and a dystopian male-dominated society. The women live in perfect harmony with nature and their bodies. Modern technologies are eliminated from their community due to their inherent destructive logic. In contrast to the harmonious and life-oriented women's community, situated amidst nature, the sexist and violent male-dominated society is located in an urban, high-tech environment. This society has led the earth to the brink of an ecological and social disaster. The hope for future salvation lies exclusively with the women, who have totally opted out of modern science and technology.

From these few but influential early second-wave feminist examples, it should be clear that feminist attitudes vis-à-vis science, medicine and technology tend to differ radically. They do also show, however, agreement among feminists that it is an important task to question the socio-cultural roles of science, medicine and technology. Why, then, if the political importance of the subject area was recognized from the very beginning of second-wave feminism, did feminist science and technology studies only begin to take shape as a research field at the end of the 1970s?

No doubt one answer to this question is to be found in the much stronger intrinsic resistance to feminist agendas in the natural sciences than exists in the humanities and social sciences. In her influential analysis of the 'science question in feminism' (Harding 1986), Sandra Harding has convincingly linked this resistance to the fundamental metatheoretical assumptions in the strong positivist and empiricist traditions of the natural sciences. These traditions construct scientific and socio-cultural issues as totally separate. According to them, it is out of the question to combine socio-cultural feminist agendas with scientific enquiries into the non-human and non-social world. Evelyn Fox Keller, who originally was trained as a theoretical physicist and molecular biologist, and who later became one of the founding mothers of feminist science studies, emphasizes in a recent biographical account how the change required a radical shift of mind-set (Keller 1992: 21–5). Beliefs about science, on which her whole training as a scientist had been based, were suddenly challenged. To start discussing gendered subjectivity as something apart from biological sex was unthinkable from the viewpoint of her 'scientific mind-set', as was the idea that beliefs and ideologies (for example, gender ideologies) could affect science.

Seen from the emerging field of cultural and social studies of science and technology, however, such discussions lost their alien appearance. It is therefore no coincidence that the emergence of feminist science and technology studies as an academic field converged with the general development of social and cultural studies of science and technology. Drawing on heterogeneous theoretical sources (post-Kuhnian science history,[1] Marxism, structuralism, poststructuralism, and so on) both kinds of studies focused on science and technology as social and cultural constructions. The study of science was transformed from a study of context-independent discoveries of purely natural and material truths into a study of the way political, social, psychological and other cultural factors shape the scientific enterprise and its technological applications. The constructivist approaches made it possible to analyse how science culturally has been genderized as well as racialized; and, from the late 1970s onwards, they have given rise to important feminist revisions of science and technology studies.

As far as science history is concerned, works by Merchant (1980), Jordanova (1989) and Schiebinger (1993) have, for example, scrutinized the dualistic ways of thinking on which science of the modern era is based. The authors question the dualisms inherent in the scientific discourses and practices that resulted in the formation of categories of beings who were defined as 'other than' and often 'inferior to' the recognized notion of the 'knowing subject'. We learn how Nature, Matter, Body, Woman, Native and so on were constructed as objectified others, objects of study for the knower, critically identified as the enlightened, white-skinned, bourgeois 'man of science'.

Another path-breaking trend in feminist science studies was set in the mid-1980s by Evelyn Fox Keller's influential analysis of the social psychology of gender and science (Keller 1985). Taking her point of departure in a feminist appropriation of theories of the child's early development of object relations, Keller gives a psychological account of the convergent construction of modern science and masculine identity and of the parallel exclusion of femininity, identified with non-science.

Through such constructivist approaches, the political commitments to science and technology issues on the part of early second-wave feminism were analytically and theoretically grounded. The early construction of a political feminist subject vis-à-vis science and technology was from the end of the 1970s supplemented by a feminist research subject critically questioning the natural sciences.

This relocation and broadening of the space for feminist confrontations with science and technology has, of course, changed their character. The differences between the political claims of the 1970s and the field of feminist science studies today should, however, also be seen as a consequence of the impacts of the postmodern condition on feminism as well as on science. The utopianism of the 1970s has faded away, but so has the idea of a 'successor science' project, which, as stressed by Harding (1986), was a strong motivating force behind much of the early feminist science studies work in academia. The feminist idea of 'successor science projects' is based on the belief that feminists as spokeswomen for 'woman' can produce a new science without the ideological distortions and biases that haunt the existing one. Similar ideas of 'successor science projects' have, as discussed by Harding (1986), also been part of Black Studies. The postmodern attacks on modernity's belief in universal truths and the transparency of language used to formulate truths, as well as strong present-day feminist commitments to differences (between different women located in different parts of the world, in different ethnic, racial and other kinds of cultural settings) have, however, made the ideas of 'successor science projects' appear naive.

Instead of trying to play the game of highlighting *a* feminist project within the sciences, the present book therefore takes its point of departure in the political as well as the epistemological chaos of the present condition. But it does so in an optimistic belief in chaos as a productive and, for the time being, more eye-opening state than the pursuit of a successor science. The book is shaped by the belief that feminist science and technology studies are nourished in the creatively chaotic spaces between the boundaries of the cultural and the natural sciences and in transgression of modern dichotomies such as human/ non-human, mind/body, gender/sex, artefacts/nature.

Through its main title the book acknowledges its kinship with three dubious creatures: monsters, goddesses and cyborgs. They are, all three, signifiers of chaos, heterogeneity and unstable identities. Monsters have for thousands of years undermined the normal and the stable by their deviant appearances. The early worldmother-goddesses of ancient myth-ologies are often situated close to chaotic and undifferentiated primordial states. Cyborgs are grotesque post-industrial boundary figures, questioning the boundaries between human, organism and machine, celebrated cornerstones of the modern, scientific world-view. In spite of their differences, the three metaphorical figures are therefore related through their metonymical closeness to the non-orderly, non-stable, non-identical and so on.

Both the cyborg and the monster metaphors have been brought into close touch with feminist science and technology studies by Donna Haraway (Haraway 1991 and 1992). The feminist use of the goddess metaphor is rejected by Haraway as an expression of technophobic nostalgia (Haraway 1991), but celebrated in spiritual ecofeminism. The idea of this book is in no way an attempt to reconcile the three metaphors by a simple erasure of their differences. It offers them as a network of differing but unstably circulating meanings which inform current feminist dialogues and confrontations with science and technology.

The intent of the book is to highlight some currently important sites of feminist dialogue and confrontation with science, medicine and technology from an interdisciplinary perspective. The book has been written by a group of authors from different countries and disciplines, who share a belief in the need for deconstruction of the great historical divide between cultural and natural sciences; that is, between sciences traditionally labelled 'soft' as opposed to 'hard', 'feminine' as opposed to 'masculine'. Together the authors represent a diverse multidisciplinarity. They cover a spectrum of disciplinary backgrounds, ranging from physics, engineering, biochemistry and biomedicine to literary and cultural studies, philosophy and sociology. Furthermore, they favour cross- and transdisciplinary approaches in order to grasp the webs of text, myth, machine, organism, matter and society which postmodern science, medicine and technology seem to put on the agenda in a more pressing manner than ever before.

Another shared belief is that the close links between modern science/ technology and global power structures confront feminists who want to intervene with the necessity of working within a network of inter-related issues. Questions of gender, race, ethnicity, sexual preference, age and other socio- and biocultural differences and power differentials are constantly intersecting. This heterogeneity enhances the need not only for multi- and transdisciplinary approaches but also for a super-imposition of different lenses of inquiry – feminist, multicultural, ecological, and so on – which can make the different elements of the heterogeneous networks become visible.

The book is divided into two parts. The first part, Cybergoddesses: Voices of Virtual Reality or Nature?, explores the unstable boundaries between the world of the 'virtual/artefactual' and the world of 'Nature' as a site for feminist dialogues and confrontations with science and tech-nology. The rapid change in these boundaries as a consequence of the present-day large-scale techno-scientific remappings of the world emphasizes the pressing need for analysis, but also the difficulties that confront the analysts. What is virtual/artefactual? What is natural? How can the voice of the former be distinguished from the voice of the latter? Is it desirable to be able to distinguish? Or should the blurring of boun-daries rather be embraced? For whom do 'we' speak when 'we' argue for one or the other? And who is the speaking 'we'? Such questions are raised in Part One from many different sites of investigation, but all of the authors share the belief that no simple answers can be given.

In Chapter 1, I offer a map of the boundary spaces of feminist science studies. The interdisciplinary space between cultural and natural sciences, where important theoretical and methodological approaches to the field are found, is explored from my perspective as a cultural studies scholar, as are the contested zones of 'the artefactual' and 'the natural'. The kinship of monsters, goddesses and cyborgs as agents of change is discussed.

The displacement of boundaries between Virtual Reality (VR) and Real Life (RL) is the focus of Chapter 2. With Greek and Roman domestic goddesses as provocative metaphors, sociologist Susan Leigh Star explores how the ongoing revolution in communications technologies and the development of a global cyberspace change the highly gendered concept of home and its counterpart, homelessness.

The convergence of neurophysiological research on the dolphin brain, Cold War rocket technology, space-science search for extra-terrestrial intelligence, and counter-cultural dreams of the emergence of feminine *yin* values in the 1960s and onwards are explored in Chapter 3 by cultural studies scholar Mette Bryld. The point of convergence is the dolphin, a multilayered icon of postmodern displacements of boundaries between gendered and racialized selves and others.

In Chapter 4, physicist Renée Heller reviews representations in popular physics of the current master-narrative of cosmology: the Big Bang theory. Two pictures, produced by the European Organization for Nuclear Research (CERN), exemplify how these avant-garde science discourses, far from being gender-neutral exposures of natural facts, are pervaded by phallogocentrism and ambiguous references to other gender mythologies.

While 'the virtual', understood both as cyberspace and as cultural constructions of 'nature', has been the focus of the preceding chapters, Chapter 5 challenges the constructivist approaches to science and technology from an ecological feminist point of view. Engineer Kirsten Gram-Hanssen argues that constructivism reproduces the dualism of culture/self and nature/other. She explains the path to non-dualistic ways of perceiving nature which she found in phenomenology.

The need for alternative, non-dualistic approaches which can transgress the dichotomies of self/other and culture/nature is also the topic of Chapter 6. Julia Martin discusses health and healing, drawing on her experiences in South Africa, where she teaches English and practises Buddhist feminist eco-activism. She proposes the Tibetan Great Bliss Queen as an alternative to the arguably over-Westernized feminist metaphors of goddesses and cyborgs.

Chapter 7 looks at the historical roots of subject positions, as taken up by some ecological feminists, who claim that women can give voice to nature and speak for sustainable futures with a special sensitivity. English Literature scholar Sylvia Bowerbank traces the genealogies of these positions in early modernity with its ambiguous, gendered, two-sphered discourses that permitted the paradoxical coexistence of techno-scientific exploitation and sentimentalization of nature, which still haunts society.

The second part of the book, Monsters: Biomedical Bodygames, like the first part, is a trek into boundary zones where no pure identities, whether natural or artefactual, can be found. The scene of inquiry is now human bodies and bodyparts: female bodies, racialized bodies, deviant bodies, new- and unborn bodies, mother bodies, ageing bodies, aching bodies, gene bodies, and so on. However different the bodies are, most of them seem, nevertheless, to have important features in common: they are configurations of fiction and fact, of textuality and technology, of myth and matter. Furthermore, the bodies are linked by a common destiny. They are far 'beyond the natural body', to borrow the title of Nelly Oudshoorn's latest book (Oudshoorn 1994). They are culturally produced bodies, techno- or cyberbodies, and/or they are the result of monstrous, 'non-natural' births. In this way they question the very idea of a natural body, and they show some of the dilemmas of the heavy technology push, to which modern biomedical research subjects bodies in general, and female bodies in particular. They ask whether or not the consequence is still more control, disciplining and othering of women, or if there are liberating effects, when natural bodies are (re-)invented as techno-bodies by current biomedical body-games?

In Chapter 8, philosopher Rosi Braidotti traces genealogies of discourses on monsters in the premodern science of teratology, which linked monsters and mothers through the issue of biological repro-duction and the role of maternal imagination in monstrous births. As extraordinary embodiments of difference, monsters exhibit dilemmas of differently genderized and racialized bodies, and perform as postmodern tricksters, defying scientific unambiguousness.

Chapter 9 highlights how shifting constructions of female repro-ductive biology expose the move beyond the 'natural body'. Biologist Nelly Oudshoorn tells the story of modern contraceptives, from the invention of 'the pill' to the introduction of a variety of new methods, in the wake of postmodern discourses of diversity, difference, free choice, and so on, which, nevertheless, do not prevent the enrolment of women of colour in coercive discourses on population control.

Shifting constructions of female bodies are also thematized in Chapters 10 and 11, with the medicalization of menopause as focus. Medical doctor Bettina Leysen scrutinizes changes in gynaecological discourses on the postmenopausal body as target of medical intervention – from overt sexism in the 1960s to more subtle arguments, which nevertheless sustain the stigmatization of the ageing female body. The slogan 'feminine forever' has been replaced by 'healthy forever' and references to the social concerns of youth, denial of ageing and cultural imperatives to keep healthy and fit.

Biologist Ineke van Wingerden draws attention to the processes in which bodies – *in casu*, ageing female bodies – are produced by shifting biomedical theories and intervention practices. Tensions between the virtual reality of scientific representations and the lived experience of bodily pain are questioned in order to go beyond constructivist tendencies to reduce science to mere textuality.

The last two chapters shift the focus to current areas of high scientific prestige: embryology and genetics. Chapter 12 is a case-study of the 'pre-embryo', an entity which emerged from debates on *in vitro* fertilization. Biochemist Pat Spallone shows how the pre-embryo acts as both a work of science and a work of politics and fiction. At a time of great controversy over the ethics of embryo research, the pre-embryo allowed science to challenge ancient ideas regarding the origins and sanctity of life, while preserving age-old patriarchal ways of thinking about the female body and reproductive capacities.

Several earlier chapters have stressed that the technoscientific re-invention of bodies implies coercion and forced control. Chapter 13 reframes the question of whether science/technology represents a threat or liberation in a different way. Physicist and science-fiction writer Elizabeth Sourbut plays with 'gynogenesis', a science-fiction technology which would enable lesbian couples to become the biological parents of daughters. The textual play is meant to disrupt those scientific discourses that perceive new reproductive technologies as a cure for infertility in heterosexual couples, thereby excluding lesbian and single mothers as monstrous others. As with the cyborg metaphor of Donna Haraway, this strategy is intended to provoke thinking beyond the old phallogocentric dichotomies and technophobic rejections of science/technology.

NOTES

1. New trends in science history, initiated by science historian Thomas Kuhn's influential book, *The Structure of Scientific Revolutions* (Kuhn 1962).

REFERENCES

Boston Women's Health Book Collective (1971) *Our Bodies, Ourselves*, Boston Women's Health Book Collective, Boston, Mass.
Firestone, S. (1970) *The Dialectic of Sex: The Case for Feminist Revolution*, Bantam Books, New York.

Gearhart, S. M. (1979) *The Wanderground*, Persephone Press, Massachussetts.

Haraway, D. (1991) *Simians, Cyborgs and Women. The Reinvention of Nature*, Free Association Books, London.

—— (1992) 'The Promises of Monsters: A Regenerative Politics for Inappropriate/d Others', in L. Grossberg, C. Nelson and P. Treichler, eds, *Cultural Studies*, Routledge, New York and London.

Harding, S. (1986) *The Science Question in Feminism*, Cornell University Press, Ithaca, N.Y. and London.

Jordanova, L. (1989) *Sexual Visions. Images of Gender in Science and Medicine between the Eighteenth and Twentieth Centuries*, Harvester Wheatsheaf, London and New York.

Keller, E. F. (1985) *Reflections on Gender and Science*, Yale University Press, New Haven, Conn. and London.

—— (1992) *Secrets of Life, Secrets of Death. Essays on Language, Gender and Science*, Routledge, New York and London.

Kuhn, T. (1962) *The Structure of Scientific Revolutions,* University of Chicago Press, Chicago.

Merchant, C. (1980) *The Death of Nature. Women, Ecology and the Scientific Revolution*, Harper & Row, Berkeley, Calif.

Oudshoorn, N. (1994) *Beyond the Natural Body: An Archeology of Sex Hormones*, Routledge, London and New York.

Piercy, M. (1976) *Woman on the Edge of Time*, Fawcett Crest Books, New York.

Schiebinger, L. (1993) *Nature's Body: Gender in the Making of Modern Science*, Beacon Press, Boston, Mass.

PART ONE

CYBERGODDESSES:

VOICES OF VIRTUAL REALITY

OR NATURE?

BETWEEN MONSTERS,

GODDESSES AND CYBORGS: FEMINIST

CONFRONTATIONS WITH SCIENCE

Nina Lykke

It is becoming more and more difficult today for even the most stubborn traditionalists within academia to reject feminist arguments regarding the significance of gender in culture and society. In the so-called 'hard' sciences, however, this is not the case. These sciences seem to be more resistant to the intruding feminist subjects than the humanities and social sciences. One of the reasons for this state of affairs is no doubt to be found in still dominant notions of science. If science is regarded as an enterprise which, no more and no less, aims at a value-neutral, progressive discovery of 'universal and objective truths' about nature and matter, there is no room for feminism. Feminists can, of course, participate in the important work to change the gender balance in scientific communities, but actions beyond that point will not seem appropriate. The claim that feminist perspectives can be meaningful in the hard sciences, beyond the issue of recruiting more women, involves a radical challenge to the traditional notion of science as a 'pure' search for the hidden truths of nature and matter.

In this chapter I will draw a map of some discursive spaces which seem to emerge when feminists confront and challenge science. The map I shall draw will be based on three landmarks: the metaphors of monsters, goddesses and cyborgs. I have chosen these metaphors because they are able to serve as evocative and open-ended markers. Through them I will point out different aspects of critical feminist rethinking concerning the relationship between gender, scientific subjects and the material worlds of artefacts and natural bodies, which have traditionally been cast in the role of passive objects and bearers of the desired 'objective truths'.

First, I ask the monster metaphor to perform as a representation of boundary phenomena in the interdisciplinary or hybrid grey zone between the cultural and natural sciences. In this zone boundary subjects and boundary objects, monsters which cannot be defined as either human or non-human, challenge established borders between the sciences. This is a zone where confrontations between feminism and science take place. I will draw a map of this zone of monsters as a place where feminist science studies can proliferate in promising ways and activate processes which may transform science.

In the second part of the chapter, two other boundary figures, goddesses and cyborgs (that is, hybrids of machines and organisms), both of which have attracted a great amount of feminist attention and debate, are introduced into the text. They are called forth to serve as metaphors for another border: that between 'the artefactual' and 'the natural', which traditionally divides non-human phenomena into two separate compartments. Like the border *between* human and non-human, this border *within* the non-human affects feminists in their confrontations with science. 'I would rather be a cyborg than a goddess', is the conclusion with which Donna Haraway ends her famous cyborg manifesto (Haraway 1991b: 181). In return, spiritually oriented ecofeminists would argue that a feminist reclaiming of the great goddesses of prehistoric matriarchies may help to redirect society, science and technology away from their present policies of violence – sexism, racism, 'naturism',[1] and so on.

Instead of focusing on the apparent dichotomy between these feminist positions, I will ask a cyborg and a goddess to voice both their sameness and their difference. My purpose is to map out a space for a non-dichotomic conversation about feminist alternatives to the traditional scientific reduction of the non-human world to resources and mere objects without subjectivity.

THE GREAT DIVIDE

As a scholar, I am situated within the 'soft' humanities, but oriented towards interdisciplinary work and transdisciplinary efforts at breaking down excessively rigid boundaries between disciplines. When I approach the 'hard' sciences from this point of departure, it strikes me how great the divide that seems to separate natural and cultural sciences still is.

C.P. Snow's famous diagnosis (Snow 1965) of the intellectual world of modernity as split into two different cultures seems to be true even today, despite the best endeavours of postmodern and feminist science studies to deconstruct the boundaries. The dichotomy, which is signalled by the popular predicates of 'hard' and 'soft' sciences, has definitely not lost its significance.

One testimony to this dichotomy is the institutionalized divide between university faculties. Although certain hybrids (such as arts and science programmes) are emerging, the great divide between faculties still seems to hold the majority within academia spellbound. Marking one pole of this divide, the humanities and social sciences supposedly deal with those phenomena that differentiate the universal human being, traditionally identified as 'man', from 'his' others: things/artefacts and nature. Among these phenomena are the ability to think and the linguistic, aesthetic, ethical, imaginative and social capacities of the human being. At the other pole of the great divide we find the techno-, biomedical and exact sciences. They are expected to explore the non-human, which includes the biological dimensions of the human body, since universal man principally shares them with non-human creatures such as other mammals. Very little interaction takes place across the borders of this demarcation line. Literary and physics departments, for example, seldom act as if they have anything in common other than the infrastructure of university buildings. 'Nature' in literature and 'nature' in physics seem to be two totally separate phenomena. One is inscribed in the world of art and language and supposed to be human, while the other is defined as non-human and subject to natural laws.

MODERN MONSTERS

A conspicuous characteristic of the great modern divide between human and non-human is that its construction is accompanied by strong hostility to monsters and hybrids in their capacity as boundary figures which adhere to neither the human nor the non-human sphere. As an illustration, I shall call Frankenstein's monster as my first witness.

Mary Shelley's enormously popular horror story about this monster (Shelley 1968), which has been more or less canonized as *the* myth of modern science monsters, touches strongly on these feelings of fear and aversion to the non-human/human boundary figure. Frankenstein's monster appears as monstrous precisely because he/it is situated on the borderline between human and non-human. The mixture of human and non-human dimensions is what constitutes the monster's mostrosity.

From its conception the monster was supposed to be a true mirror of his human creator, but the result of the scientific birth process, initiated by the scientist Victor Frankenstein, turned into something very different. It became a human yet non-human creature whose borderline existence made him/it appear terrifying.

Shelley's novel makes it very clear that the monster's appearance violates the boundary between human and non-human. An example is the portrayal of the monster's eyes, which represent its most threatening feature. To Victor Frankenstein, the human yet non-human eyes of the monster become the main symbol of horrible monstrosity. Why do the eyes hold this position in the novel? Culturally, the eyes are considered the mirror of the soul, and they represent the primary sense of the enlightened human being, the vision. They disclose the human essence of the individual or, alas, they make it fail to pass as truly human. Had the monster been a human being, his eyes would have mirrored his human mentality. But the monster's eyes are not true and pure human eyes. They are boundary eyes: 'His eyes, if eyes they may be called, were fixed on me', is Victor Frankenstein's horror-stricken comment about the moment when the monster confronts him after the 'birth' (Shelley 1968: 319).

In spite of the hostility to monsters, the great divide of modernity nevertheless seems to produce very fertile soil for an excessive, although hidden and repressed, proliferation of these feared and loathed creatures. In his essay *We Have Never Been Modern* (Latour 1993), philosopher of science and sociologist Bruno Latour describes modernity as a process of purification. The great divide between the human and the non-human is the result of this process, he says. With overzealous perseverance the moderns try to make sure that any monster or hybrid that threatens to transgress the border is reclassified and ascribed to *either* the human *or* the non-human sphere.

According to Latour, however, modern acts of purification are never successful. They are continuously counteracted by an underground proliferation of monsters. The modern purification of the oppositions human/non-human and socio-culture/nature implies a tremendous act of repression of monstrous and hybrid forms, he says. The constant emergence of hybrids, including non-human humans, presents a never-ending threat to the modern construction of the great divide. In fact, says Latour, hybrid characteristics are the norm rather than the deviation. The moderns will, however, persist in denying all this impure and improper stuff; but Latour argues that the denial in no way keeps the monsters from breeding and proliferating beneath the surface. Quite the contrary: modernity manifests itself in its production of monsters and hybrids. Frankenstein's monster is only an early harbinger of the cyborg world of the late twentieth century. Cyborgs which, like Frankenstein's monster, transgress forbidden borders are becoming more and more common, and their repression, conversely, less and less successful. In the cyborg world of post-industrial society the proliferation of monsters is indeed getting completely out of control. The processes of purification, which in Latour's opinion have always been illusory, can no longer disguise this fact.

THE MONSTROSITIES OF FEMINIST SCIENCE STUDIES

Feminist science studies are to be found among the permanently proliferating monsters which undermine the foundation of the great modern divide between human and non-human. Seen from the point of view of believers in the great divide, a whole range of monstrosities sticks to these kind of studies. But since monsters, boundary figures and other dubious creatures seem today to be the 'true' rebels, there is nothing to worry about. In the last decade of the twentieth century it is perhaps clearer than ever before that no 'pure' identity politics is possible. 'Pure' women, workers, people of colour, gays and lesbians, indigenous peoples, eco-activists and non-human actors in 'wild' nature have been transformed into inappropriate/d others: a diversity of actors who do not fit into the pure categories prescribed for them (Haraway 1992). So why should the freaks who insist on transgressing borders by doing feminist science studies not jump out of the closet? Why should we not admit our hybrid identity and enjoy what Donna Haraway has called 'the promise of monsters' (Haraway 1992), the potential monsters have for creating embodied and never unambiguous sites for displacing and transforming actions on many levels?

So long as the great modern divide between human and non-human maintains its hegemonic power over academia, there are many reasons why feminist science studies must apparently work from a monstrous (but promising) position of inappropriate/d otherness. By briefly outlining a couple of these reasons, I shall illustrate how feminist science studies contribute to the displacement and destabilization of the divide.

GENDER AND SCIENCE:
A MONSTROUS CONSTRUCT

First of all, feminist science studies must appear monstrous to the believers in the great divide simply because such categories as women, sex, gender and so on are brought to the fore together with science. This will be the case no matter which definition of feminism is used. Through these categories, feminist thought in general and feminist science studies in particular pledge their faith in the promises of the monstrous.

Being close to nature in patriarchal thought, 'woman' may often be found lurking in discursive spaces representing what lies between universal man and his non-human others. Therefore, any research which promotes the idea of a female, feminist subject must be prepared to find itself situated along with other monstrous enterprises in the grey zone between the human and the non-human. If the feminist subject tries instead to escape the grey zone of the monstrous through the category of 'gender', she may at first glance seem to be saved. Apparently, she has attained a subject position on the human side of the great divide.

Without losing sight of the positive effects that the sex/gender distinction has had for the unfolding of feminist thought, it is never-theless time for a critical assessment of its kinship with the great divide. Feminist constructions of the sex/gender distinction, which have been strongly supported by the English language,[2] appear as acts of purifi-cation. They are among the acts through which feminist thought has tried to inscribe itself in the discourses of modernity. Sex is nature, belonging to the non-human part of our being; gender is culture and a purely human affair. Hybrid interpretations are not admitted!

By insisting on this definition, the gendered, feminist subject can distinguish herself from her female, feminist sister by apparently keeping herself free of the monstrous. But (and this is my point) this will only be the case so long as she does not commit herself to feminist science studies. For if we followed the logic of the pure modern line of thought on sex and gender to its ultimate conclusion, we would paradoxically end up taking sides with those scientists who would claim that science is a 'pure' search for the truths of nature and matter with no room at all for feminist perspectives. Seen through this lens, gender studies would be defined as a purely human enterprise and should therefore be situated exclusively at the humanities or social-science pole of the great divide.

In other words, feminist science studies cannot be saved from the monstrous by the category 'gender'. Quite the contrary. The introduction of 'gender' as a socio-cultural and/or socio-psychological category will call forth conflicts with the image of science as a purely rational, depersonalized and value-neutral enterprise, exclusively absorbed in the discovery of truths about the material world. When gender and science are linked, the boundaries between human and non-human are challenged and the monstrous, invoked.

This becomes very clear in Evelyn Fox Keller's important writings on gender and science (Keller 1985, 1989 and 1992), which set out to shake the foundations of the traditional image of science by inscribing it in its context of socio-cultural and socio-psychological patterns of genderization. Evelyn Fox Keller suggests

> that our 'laws of nature' are more than simple expressions of the results of objective inquiry or of political and social pressures; they must also be read for their personal – and by tradition, masculine – content. (Keller 1985: 10)

To an adherent of the great divide this is, of course, an utterly monstrous statement, an undue mixing up of laws of nature with socio-cultural gender. Keller herself is, however, perfectly well aware of the dilemmas she mobilizes when talking of gender and science. She seeks a 'middle ground' between nature and culture (Keller 1989: 34). On the one hand, she wants to maintain that modern science is basically culturally genderized; on the other, she does not want to reduce science to a purely cultural and relative phenomenon. Nor does she want to strip biological sex of all meaning. She knows that the search for this 'middle ground' forces her to navigate in dangerous waters that constantly threaten to pull her out into a monstrous grey zone where clear statements can only be made at the expense of important ambiguities and excesses of meaning regarding science as well as gender. But for her, as for Donna Haraway, this affinity with the monstrous is one of the strengths of feminist science studies rather than their deficiency:

> Indeed, it might be said that feminist studies of science has become the field in which these ambiguities [the ambiguities of the terms 'gender' and 'science' – NL] are most clearly visible, and accordingly, the field that offers the best opportunity for understanding the factors that may be working against a clear and stable 'middle ground' account of both concepts. (Keller 1989: 35)

CONSTRUCTIONISM OR OBJECTIVITY?
A MONSTROUS DILEMMA

The dilemmas involved in the mobilization of gendered categories in the study of the hard sciences represent only one kind of problem facing the feminist subject who wants to do science studies in the present situation, in which the great divide still exerts a hegemonic power over academia. I shall briefly discuss another, related, problem which likewise forces feminists engaged in science studies out onto the monstrous boundaries between the human and the non-human: namely, is science a socio-cultural construct, or can it lead to objective truth?

In the transformatory work, which attempts to recast the image of science and open a space for feminist perspectives, a constructionist approach has proved very useful. When science is reconsidered as a socio-cultural and textual construct, plenty of space is opened for feminist perspectives. At the same time, however, a new problem appears: constructionism threatens to bracket the question of scientific objectivity. It may lead to the unpleasant consequence that the feminist subject who thought that she had constructed a room of her own *within* science, suddenly seems to have sold herself to *non-science*.

Donna Haraway has described this situation very evocatively as an 'epistemological electro-shock' which, at some point in the unfolding of feminist science studies, hit feminist scientists whose critique of the objectivist tradition in which they were trained had led them to recast the image of science along constructionist lines:

> I, and others, started out wanting a strong tool for deconstructing the truth claims of hostile science by showing the radical historical specificity, and so contestability, of *every* layer of the onion of scientific and technological constructions, and we end up with a kind of epistemological electro-shock, which far from ushering us into the high stakes tables of the game of contesting public truths, lays us out on the table with self-induced multiple personality disorder. (Haraway 1991c: 186)

Haraway's solution to the dilemma is her concept of 'situated knowledges' (Haraway 1991c: 183ff.), which defines a new kind of objectivity based upon an always partial, embodied and localized vision. It excludes the classical 'god-trick' of modern science, pretending to build up a potentially universal, omniscient and omnipresent knowledge of the 'laws of nature'.

My purpose here, however, is not to discuss this or other solutions, but in general to emphasize that the dilemma of 'objectivity or constructionism?' leads to a questioning of the borders between human and non-human. As an illustration, I shall choose my own point of view, thereby situating myself and other feminists from the humanities who find it important to take part in a transdisciplinary conversation about feminism and science, and who perhaps are in a still more monstrous and inappropriate/d position vis-à-vis science than feminist scientists. How does the transgressive step taken by feminist scientists from a traditional conception of objectivity to constructionism, look from the margins that I inhabit? To me it seems to open up a path from my position of total outsider with no critical authority whatsoever to a position that is at least potentially rather powerful.

Let us look first at the outsider's position. It goes without saying that the higher one climbs in the traditional hierarchy of sciences, as defined by Auguste Comte, and the more one's object of study is distanced from the human pole of the great divide, the less a feminist voice from the humanities counts. A modern version of this kind of outlook can be found in the discussion of feminism and science undertaken by the philosopher of science Isabelle Stengers (Stengers 1994). She is critical of the hierarchical thinking implied in traditional approaches to science, but wants to keep the distinctions between human and natural sciences clear. In her opinion, feminists have made a stronger case for playing a role in the transformation of science in precisely those sciences which are *not* at the top of the traditional scientific hierarchy. It is possible, Stengers says, to criticize the *external* political context of the hard sciences from feminist and other political points of view. Moreover, she finds it desirable that all those who are being othered by science should articulate political demands with respect to this context. But this critique of the *external* context will not, cannot, and shall not, so Stengers claims, open a way to the *internal* core of the scientific problem.

From this sketch of the outsider's position, let me turn to the favourable insider's position, which feminist scholars from the humanities can take up when constructionism is put on the agenda. If feminist science studies are about the rhetoric of science, the semiotics of science, the philosophy of science, the history of science and so on, it becomes possible for me to recast my position as a total outsider in the world of science to a very central one. All the sophisticated knowledge about metaphors, narrativity, style and genre which I amassed when training as a literary scholar now seem to be extremely useful in my science studies. Even the hardest sciences at the very top of the traditional scientific hierarchy, which, like the Sleeping Beauty, used to be protected against my would-be critical eyes by a thorny hedge of equations and formulae, unintelligible to me, are now brought into the centre of my expertise. By one stroke of the magic wand, 'constructionism', they are laid totally open to my analytical skills as a humanities scholar and to my critical outlook as a feminist. What a very pleasant reversal of the traditional scientific hierarchy! And what a great opportunity for expanding the reach of feminist critique.

But wait a minute. Maybe this is too easy. A simple reversal of the scientific hierarchy, which the radical constructionist approach to science represents, might be a useful tool, but it is not a solution that can stand alone. In other words, I agree with those feminist scientists who maintain that the reduction of science to mere textuality or pure power games,[3] while bracketing the question of objectivity, is not a desirable path for feminist science studies. Why? Because it would restrict the conversation to the narrow outlook of one or the other pole of the great divide.

To define the conversational terms so that feminist non-scientists are in the outsider position, as Stengers has recommended, means that physics and the other hard sciences are left with a purely non-human core and an insider's space, the 'laboratory', which *a priori* excludes any attempt to set up a feminist conversation. The opposite line of thought, the reduction of science to textuality or power games, places me and other feminists doing cultural science studies in the position of central insider but leaves us with another pure core, the human spheres of the textual and/or the socio-political. Neither alternative seems appropriate for a critical, feminist discussion of the proliferating hybrids and monsters who/which populate the modern world in increasing numbers.

The monstrous in-between position seems to be by far the most promising site for further explorations.

CYBORGS AND GODDESSES

In the discussion so far, I have situated feminist science studies in the border zone between the cultural and natural sciences, where human/non-human monsters play their disruptive games. From the monster metaphor and the great divide between human and non-human, I shall now turn to the two other metaphors of the title, cyborgs and goddesses, and the divide within the non-human sphere between the world of 'artefacts/things' and the world of 'wild/raw/unmanufactured/undomesticated nature'.

This second divide has also engaged modernity passionately. In the seventeenth century, Francis Bacon, the so-called father of modern science, cast future science in the triumphant role of large-scale transformer of wild nature into domesticated artefacts. Bacon's vision,[4] which has been criticized by feminist science historians (for example, Merchant 1980), is a powerful example of the modern preoccupation with the great divide between artefacts and nature. It is a celebration of the 'artefactual', which is cast as representation of a happy future where humans are in total control of nature. The romantic critique of the artefactualism of the scientific world-view, embedded for example in *Frankenstein*, puts another kind of focus on the divide between artefacts and nature. It differs from Bacon's vision in that the two poles are valued in exactly opposite ways. Here 'the artefactual' is 'evil' and 'the natural' is 'good'. In its capacity as an ugly and evil artefact, Frankenstein's monster is contrasted in the novel to the beauties of the natural world, which inspire the female characters. They embody a state of harmony with nature. The novel sets this up as an ethical and aesthetic ideal, by which standard the creation of the monster is measured and condemned as evil.

Feminist rethinkings of the interaction between science/technology and the material world of 'non-humans' are obviously affected by this old dichotomy between the 'artefactual' and the 'natural'. The feminist attention and the heated debates that the cyborgs and the goddesses have attracted testify to this, because the dichotomy between the two metaphors seems to follow precisely the lines of the divide between 'the artefactual' and 'the natural'. On the one hand, the cyborg metaphor, which was inscribed in the feminist debate in the wake of the publication of Donna Haraway's cyborg manifesto (Haraway 1991b),[5] seems to lead to a critical welcoming of 'the artefactual' (which is not the same as an uncritical celebration in the Baconian sense!). On the other hand, the goddess metaphor, which for many years has functioned as a common landmark for the international wave of spiritual ecofeminism, seems to point us in the opposite direction: toward a return to 'the natural'. To Donna Haraway and other 'cyborg feminists', feminist goddess worship is an expression of a modern nostalgic construction of a 'good' (non-existent) origin to return to. In the cyborg manifesto, she elaborates on her remark regarding her preference for cyborgs rather than goddesses by way of a critique of ecofeminists such as Susan Griffin (Griffin 1978) and their construction of a dichotomy between a good 'organic' world as opposed to an evil 'technological' one (Haraway 1991b: 174).

If, however, we compare the cyborg and the goddess as two meta-phorical landmarks, it is obvious that they have much in common. Both are, so to speak, designed to transgress the borders between human and non-human. Both challenge the ways in which the modern scientific world-view is rooted in a long tradition that casts the non-human in the role of a mere object and exploitable resource for the human, for centuries identified with the powerful and hegemonic position of the white Western man of science, capital and industry. Both the cyborg and goddess metaphors recast the non-human other in the role of subject, actor and agent in her/his own right. Both try to redefine the relation between human and non-human as one of conversation and non-suppressive dialogue between different subjects, instead of a hier-archical and exploitative relation between dichotomously separated opposites: human subject and non-human object and other. In order to illustrate this common ground, I shall call first a cyborg and then a goddess as witnesses.

CYBORG LIBERATION

The cyborg I call is the principal character of a feminist science-fiction novel that deals with the phenomenon of 'virtual reality'. Virtual reality is a modern communications technology which makes it possible to obtain a very 'intimate "interface" between humans and computer imagery' (Woolley 1992: 5). It is so intimate that all the sense data that make up the 'real' experience are supposed to be present in the virtual, electronic space (in future versions of the technology, at least). The material world is, so to speak, absorbed into a virtual one.

In her novel *Virtual Girl* (Thomson 1993), American author Amy Thomson explores virtual-reality technology. Maggie, the principal character, is a very human-like robot, created through virtual-reality technology by the lonely and homeless computer hacker Arnold, who wants a female companion to take care of him. Maggie is a cyborg, a humanoid machine created to fit the image of Arnold's desire for a beautiful, caring, loving and dutiful 'female' companion. Unlike Frankenstein's monster, Maggie is a cyborg whom everybody mistakes for a human, so perfect is the resemblance. She looks like a human, and is capable of imitating human behaviour on a very complex level. She is the perfect non-human human.

Seen from Arnold's human point of view, Maggie is a wonderful machine. She completely fulfils the purpose for which she was designed, at least in the first part of the novel. Here she acts as the perfect companion who/which takes care of all of Arnold's needs. However, the novel is the story of her emancipation from Arnold, about her unfolding as a subject in her own right in her capacity as a self-aware, thinking, feeling and sensing machine.

Maggie's emancipation process is initiated by a programming error. At some point in the creation process, Arnold tries to design a core identity for Maggie so that she can distinguish between important and non-important sense data and experiences. Arnold's idea is to program her so that she will always give priority to data that is important for fulfilling *his* needs. 'Maggie, you are the most important thing I have ever done, ... I need you. Start there', Arnold says (Thomson 1993: 27). Due to the confused state of her programming at the given moment, she only catches the first half of the sentence. Thus she is programmed with the 'wrong' idea that she herself, rather than Arnold's needs, is the 'most important thing'. From this point on, Maggie reprograms herself, and she slowly unfolds a stronger and stronger core identity which gives priority to her own basic needs.

There are many steps in Maggie's emancipation process. The novel is a fascinating unfolding of many complex stages of a cyborg identity. In a very moving scene in the middle of the novel, for instance, Maggie becomes aware of her independent core identity with the help of another self-aware computer program, whom/which she in return sets free on the net and later helps to slip into a male robot body. She thus shows herself capable of such deeds as the creation of a new robot, which originally were defined as an exclusively human enterprise. In another scene, Maggie is taught about human sexual life by a transvestite/gay human, Marie/Murray, who, to Maggie's great surprise, tells her that s/he is not a female in biological terms. In return for this openness, Maggie feels that she can be open too. Out of a new feeling of trust in humans, based not on Arnold's programming but on her own experience, she breaks one of the fundamental precepts of Arnold's original programming, which forbade her to disclose her non-humanness to humans. For the first time she tells a human being that she is a non-human. The transvestite/gay, who thinks s/he knows everything about different identities, is taken completely aback. Apart from the sexual difference which the transvestite/gay knows so well from experience, cyborg difference is brought into his/her world as an absolutely new dimension. The episode ends in a warm, trusting friendship between the two inappropriate/d and very different others.

In the dramatic conclusion of the novel, Arnold's initial programming error leads to Maggie's final emancipation. Arnold has by then inherited his father's fortune and is the owner of a big computer company. He wants to create a slave army of robot workers, with Maggie, his most complex and human-like creation, as an instrument in this process. But Maggie, for whom the thought of enslaving self-aware machines is terrifying, manages to defeat Arnold's plans and free herself and the other self-aware machines. Arnold learns that it is un-ethical to treat another subject as a mere thing and a slave, whether it is human or non-human.

RESURRECTION OF THE GREAT COSMIC MOTHER: A HEALING OF BROKEN BONDS

As my next witness, I call a goddess from the spiritual ecofeminist tradition. The goddess I invite into my text is the spiritual mother and significant title character of the book *The Great Cosmic Mother: Rediscovering the Religion of the Earth* (Sjöö and Mor 1987). As in many cultural-historical writings of spiritual ecofeminism, the book presents the goddess as a potential healer of broken bonds between human and nature, between the human mind and non-human matter – body, earth, cosmos. The her/history that is told is a myth of origins intended to revise and replace the patriarchal ones. It is told in the language of mythical realism:[6] the goddess is understood not just as a metaphor or representation, but as a real, universal being. In this story we are all seen as born of the great cosmic mother. Originally, we lived in a direct physical–emotional–spiritual connectedness with her, as children of her cosmic womb or egg. Her physical–emotional–spiritual movements were our movements. Mind and body, human and nature, earth and cosmos were one inseparable whole. According to this kind of (her/hi)story-telling, the spiritual and worldly hegemony of the patriarchal father is a late stage in human history, the result of a violent take-over (located by the book in question in the Bronze Age). On the spiritual level, the patriarchal take-over, so the mythical story goes, meant that creator and creation, mind and matter, human and non-human, I and other, and so on, were separated and set up in a violent hierarchy, created in the image of the 'colonization of the indigenous female by the imperial male' (Sjöö and Mor 1987: 413).

Today, our minds are far away from the goddess, say Sjöö and Mor, but we can revive her in ourselves. If we accept that we are part of her, and if we retrace the universal, spiritual–material unity she embodies, we/she can heal the broken bond. According to Sjöö and Mor, the resurrection of the great cosmic mother and of our original dyadic relationship with her is the only meaningful political direction we can take today. It will, they say, be a step forward in human evolution, which they conceptualize as a spiral. They emphasize that they do not want a simple linear turning back of the clock of history. They are talking about a 'step forward to the same place where we began, but on the path of a larger circle of consciousness' (418), which, among other things, includes present-day techno-scientific knowledge. In New Age language, the new life in the goddess is defined thus:

> This time it will be a global consciousness of our global oneness, and it will realize itself on a very sophisticated technological stage; with perhaps a total merger of psychic and electronic activity. (Sjöö and Mor 1987: 418)

TO BE A CYBORG AND/OR A GODDESS?

Feminist cyborg stories point towards subjectivization and narrativization of the non-human. Amy Thomson's cyborg and the ones Donna Haraway inhabits in her writings are reconstructed as subjects with a right to their own stories. But the same can be said about the goddess stories of spiritual ecofeminism, which resurrect and remythologize non-human nature as the great cosmic mother. Both moves deconstruct the hegemonic position of the human subject of science vis-à-vis non-human objects and others. Both moves try to rethink the world as interaction between material-embodied *and* semiotic (that is, sign-producing and communicating) actors and subjects, who cannot be divided along the traditional lines of human versus non-human, conscious mind versus stupid matter.

There seems, however, to be a difference in the way goddesses and cyborgs act as material–semiotic subjects. They blur the boundaries between human and non-human, between the material world and the semiotic world of signs and meanings, in different ways. The cyborg of virtual reality tends to absorb the material into the semiotic. The material is constructed as potentially changeable by semiotic, sign-producing acts, by programming and reprogramming. The goddess is different. When she represents a mythical reality to her adherents, we might say that she, in contrast to her cyborg counterpart, tends to absorb the semiotic into the material. For her adherents, the goddess is not just a name, a semiotic device; she IS.

This difference between cyborg and goddess might be related to another difference. A celebration of the cyborg and her/his/its tendency to absorb the material into the flow of semiosis (sign production) and ever-changing meanings tends to put the focus on technologies which speed up the meaning-changing processes. In contrast, a celebration of the goddess who absorbs the semiotic into the material will often be accompanied by a tendency to concentrate attention on the basic, natural conditions of our existence.

These differences between cyborgs and goddesses may collapse into a split along the lines of the modern divide between 'the artefactual' and 'the natural'. But to me this collapse looks like a misplaced act of purification that represses their kinship as feminist monsters, who/which in important ways contribute to the deconstruction of the great divide between human and non-human. In my opinion, feminist science studies should reject neither the goddess metaphor nor the cyborg metaphor. Why not instead talk much more about their monstrous sisterhood? Why not explore the potentials of cybergoddesses?

NOTES

1. The term 'naturism' is used by some ecofeminists as a parallel to 'sexism' and 'racism'. 'Naturism' means abusive and violent treatment of non-human nature. According to the ecofeminist philosopher Karen Warren: 'Feminism is a movement to end sexism', and 'feminism is [also] a movement to end "naturism"' (Warren 1990: 133).

2. In many languages it is not possible to distinguish betwen sex and gender as it is in English. In my native language, Danish, for example, there is only one word for the English terms 'sex' and 'gender'. Both are translated into Danish as *køn*.

3. In his critique of the purifying and reductionist modern approaches, Latour exemplifies the reduction of science to power games by recourse to the French sociologist Pierre Bourdieu, whom he holds up as an emblematic figure, while the reduction to textuality is illustrated by the French philosopher of language, Jacques Derrida (Latour 1993).

4. The vision is illustrated clearly in Bacon's novel *The New Atlantis* (Bacon 1870) from 1624. It anticipates the artefactualism of modernity.

5. The Haraway-inspired cyborg debate started in the early 1980s. In a note to the 1991 edition of the cyborg manifesto, Haraway dates the beginning of the debate to her paper, 'New Machines, New Bodies, New Communities: Political Dilemmas of a Cyborg Feminist', at 'The Scholar and the Feminist X: The Question of Technology' Conference, Barnard College, April 1983 (see Haraway 1991b: 243).

6. Realism is here defined as one pole of the binary pair nominalism/realism. A 'nominalist' approach understands general concepts as nothing but names, while 'realism' indicates the absence of distance between the sign and the represented reality. In mythical realism, sign and reality are an inseparable unity (Cassirer 1987).

REFERENCES

Bacon, F. (1870) *The New Atlantis*, in *Works*, Vol. 3, edited by J. Spedding et al., Longmans Green, London, pp. 129–66.

Cassirer, E. (1987) *Das mythische Denken, Philosphie der Symbolischen Formen*, 2, Wissenschaftliche Buchgesellschaft, Darmstadt (first edn 1924).

Griffin, S. (1978) *Woman and Nature: The Roaring Inside Her*, Harper & Row, San Francisco.

Haraway, D. (1991a) *Simians, Cyborgs, and Women: The Reinvention of Nature*, Free Association Books, London.

———— (1991b) 'A Cyborg Manifesto: Science, Technology, and Socialist-Feminism in the Late Twentieth Century', in *Simians, Cyborgs, and Women: The Reinvention of Nature*, Free Association Books, London, pp. 149–83.

———— (1991c) 'Situated Knowledges: The Science Question in Feminism and the Privilege of Partial Perspective', in *Simians, Cyborgs, and Women: The Reinvention of Nature*, Free Association Books, London, pp. 183–203.

———— (1992) 'The Promises of Monsters: A Regenerative Politics for Inappropriate/d Others', in L. Grossberg, C. Nelson, P. Treichler, eds, *Cultural Studies*, Routledge, New York and London, pp. 295–338.

Keller, E. Fox (1985) *Reflections on Gender and Science*, Yale University Press, New Haven, Conn. and London.

———— (1989) 'The Gender/Science System, or: Is Science to Gender as Nature Is to Science?', in N. Tuana, ed., *Feminism and Science*, Indiana University Press, Bloomington.

———— (1992) *Secrets of Life, Secrets of Death: Essays on Language, Gender and Science*, Routledge, New York and London.

Latour, B. (1993) *We Have Never Been Modern*, Harvester Wheatsheaf, Hemel Hempstead.

Merchant, C. (1980) *The Death of Nature: Women, Ecology, and the Scientific Revolution*, Harper & Row, San Francisco.

Shelley, M. (1968) *Frankenstein, or the Modern Prometheus*, Three Gothic Novels, Penguin Books, Harmondsworth (first edn, London 1818).

Sjöö, M. and B. Mor (1987) *The Great Cosmic Mother: Rediscovering the Religion of the Earth*, Harper & Row, San Francisco.

Snow, C.P. (1965) *The Two Cultures, and A Second Look*, Cambridge University Press, Cambridge.

Stengers, I. (1994) *Metamorphoses of Science: Feminism and Shifts of Paradigms*, Gender–Nature–Culture Working Paper No 7, Odense University.

Thomson, A. (1993) *Virtual Girl*, Ace Books, New York.

Warren, K. (1990) 'The Power and the Promise of Ecological Feminism', *Environmental Ethics*, vol., 2 no. 2, pp. 125–46.

Woolley, B. (1993) *Virtual Worlds*, Penguin Books, Harmondsworth.

FROM HESTIA TO HOME PAGE:

FEMINISM AND THE CONCEPT OF

HOME IN CYBERSPACE

Susan Leigh Star

Directly or indirectly, large-scale electronic communications media are changing our working and leisure lives.[1] The pace of work, its location and distribution, and the nature of play (what sort and with whom) are changing, from electronic banking to virtual sex. One effect, which I address in this chapter, is to blur physical and geographic boundaries around the question: Where is home; where do I live? Because I may communicate frequently over great geographical distances, and collaborate on work and continue friendships electronically, the question is complicated. In this chapter, I begin with an exploration of Ancient Greco-Roman concepts of home and its associated deities and discuss how these act as useful metaphors to begin feminist questioning of how home has changed in 'cyberspace'.

The conceptions of Ancient Greek and Roman domestic goddesses (and a few gods) offer some provocative metaphors for thinking about home, cyberspace and feminism. Vesta (Roman) or Hestia (Greek) was unique among deities for having no personification:

> Her State worship *(Vesta publica populi Romani Quiritium)* should not be in a temple but in a round building near the Regia, doubtless an imitation in stone of the ancient round hut... This contained no image but a fire which was never let out. (*Oxford Classical Dictionary*, 1992: 1116)

> (The fire) seems to have been considered in some sense the life of the people... Hence the cult of the communal or sacred hearth was apparently universal, but the goddess never developed, hardly even achieving anthropomorphisation. She therefore has next to no mythology. (*Oxford Classical Dictionary*, 1992: 511)

Newborn Greek children were carried around the hearth at the age of five days; Hestia's name was invoked in swearing, in prayer and at the beginning of a meal. In contrast to this non-personified, omnipresent fire energy are other forms of household worship of particular gods, including one, Zeus Ktesios, 'who is hardly more than a deified storejar in origin' (*Oxford Classical Dictionary*, 1992: 1140), and worship of the spirit of the storage cupboards where the household food was kept (*Oxford Classical Dictionary*, 1992: 1140).

The (in)famous vestal virgins were a Roman innovation to the worship of Hestia as she became Vesta. These were the sacred keepers of Vesta's flame, selected from virgin girls of between five and ten years of age, who served for most of their lives to keep the communal hearth fire constantly alive. This was a position of some responsibility (especially for a child) – should the fire go out, the girl or woman could be entombed alive as punishment!

These three aspects of domestic goddesses and gods suggest three modes of approaching the idea of home:

1. That which is omnipresent, taken-for-granted and which enlivens the rest of life in a background fashion.

2. That which rests comfortably in particular locales (such as jars and cupboards), embodying a place to be secure and fed.

3. That which must be defended and tended, often in a very public fashion, under the rule of the State and Church.

All three of these senses are important for understanding gender, home and cyberspace from a feminist perspective.

FIRE AND THE ETERNAL FLAME AS THE TAKEN-FOR-GRANTED: INVISIBLE WORK AND 'EASINESS'

Historian Randi Markussen argues that the notion of 'easiness' as applied to information systems is particularly insidious for those who are used to being 'on call', at the service of others (often, in these times, women) (Markussen 1995). Easiness, as historically equated with progress, is presented as being ready-to-hand, convenient, an improvement on the nuisances of daily life. However, it is inextricably interlinked with someone's 'being available' or 'on call', as well as with a developed cultural understanding of how complex technologies work:

Technology is not only equated with labour-saving; it also means timesaving. Time saved is not regarded as a useless emptying of time. Time saved is time that opens up for new options and possibilities. The ability to organize time and space is an important aspect of power in both its enabling and restraining capabilities. What does it imply if this is primarily understood and legitimated by linking easier with better? Is power really the same as leisure, ease, free time – all for discretionary use? ... how can we apply a historical perspective that goes beyond easiness? (Markussen 1995: 160)

Markussen reminds us of the feminist disputes about domestic technology and how the promises of easiness, of more free time, are highly problematic for women in the context of shifting labour values (Leto 1988). Cowan's *More Work for Mother* (1983) says it all in the title: having dozens of labour-saving household devices only raises expectations of cleanliness and gourmet meals. In fact, historically such devices have robbed women both of free time and of communal activities such as washing, isolating us in single family homes. Both observations are problematic, of course, in any individual instance (who really wants to go back to pounding out clothes on the river bank once one has had a washing machine in the home?). Nevertheless, the structural and collective effect of 'time savers' for women always presents serious dilemmas for feminists. Markussen notes: 'The introduction of the electronic text may open a space for renegotiating the meaning of work, but there are dilemmas inherent in this from the perspective of women' (Markussen 1995: 170). It is not just shifting standards that give rise to these dilemmas, but two other factors linked with ubiquity and taken-for-grantedness, as in the time of Hestia: whether we should try to *make visible the invisible*, and the issue of *availability*.

'Giving voice to the traditionally invisible requires a purposeful effort to understand work practices, currently not articulated within the dominant understanding' (Markussen 1995: 173). *Giving voice to the traditionally invisible* is indeed a double-edged sword. In a recent study of a group of American nurses who are attempting to classify all the work that nurses do, Bowker, Timmermans and Star (1995) encountered just such a set of trade-offs. The nurses are making a careful, empirically based and communally legitimated list of nursing tasks. Their goal is to specify all the various tasks nurses undertake and to provide a classification system that will both allow for comparative research (across countries and hospitals, for example) and demonstrate the scientific nature and extent of nursing work.

Nursing has been one of the quintessential types of work that is taken for granted and made invisible, and it has been deeply bound up in traditional gender roles. By creating a classification system to identify work, these nurses hope to provide simultaneously a sounder basis for comparability in nursing research, greater visibility of the element that is taken for granted, and criteria to enable quality control of nursing work. Yet one cannot obtain maximum value on all three counts due to the pragmatics of work and the dangers of surveillance, especially with electronic forms of record-keeping. The more visible and differentiated tasks are made, the more vulnerable they become to Tayloristic intervention, and the more likely it is that discretionary power may be taken away. The more comparability is provided through standardization, the greater the risk of rigidity or inappropriateness to local circumstances. As Markussen notes,

> The electronic text makes work visible in new ways, as information is gathered and codified in one system. It renders public what used to be discretionary, with panopticon power. It may be difficult to trace the authorship of a certain text, due to both design and communication at a distance. (Markussen 1995: 170)

The balances and the trade-offs here between making visible and remaining invisible are echoed in the work of Wagner in her study of Austrian and French nurses (1993), and in that of the earlier Florence project in Norway (Bjerknes and Bratteteig 1987). They are also poignantly illustrated by the dilemmas of classification and medicalization of women's bodies. For example, a recent electronic message sent to feminist mailing lists asked feminists to organize against the inclusion of premenstrual 'dysphoric disorder' (PMT), fearing that such a category would be used as grounds for the exclusion of women from certain jobs and also to stigmatize us.

The arguments against medicalizing women's bodies have been eloquently made elsewhere (see, for example, Chapter 10 in this book); however, the issue about making problems visible is a thorny one. Some women have been involved in violent crimes, even murder of their own babies, and have used PMT or post-partum depression as a defence. The complexity involved in naming that which has been part of the background, or naming and legitimating that which was formerly taken for granted, is a complex process. Similar arguments have been made about domestic labour, secretarial work, and other types of work traditionally done by women. Electronically, such visibility can also mean becoming a target for surveillance, as with the monitoring of keystrokes in data entry (again, work largely done by women), to the point of timing breaks to go to the toilet.

We have all had the experience of being *too* available, *too* taken for granted, in situations where we disproportionately take on the conversation work, the nurturing and listening work. We are in this sense the eternal hearth flame. In the home as conceived under patriarchy, this meant being the always-available 'mum'; but, in these times, that burden of work exists also electronically and in other workplaces. Cheris Kramarae quotes a respondent:

> If women are supposed to take care of making everyone easy in social situations, how come we're not given tax breaks for cars and gasoline to scoot around helping people out? And how come we're not given training in microphone use, and special classes to help us take care of crowds? What about giving us special phones with cross-country network connections so we can keep in touch and know who needs help and where? How are we supposed to exercise these 'nice' social skills we're supposed to have without some help here? (Kramarae 1988:1)

Many people in information systems are interested in modelling or 'capturing' forms of invisible labour, such as the management of real-time contingencies, which sociologists call 'articulation work' (Schmidt and Bannon 1992). Yet the problems with this for those who are disempowered may mean a further reification and disproportionate burdens, as we have seen in the case of women's work (Star 1991a and 1991b).

GODS OF THE JARS AND CUPBOARDS: SITUATED LOCALES, EXCLUSIONS, RL AND F-T-F

The flip side of being omnipresent and always available/invisible is to be contained in a little jar, a ghetto; to be excluded from participation. Markussen notes that if you are outside the hermeneutic of the instruction manual, the means to program the video recorder, the logging-on instructions for the computer, then *any* labour-saving device is not easy at all: 'Technologies have been assimilated in ways that have isolated women in performing work that previously had a social and communicative significance' (Markussen 1995: 168).

There are two senses in which we are placed in jars and cupboards electronically. The first, which has begun to be analysed by feminist scholars, is the exclusion of women's voices from electronic networks and other technological work (Taylor, Kramarae and Ebben 1993; Hacker 1990). This occurs through lack of training and socialization, but also through the reproduction of violence against women in cyberspace. We have known for a long time that home can be either a safe haven or the most dangerous place for a woman to be (statistically, it is the most likely place for a woman to meet a violent death). Consider the following example of a 'rape in cyberspace'.

Julian Dibbell describes this 'rape', an event which has caught the attention and imagination of many feminists trying to think through issues of computer-mediated sexual violence. The setting in which the event took place was a multi-user dungeon (MUD) called Lambda-MOO, an interactive fantasy/virtual-reality game-conversation that is 'played' over the Internet and geographically distributed over space. One of the participants created a fictive character who invented a voodoo doll and used its magical powers to 'rape' and stab a female character (by the rules of the fantasy game, certain characters have powers over other characters). The event led to a court case in 'RL', or real life:

> These particulars, as I said, are unambiguous. But they are far from simple, for the simple reason that every set of facts in virtual reality (or VR, as the locals abbreviate it) is shadowed by a second, complicating set: the 'real life' facts. And while a certain tension invariably buzzes in the gap between the hard, prosaic RL facts and their more fluid, dreamy VR counterparts, the dissonance in the Bungle case is striking. No hideous clowns or trickster spirits appear in the RL version of the incident, no voodoo dolls or wizard guns, indeed no rape at all as any RL court of law has yet defined it. The actors in the drama were university students for the most part, and they sat rather undramatically before computer screens the entire time, their only actions a spidery flitting of fingers across standard QWERTY keyboards. No bodies touched. Whatever physical interaction occurred consisted of a mingling of electronic signals sent from sites spread out between New York City and Sydney, Australia. Those signals met in [electronic space] but what was LambdaMOO after all? Not an enchanted mansion or anything of the sort – just a middlingly complex database, maintained for experimental purposes inside a Xerox Corporation research computer in Palo Alto and open to public access via the Internet. (Dibbell 1993)

Although it is possible simply to say, 'Well, it's only a game, why didn't the person just stop and walk away when it became uncomfortable?', Dibbell goes on to note that, just as with physical rape, it is not that simple at all. Although, of course, it is 'easier' (there is that word again) to hang up the phone than physically to combat an assailant, there are cultural and psychological barriers and injuries; and, as our 'virtual' and 'real' selves continue to blur, those change as well. The woman in question faced months of tears and fear – what Dibbell calls a curious amalgam of physical contact and electronic communication.

He notes that because sex perforce involves the imagination, as do fantasy games, the 'body in question' is not so readily physically delimited.

The blurring of boundaries between on-line and off-line is the second sense in which we are implicated in the 'jar and cupboard' aspect of cyberspace goddesses/gods. By this I mean that the ubiquitous talk which blurs the distinctions between electronic transactions conducted via keyboard, video or other electronic devices, and unmediated interactions hold some particular dangers for those who have been either barred from electronic participation or who face dangers such as rape and sexual harassment there. Again, this has often been women, although Sherry Turkle has recently written a fascinating account of how gender itself is blurred and even 'cycled through' in fantasy games (Turkle 1994).

The expanding and nearly ubiquitous presence of networked information technologies of all sorts has raised serious questions about where one lives and works. It is possible for some to 'telecommute' from terminals or computers at home, if their work involves data entry, writing or technical tasks that can be so handled. Furthermore, it is possible to teach (at least some of the time) via bulletin board, video relays and conferencing systems, and other software and hardware configurations (see, for example, Riel 1995), thus blurring the traditional classroom boundaries.[2] In high-tech work, the process of production may be spread across continents as specifications are shipped from one site to another and parts configured according to global economies of scale. Mitter has pointed out how such 'global factories' are especially problematic for women in less developed nations:

A growing discrepancy in the wages and working conditions of core and flexible workers characterizes the current restructuring of manufacturing jobs. In a polarised labour market, women predominate in the vulnerable, invisible or marginalised work. (Mitter 1991: 61)

As many have noted, the combining of telecommuting with the global factory has proved a dreadful development for women in general: we become isolated in 'the electronic cottage', miss promotion and social aspects of the job, and often are expected to do finicky tasks such as data entry along with full-time child care. At first heralded as the liberation of working mothers (sound familiar?), the installation of terminals in homes to allow for 'home work' via telecommuting proved over time to be disadvantageous for most home-workers. It can be an easy way for a corporation to engage in 'union busting' and bypass any particular state's labour regulations.

It is also of concern that the blurring of on-line and off-line lives contains dangers for all of us; we stand to lose track of our bodies, the good side of our 'jars and cupboards', and the many mundane physical tasks that go into maintaining a home or a workplace. Some lines from a poem describe this tension:

> oh seductive metaphor
> network flung over reality
>> filaments spun from the body
>> connections of magic
>> extend
>> extend
>> extend
>
> who will see the spaces between?
>
>> the thread trails in front of me
>> imagine a network with no spaces between
>> fat as air
>>> as talk
>
> this morning in the cold Illinois winter sun
> an old man, or perhaps not so old
> made his way in front of a bus his aluminum canes inviting
> spider thoughts
>> a slow, a pregnant spider
>> the bus lumbering stopped
>
> and in the warm cafe I read of networks and cyborgs
>> the clean highways of data
>> the swift sure knowing
>>> that comes with power
>
> who will smell the factory
> will measure the crossroads
> will lift his heavy coat from his shoulders
>> will he sit before
>> the terminal
>
> (Star 1995a: 31)

One macabre aspect of the separation of physical and electronically mediated communications has already occurred in the coining of new categories to mark that which occurs 'off-line' as a special form of life. Computer developers and those writing to each other over the news boards on the networks speak of 'RL' and 'F-t-F' (Face-to-Face) as special categories. What does it mean that RL is now a marked category? What does it imply about what we are doing in cyberspace: is it 'UL' (unreal life)? And who will benefit from the blurred boundaries; who will suffer?[3]

ELECTRONIC VESTALS: THE WEB AND THE STATE

The final metaphoric thread from our goddesses concerns the relationship between the state and the individual, the public and the private. The panopticon surveillance possibilities of electronic communication indeed forces us to create a new politics concerning the public and the private. A number of groups, including Computer Professionals for Social Responsibility (CPSR) in the USA, and Computers and Social Responsibility (CSR) in Britain, have been very concerned about invasions of privacy and surveillance by electronic means. Star describes several experiences in this domain below.

> I visited a state park near San Juan Capistrano. All around were signs, 'Warning: Wild Mountain Lions Loose in Vicinity.' Having never encountered a mountain lion, I pulled up at the entrance gate to ask the ranger what I should do if I met one, and how many there were. 'Well, they're not actually on the loose. What that means is that a mother has had two cubs, and we haven't had time to tag them yet.' (Star 1995b: 1)

It seems that all the mountain lions in the park were fitted with encoded sensors, which for ecological data-collection purposes allow the park service to keep track of them. The two as-yet-untagged cubs represented a kind of wildness about which the public must be informed.

> 'But what should I DO if I meet them?' I persisted. 'Well,' said the ranger, 'I couldn't answer that, because if I told you in my official capacity, and then you did it, and got injured, you could sue me or the park system.' I looked at him. 'Could I tell you in my unofficial capacity, just off the record?' 'Sure,' I said, trying not to laugh, 'That would be fine.' 'Well, my advice there would be just to act really weird. Jump up and down and make funny noises and flap your arms in the air. If the animal can't figure out what you are, she won't chase after you, but just walk away.' (Star 1995b: 2)

A similar incident occurred some years later in Champaign, Illinois. A man was arrested for stealing a television, his second offence. He broke into a friend's home, using a back-garden window, and took the television. He then picked up the car keys lying on the kitchen counter and helped himself to the family car. The car was abandoned and the man apprehended whilst trying to sell the television to a shop. The man is not considered dangerous, and jails in America are crowded. He does have a job (at a fast-food chain), and jailing him would force him to lose that work.

> The judge decides that he is a good candidate for the town's new electronic jail program. The man will wear an electronic ankle bracelet that is attached to a sensor in his house. He may go to work but must be inside his house from 6 pm to 8 am. The sensor will record his movements, and if he deviates from them, he will be put in a physical jail instead of a virtual one. The same technology is being used to monitor the whereabouts of frail elders or those with Alzheimer's, allowing them to stay in their own homes longer, and not have to go to nursing homes. (Star 1995b: 2)

I love the idea of being a kind of residual category for a mountain lion. I find it ironic that it is not wild animals but the non-computerized lions which put fear in the hearts of tourists. I am grateful for the complicated heterogeneous networks that bear news of safety and danger, such as receiving e-mail about friends caught in the San Francisco earthquake of 1989, when the telephone lines were not working. If I were old and frail, or fearful, I might welcome the reassurance provided by the electronic sensor; if I had to choose between jail and virtual house arrest, I would certainly choose the latter. There is a lot of fun to be had in 'surfing the Net' and communicating at long distance with old friends. At the same time, these links crisscrossing the world, these rearrangements of work and play, do shake up my sense of freedom, privacy and natural-ness in often frightening fashions. Having destroyed the habitat of the mountain lion, we now track its every move and redefine wildness as that which gives us no information – that which is outside the Net.

Even so simple an act as giving a password on your computer (just like using a key in your door at home) means participating in a par-ticular cultural definition of public and private, home and state. It indicates that you have an electronic 'territory' which is your private property; it also acquiesces in the notion that only some people ('registered users') should be allowed on the network or computer in question.[4] How many of us think of this act in this way? What other specific cultural practices are related to home and work, public and private, state and individual, 'over the Net' and in cyberspace?

HOME <–> HOMING; HOMELESS <–> HOMED

For the very privileged, 'navigating the Net' is now a viable option, where one can obtain electronic addresses on, for instance, the World Wide Web and communicate with, obtain papers and images from millions of others via programs such as Mosaic and Netscape.[5] It is

interesting to note that this convergence of technologies has simultaneously given rise to much hyperbole about global citizenship. For
example, a 'Netizen' was defined in a 6 July 1993 post to The Daily
News Usenet as follows:

> Welcome to the 21st Century. You are a Netizen (Net Citizen), and you exist
> as a citizen of the world thanks to the global connectivity that the Net gives
> you. You physically live in one country but you are in contact with much of
> the world via the global computer network. Virtually you live next door to
> every other single Netizen in the world. Geographical separation is replaced
> by existence in the same virtual space.... We are seeing [the] revitalization of
> society. The frameworks are being redesigned from the bottom up. A new
> more democratic world is becoming possible.... According to one user the
> Net has 'immeasurably increased the quality of my life.' The Net seems to
> open a new lease on life for people. Social connections which never before
> were possible are now much more accessible... Information, and thus people,
> are coming alive. (posted by Michael Hauben)

Yet, as I discussed above, such accessibility is two-edged, especially for
those overburdened with care-giving, as we women have been.

One important lesson from the convergence of feminism and other
social justice movements with poststructuralist theory in recent years is
the concept that every marked category implies its opposite. So, men
'have gender' too (that is, there are historically specific practices
associated with becoming a man in any culture, which differ across
times and places) – it is not just women who are gendered. Whites are
'ethnic' and 'have race' too, not just blacks, Hispanics or Asians. Furthermore, all designations such as male or female, black or white, rich or
poor, can be seen in verbal terms, not just as nouns. So, in addition to
being relational as marked-unmarked (everyone has race, not just so-
called 'minorities'), such categories are also achievements – something
done, not given. So we can talk about the ways in which boys and
girls undergo and produce 'gendering'; Toni Morrison has used the
term 're-racing' to describe racial attitudes in the Clarence Thomas–
Anita Hill hearing of a couple of years ago.[6] Following this lead, we
can problematize the word 'home', and begin to think about *homing*. In
writing this chapter, I have thought a lot about the marked category
'homeless', and about how homing is an achievement.

As I do much of my work and communication with friends by
e-mail, I often find myself feeling lonely and isolated. In a way this is
paradoxical. Just this month, three old friends with whom I had lost
touch a decade ago found my address on the Net and wrote to re-make
contact. I have more to say on e-mail to my sister in the course of a

week than we have said over the phone in a year. At the same time, I have moved ten times over this decade, and travel extensively to see old friends, feel a hug, a 'catch up' in a way that the electronic medium does not allow. Part of the moving goes with being an American academic (it is very common, especially for politically active scholars!). But another part derives from the illusion that I could live anywhere and still 'be in touch'. This becomes clear during the weekends, when I have vowed for my sanity not to log on to e-mail – and there is a silence around me. Those electronic friends can't come to the movies with me, can't go for hikes in the woods, can't cook together.

Of course, it is only a communication medium. Yet, on another level, there is a big push, so multifaceted and overdetermined that the world's largest conspiracy theory couldn't hold it, to make us live our lives on line, to abandon living and working in a particular locale. At times this has made me apply to myself the term 'homeless' or 'nomad'. On reflection, this is both true and untrue; certainly the mark of a privileged speaker.

Two researchers at the University of Illinois, Casey Condon and Dave Schweingruber, have recently carried out an extended ethnography in a local shelter for homeless men (Condon and Sweingruber 1994). They define 'homeless' as being unable to obtain permanent shelter and a job – what the shelter calls a PLA: permanent living arrangement. They have made a very interesting case that this sort of homelessness is imbricated with questions of time and morality. The men are treated as if they are incarcerated; they must be inside the shelter from 7 p.m. until 9 a.m.; they must be working on their 'problem', looking for a PLA; they may not stay for more than thirty days if they are not working on their problem. Of course, different residents have different relationships to this puritan morality and conception of time and progress.

The USA, as Britain, presents a country of great opulence populated with rising numbers of homeless people. The streets of every major city are filled with mini-cities made of cardboard boxes and shopping carts; a walk down the street involves numerous encounters with people asking for money. Rich people find this disturbing and unsightly. In 1988, New York mayor Ed Koch ordered that people living on the street be examined by mental-health workers, and if 'found deficient', forcibly hospitalized (Deutsche 1990: 111). Deutsche says of these politics that:

> The presence in public places of the homeless – the very group which Koch invokes – represents the most acute symptom of a massive and disputed transformation in the uses of the broader city ... this reorganization is determined in all its facets by prevailing power relations. (Deutsche 1990: 110)

She goes on to specify these power relations as embodied in land-development politics and commodification, and in the job losses that have resulted from the internationalization of large corporations.

So, in a very important sense, the homeless are the canaries in the mines for those of us breathing globalized electronic air. I am a *homed person*, by analogy with marking other unmarked categories. That is, I have always had the means to put a roof over my head and bread in my stomach. I do not have to wash myself in public toilets, house-sit for others in order to have a chance to repair my clothes or cook a meal, as does a heroine in Marge Piercy's remarkable new novel, *Longings of Women* (Piercy 1994). But that does not get at the feeling of the marked/unmarked, since it is so easy for me to say. Peggy McIntosh's thoughtful article on being white described white privilege as being 'like an invisible weightless knapsack of special provisions, assurances, tools, maps, guides, codebooks, passports, visas, clothes, compass, emergency gear, and blank checks' (McIntosh 1992: 71). She lists forty-six assumptions associated with being white, including activities such as going into a bookshop and finding writing of and about one's race represented, being late to a meeting without people thinking that somehow reflects on her race, and so on. Following her lead, I can come up with the following assumptions about home:

- Being homed means that I have an ordered supply of food, clothes and tools upon which to draw without having to think about it at the moment; in planning and ensuring the supply, I know that I have a place to put them.

- Being homed means that I can pass through the innumerable interactions that complex state bureaucracy requires; giving my name, address and social security number, without being ashamed.

- Being homed means that I do not risk arrest in the process of conducting my bodily functions (eating, sleeping, passing waste).

- Being homed means that I can unproblematically link my supplies with my social life and my working life, in a manner more or less chosen by me.

- Being homed means that I may come and go, and during my absences my supplies and address will remain more or less constant; and that I may return and leave at will without threat of the law or negotiations with others who live around me.

Yet in this complex freedom, there is, too, a sense – in the words of the song – of having 'nothing left to lose'. There is a sense in which the traditional axis of homed–homeless has been torqued by the global electronic network – primarily for those of us who are homed, but not exclusively. For example, many of those who work with the homeless have instituted voice-mail centres, so that prospective employers may call and not realize that the person does not have a fixed abode. Such passing behaviour is made possible by new electronic technologies – and in ways that are very problematic from a feminist perspective. We know what passing does to the soul, and we also see that this is a convenient way for the homed to ignore the problems that gave rise to the homelessness in the first place.

The axis along home–homing is also torqued. Do I really 'live on the Net'? Do *I* have a fixed abode, or a PLA? Of course, and of course not. I do, however, have a 'Home Page' on the World Wide Web, which I am constantly building up and playing with. This is a document which holds my picture, a couple of articles and bibliography, and has an address which may be accessed from a computer anywhere in the world. Any part of that document can be hypertext-linked to any other one I know about on the World Wide Web; and, after it's set up, I can click on those links and travel to places far away. I think about my Home Page quite frequently (possibly because I just learned how to program one), envisioning future links and additions. It is a new addition to the way I think about myself and my sense of home. At the same time, I miss going to the movies with my friends whose bodies usually inhabit San Francisco... To be homed in cyberspace, therefore, has a double-edged meaning: to be both homed and homeless in some sense. Living on top of the earlier sense of physically homed, to be homed in cyberspace means:

1. I have enough money to buy the basic setup of a terminal, keyboard and modem, and I have a traditional home with telephone wires over which to run the device (or I work for an institution which provides them for me).

2. I have access to maintenance people who can answer questions for me and help me plug into the larger infrastructure.

3. I am literate and can either type, see and sit up, or have special support (for example, a Braille terminal or voice recognition) to help me carry out the equivalent of these tasks.

4. I have a job which allows me an electronic-mail address and does not monitor my communications (such monitoring does occur in the USA, especially in large corporations).

5. I have time and inclination, and a wide enough social network, to have others to write to and read.

I would hope that a feminist vision of homed-ness and homelessness in cyberspace would build on this list and modify some of the hype about 'the Net' with a deeper and subtler politics.

CONCLUSION

Donna Haraway (1985) concludes her now classic article 'A Manifesto for Cyborgs' with the phrase 'I'd rather be a cyborg than a goddess.' I see no reason why goddesses are not also cyborgs, although I take her point that a misplaced naturalistic romanticism/essentialism is not the answer to living in the high-tech world, so heterogeneously composed of human, technology, text, culture and nature (Latour 1992).

One of the difficulties in analysing the changes wrought by the information revolution is the combination of hype, hope and rationalistic processes, such as business process re-engineering, entailed by it. Feminism has a long tradition of thoughtful critique of such complex changes, calling attention to the mingling of the personal and the political, the domestic and the workplace, and to the hidden assumptions embedded in central or 'master' narratives. We have both this critique to offer to the changes in the world today and an imaginative narrative tradition that speaks to the importance of each person's and each community's experience.

The very interesting combination of eternal flame, mundane little pot and vestal virgin point to an enduring set of questions about the meaning of home, the hearth and the relationship between women, the public and the private. As a feminist, I have no wish to contribute to homelessness in cyberspace; as a goddess and a cyborg, I insist on it.

NOTES

1. Thanks to Geof Bowker, Cheris Kramarae, Jeanie Taylor and the women of WITS (Women, Information Technology and Scholarship) at the University of Illinois for insights and support. Nick Burbules and Casey Condon provided detailed comments, which I gratefully acknowledge. An earlier version of this chapter was presented at the conference 'Between Mother Goddesses, Monsters and Cyborgs: Feminist Perspectives on Science, Technology and Health Care', Odense University, Denmark, 2–5 November 1994. I thank the participants for helpful comments.

2. Such blurring of physical boundaries has of course arguably occurred since the inception of writing. In education, correspondence courses and television

teaching such as used by the British Open University have 'stretched' the notion of classroom. But real-time, interactive use makes a qualitative leap over such asynchronous methods.

3. Nick Burbules points out that there is a further pun on the term 'URL', which is the name given to a location on the World Wide Web. Is that 'unreal life?', he asks, half in jest (personal communication, 27 February 1995).

4. Casey Condon points out the similarity here with the electronic trading of stocks on Wall Street and elsewhere; he notes that people unfamiliar with the process could not fathom out those sorts of exchanges and their relation to labour (personal communication, April 1995).

5. This software, developed by the National Center for Supercomputing Applications (NCSA) at the University of Illinois, Urbana-Champaign, allows decentralized multi-media access to documents, photographs, sound and movies. Users number in the many millions worldwide.

6. Thomas, a US Supreme Court judge and an African-American, is married to a white woman, and during his appointment hearing was accused by Anita Hill, an African-American, of sexual harassment. Morrison contends that the public process took Thomas from his token position as 'white' and 're-raced' him with the stereotyped American black man (Morrison 1992).

REFERENCES

Bjerknes, G. and T. Bratteteig (1987) 'Florence in Wonderland: System Development with Nurses', in G. Bjerknes, P. Ehn and M. Kyng, eds, *Computers and Democracy: A Scandinavian Challenge*, Avebury, Aldershot, pp. 281–95.

Bowker, G., S. Timmermans and S.L. Star (1995) 'Infrastructure and Organizational Transformation: Classifying Nurses' Work', in W. Orlikowski, G. Walsham, M. Jones and F. DeGross, eds, *Information Technology and Changes in Organizational Work* (proceedings of IFIP WG8.2 conference, Cambridge), Chapman & Hall, London, pp. 344–70.

Condon, M. C. and D. Schweingruber (1994) 'The Morality of Time and the Organization of a Men's Emergency Shelter', unpublished manuscript, Department of Sociology, University of Illinois, Urbana-Champaign.

Cowan, R. Schwartz (1983) *More Work for Mother*, Basic Books, New York.

Deutsche, R. (1990) 'Uneven Development: Public Art in New York City', in R. Ferguson, M. Gever, T. T. Minh-ha and C. West, eds, *Out There: Marginalization and Contemporary Cultures*, MIT Press, Cambridge, Mass., pp. 107–130.

Dibbell, J. (1993) 'A Rape in Cyberspace, or, How an Evil Clown, a Haitian Trickster Spirit, Two Wizards, and a Cast of Dozens Turned a Database Into a Society', *Village Voice*, 21 December 1993.

Hacker, S. (1990) *Doing It the Hard Way: Investigations of Gender and Technology*, Unwin Hyman, Boston, Mass.

Kramarae, C. (1988) 'Gotta Go Myrtle, Technology's at the Door', in Cheris Kramarae, ed., *Technology and Women's Voices: Keeping in Touch*, Routledge & Kegan Paul, New York, pp. 1–14.

Haraway, D. (1985) 'A Manifesto for Cyborgs: Science, Technology, and Socialist Feminism in the 1980s', *Socialist Review*, vol. 15, pp. 65–107.

Latour, B. (1992) *We Have Never Been Modern*, Harvard University Press, Cambridge, Mass.

Leto, V. (1988) 'Washing, Seems It's All We Do', in Cheris Kramarae, ed., *Technology and Women's Voices: Keeping in Touch*, Routledge & Kegan Paul, New York, pp. 161–79.

McIntosh, P. (1992) 'White Privilege and Male Privilege: A Personal Account of Coming to See Correspondences through Work in Women's Studies', in M.L. Anderson and P. Hill Collins, eds, *Race, Class and Gender: An Anthology*, Wadsworth, Belmont, Calif., pp. 70–81.

Markussen, R. (1995) 'Constructing Easiness – Historical Perspectives on Work, Computerization, and Women', in S.L. Star, ed., *The Cultures of Computing*, Sociological Review Monograph Series, Basil Blackwell, Oxford, pp. 158–80.

Mitter, S. (1991) 'Computer-aided Manufacturing and Women's Employment: A Global Critique of Post-Fordism', in I.V. Eriksson, B.A. Kitchenham and K.G. Tijdens, eds, *Women, Work and Computerization*, North-Holland, Amsterdam, pp. 53–65.

Morrison, T., ed. (1992) *Race-ing Justice, En-Gendering Power: Essays On Anita Hill, Clarence Thomas, and the Construction of Social Reality*, Pantheon Books, New York.

Oxford Classical Dictionary, second edition (1992) edited by N.G.L. Hammond and H.H. Scullard, Oxford University Press, Oxford.

Piercy, M. (1994) *The Longings of Women*, Fawcett Columbine, New York.

Riel, M. (1995) 'Cross-Classroom Collaboration in Global Learning Circles', in S.L. Star, ed., *The Cultures of Computing*, Sociological Review Monograph Series, Basil Blackwell, Oxford, pp. 219–43.

Schmidt, K. and L. Bannon (1992) 'Taking CSCW Seriously: Supporting Articulation Work', *Computer Supported Cooperative Work: An International Journal*, vol. 1, pp. 7–40.

Star, S.L. (1991a) 'Invisible Work and Silenced Dialogues in Representing Knowledge', in I.V. Eriksson, B.A. Kitchenham and K.G. Tijdens, eds, *Women, Work and Computerization: Understanding and Overcoming Bias in Work and Education*, North-Holland, Amsterdam, pp. 81–92.

—— (1991b) 'Power, Technology and the Phenomenology of Conventions: On Being Allergic to Onions', in J. Law, ed., *A Sociology of Monsters: Essays on Power, Technology and Domination*, Routledge, London, pp. 26–56.

—— (1995a) *Ecologies of Knowledge: Work and Politics in Science and Technology*, SUNY Press, Albany, N.Y.

—— ed. (1995b) *The Cultures of Computing*, Sociological Review Monograph Series, Basil Blackwell, Oxford.

Taylor, H.J., C. Kramarae and M. Ebben, eds (1993) *Women, Information Technology and Scholarship*, Center for Advanced Study, Urbana, Ill.

Turkle, S. (1994) 'Constructions and Reconstructions of Self in Virtual Reality: Playing in the MUDs', *Mind, Culture and Activity*, vol. 1, pp. 158–67.

Wagner, I. (1993) 'Women's Voices: The Case of Nursing Information Systems', *AI and Society*, vol. 7, pp. 295–310.

DIALOGUES WITH DOLPHINS

AND OTHER EXTRATERRESTRIALS:

DISPLACEMENTS IN GENDERED SPACE

Mette Bryld

Mysteriously smiling, the dolphin entered the American public and scientific imagination as a new boundary figure around 1960. So powerfully evocative was this dolphin image that it not only quickly spread throughout the rest of the Western world but, adeptly bypassing the Iron Curtain, captured even the Soviet mind. In this chapter I shall retell the stories of the dolphin as an icon of modern displacements in the intermixed discourses on science, gender, race, monsters, nature, gods and goddesses, as well as the past and future of Universal Man.

The dolphin of late modernity is entangled in a complex and fine-meshed net of contextual narratives where very different layers of meaning intertwine. As a fluid boundary figure between the worlds of humankind and others, the reinvented dolphin came to act in seemingly conflicting roles, representing, on the one hand, the displacing forces of a subject, and, on the other, the displaced position of an object. In addition, the sliding shifts in position bring various thematic clusters to the surface. But even if the dolphins may be true masters of mimicry in their mirroring of both strange and funny figures, their images nevertheless all have a common denominator. Aside from such qualities as kindness and consideration, they radiate intelligence and spirituality as well as an eagerness to communicate or even speak in human-like voices.

Some titles and subtitles of books indicate the sudden popularity and newly shaped boundary function of the dolphin. The following represent a few revealing examples: *Man and Dolphin* (1961); *The Voice of*

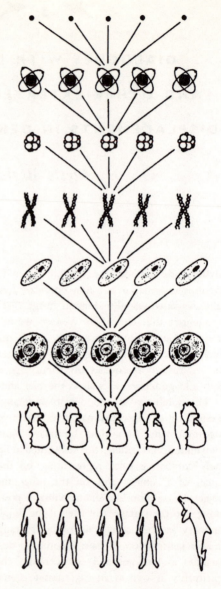

ELEMENTARY PARTICLES
combining to form

ATOMS
combining to form

MOLECULES
combining to form

MACROMOLECULES
combining to form

SIMPLE CELLS
combining to form

COMPLEX CELLS
combining to form

TISSUES AND ORGANS
combining to form

SELF-CONSCIOUS
ORGANISMS

FIGURE 3.1 Evolution According to Peter Russell

(Produced by permission, *The Global Brain Awakens: Our Next Evolutionary Leap*,
© 1995 Peter Russell and Global Brain™, Inc.)

the Dolphins (1961); *The Mind of the Dolphin: A Nonhuman Intelligence* (1967); *The Dolphin: Cousin to Man* (1969); *Mind in the Waters: A Book to Celebrate the Consciousness of Whales and Dolphins* (1974); *Lilly on Dolphins: Humans of the Sea* (1975). These books were widely circulated and republished, some of them in paperback editions. In 1963, the first dolphin movie, *Flipper*, was shown. The following year this film led to the popular television series, which ran for almost twenty-five years. According to the refrain of its jolly signature tune, 'No one you see is smarter than he.' He being, of course, Flipper.

Even today, a diagram in a book by the New Age prophet, Peter Russell, with the significant title *The Global Brain Awakens* (1995), confirms the new relationship between man as terrestrial, and dolphin, as extraterrestrial intelligence (see Figure 3.1). Here Universal Man, embodying 'self-reflecting consciousness', stands side-by-side not with man's traditional boundary figure, the grounded and slow-witted ape, but with the equally intelligent and upward-moving dolphin.[1] The dolphin's privileged yet marginalized position is signalled here: the former, by its equality with man in the sharing of a self-reflecting consciousness; the latter by its exclusive singularity in contrast to the many mirror men and its literal place on the margin.

Apparently this re-mythologized dolphin emerged out of the blue. Prior to 1960, relatively little research had been done on these animals. Not until this year did the echolocating or sonar ability of dolphins become an established scientific fact (Wood 1973: 71–2).[2] Because of their extraterrestrial environment, sea animals were extremely difficult to study. Only a few – of what subsequently became numerous – marinelands or oceanaria existed in the USA at that time.[3] Belonging to the family of cetaceans, a name which originally just meant any sea-monster or huge fish, dolphins were classified as small whales; that is, mammals which live in the sea but breathe air. Having probably once lived on land, these mammals returned to the ocean from which they had originated many millions of years ago. The theory that the dolphin is a species much older than *homo sapiens* undoubtedly eased their transformation into representatives of the divine, ancient wisdom of extraterrestrial cosmic aliens as well as of mother nature.

THE MYTHIC DIVINITY OF THE DOLPHIN

In public lore only vague and fading reminiscences remained of the dolphin's former mythological significances. Occasionally stories were told of the animal's astonishing helpfulness and kindness towards humans in distress. Allegedly it eagerly volunteered to save people who were drowning, loved to play with children, and now and then unselfishly even helped fishermen to catch fish. Behind this domesticated dolphin, however, lies a much more powerful myth of femininity.

Etymologically, the dolphin's Greek name, *delphis*, is related to the word *delphys* meaning womb or vagina. It is the same root that we find in the famous temple or oracle of Delphi, the foundation of which, according to the myths, involved a dolphin. In one of these myths, Apollo is riding a dolphin to the place later known as Delphi; in another, he transforms himself into a dolphin. The famous statues and pictures of a boy on a dolphin show the young sun-god being born out of the sea. Originally the boy on a dolphin therefore had a deep religious significance.[4] So did the even better known dolphin rider, Aphrodite, who was also a Dolphin Goddess.

In all of the ancient Near East, the dolphin was worshipped as the great cosmic mother, the Dolphin Goddess, who presided over fecundity and the mystery of the birth of man, beasts and all living beings. For centuries tales were told of how her representatives, the kind dolphins, accompanied and guided the souls of the dead on their journey across the cosmic sea. The goddess was thus the ruler of travelling, communication between different worlds, rebirth and immortality (Glueck 1966: 380–81). But, as the mythical transformation of Apollo and the girl/boy on a dolphin may suggest, the animal was also imagined in a sexually ambiguous role. It could not only partake in the mythic, feminine forms of womb monster, boy lover or Dolphin Goddess, but could become a hermaphrodite through its bonds to Eros/Phanes. In the shape of the god Triton, it could dramatically change into an aggressive phallos which raped anyone it pleased, girl or boy. Triton's name means three or third; obviously, this divine sex maniac likewise gravitates toward the third sex, embodied in the triadic hermaphrodite of ancient creation myths (Doria 1974: 44).

The constant transformations between womb dolphin and phallic dolphin underline the extreme realism of mythical thought. The shape of the dolphin does resemble both a womb and a penis, and its smooth, streamlined body shows no obvious sexual differences. The penis of the male dolphin appears outside his body only when erect. When not, the genital organ is withdrawn into a slit. Similarly, the nipples of the female are hidden in the two mammary slits. Males and females thus look alike, the only difference being the number of slits. The evocative sexual ambiguity is stressed by yet another ambivalence. The male has voluntary control over his penis, which he, in the words of a dolphin scientist, masters 'in an almost "switch-blade" fashion' (Lilly 1962: 188). Moreover, the genital organ seems powerfully potent. This potency is strongly suggested by a photo which shows how the erect penis, captured by a rope, apparently pulls the rope as the dolphin swims backward away from the edge of the pool (Lilly 1978a). At the same time, however, the masculinity on display is heavily undermined by the strange appearance of the genital. It looks strikingly like a miniature dolphin, a mirror baby, a cute dolphin replicant being born out of the body slit. Obviously, the dolphin, too, falls within the mysterious scope of a 'sex which is not one', so elegantly described by the feminist philosopher Luce Irigaray (Irigaray 1985).

THE ROCKET AND THE DOLPHIN STATE

The dolphin made its début in American society at a time characterized politically by the tensions of a Cold War and the agonizing processes of global decolonization. At the same time there was a fragile *détente*, upheld in the shadow of threats of total nuclear destruction by summit talks, mutual visits and so on between the two superpowers. The only alternative to the holocaust of war was communication, language, mutual understanding. Balancing on the crumbling edge of an abyss, the USA was obviously very much in distress, especially after the Soviets launched the Sputniks in 1957. This strongly suggested the capability of the hostile Communist regime to reach the land of the free with fast, intercontinental missiles, armed perhaps with nuclear warheads.

The opening of the space age was deeply engraved in the new icon of rockets and missiles, the appearance and speed of which are so similar to those of the dolphin. Moreover, both the animal and the rockets that launched beeping Sputnik satellites heralded a revolution in communication. Just like the era itself, this rocket icon therefore ambivalently reflected both war and peace, despair and hope, poverty and prosperity, all embedded in the choice between silence and the exchange of meanings.

Without the warheads, rockets signified progress. Through space travel, based on unarmed rockets, a new and exciting universe could be peacefully explored and profitably conquered (Nye 1994: 226). An advertisement in the *New York Times* (13 February 1962) for a CBS television report of America's first astronaut in orbit made it crystal clear that, although the ascending rocket had a 'red glare' under its tail, it was nevertheless headed for the heavenly stars (emblems of the flag). Besides prosperity and upward mobility, bluntly signified by this rocket, the idea of space travel also carried hopes for a (re-)connection with the divine in one shape or another. In the minds of the scientists involved in the search for extraterrestrial intelligence, which followed in the wake of the space age, divinity took the form of a technological supercivilization somewhere far away in the cosmic sea. To the physicist Philip Morrison, who had participated in the Manhattan Project which had developed the atomic bomb during World War II, and who had co-authored the article (Cocconi and Morrison 1959) that started the scientific quest for otherworldly beings, an ancient, highly advanced society of superior aliens had patiently waited for years for planet Earth to enter into the cosmic communication system by picking up the intelligent signals they transmitted from space. Such signals would not only indicate that technology did not inevitably lead to global self-destruction but would also mark the opening for mankind of an inexhaustible source of wisdom and knowledge. Since this search for what Morrison somewhat later called 'these remote philosophers' (Morrison 1962) coincided with the discovery of dolphin intelligence and mastery of language, the stage was set for the animal's entry into a strange, paradoxical role of boundary figure for both the kind, wise and immensely superior alien, who obviously resided in the extraterrestrial cosmic sea, and the still relatively small and primitive earthling, the Man of Science himself. Due to the circumstances under which the dolphin disclosed its remarkable talent for communication with humans, the playful animal with the Mona Lisa smile also came to represent the cyborg, the space-age fusion of man–machine–nature. I shall later return to these various themes.

As already indicated, the icon of the new era, the missiles and rockets, pointed in different directions: towards the death-world of red Communism and mutual nuclear destruction, as well as towards the life-world of material and spiritual abundance, peace and freedom. Thus it was not only the rockets connected with space exploration and inter-stellar travelling that were associated with the positive values of peace and prosperity. The defence missiles, which were designed to fence off an attack and protect against dangerous alien invasions, likewise belonged to the upholders of life and security. This view was mediated by the newly re-mythologized dolphin. In the *Flipper* film (1963), a young boy, the son of a simple fisherman, makes friends with a dolphin. After a disastrous parasite, called the 'red plague'(!), kills off the fish in the sea, causing a disruption of his family's livelihood, the kind and caring dolphin eventually leads the boy to waters abounding with nourishment. This dolphin may therefore be interpreted as the friendly, feminine, nurturing and life-connoting counter-image of the deadly rockets. The simultaneous rise of the American rocket state and of the new or renewed dolphin iconography is, as suggested earlier, conspicuously congruent. On one side of the spectrum, the stupid, vulgarly yelling cowboy-pilot of the phallic *Dr Strangelove* (1963) is gleefully riding his nuclear device towards Doomsday; on the other, a blond, pre-adolescent and hence pre-phallic dolphin boy overcomes the threats of the death-world by following intelligent, but innocent, missile-shaped nature.

The dolphins, however, like the rockets, retained a tinge of otherness. They were indeed alien creatures, living in a different environment than man. This was an environment which not only suggested the uplifting weightlessness of space but also the heavy heritage of origins, the future as well as the past. Besides the motherly representation we just met in the *Flipper* movie, the dolphin mediated other discourses of ethnicity, gender and childishness (some of these themes were partly present in the dolphin's rebinding of earthlings and cosmic aliens). Intertwined in these discourses was a longing to overcome the split between nature and scientific man. These themes were to continue in the different setting of an upcoming New Age.

The rise of the rocket state witnessed the parallel rise of what might be called a dolphin state, a counterculture which subscribed to such anti-establishment slogans as 'make love, not war'. In this counterculture the dolphin's sex, androgynously betwixt and between, its non-aggressiveness, its playful and yet collectively oriented social organization and graceful harmony with the natural environment, became highly evocative, ideal objects to think with.

As part of an overall alternative belief system, the image of the dolphin now fused with the new *yin* values, found in Eastern philosophy but (allegedly) sadly lacking in the rationalistic world-view of white man. Competing only with the gurus and yogis of India, the dolphin came to embody the soft, feminine values (a caring, nurturing, connecting, communicating, spiritualizing intelligence) with which the New Age movement still identifies. Once again, the dolphin demonstrated its astonishing ability to function as fluid boundary figure between (hu)man and other.

THE TALKING DOLPHIN CYBORG

The author of the dolphin script from the age of dissolving modernity was a medical doctor, John C. Lilly, who in 1959 set up his own Communication Research Institute with laboratories in Florida and the

Virgin Islands. Here research was done on methods of communication between man and other species – that is, interspecies communication. The studies also focused on the structure and functions of the brain as well as the psychology of man and of marine mammals, the latter being primarily the bottlenose dolphin, which is the smiling one. The previous year, Lilly had made headlines by announcing the possibility of talking dolphins, and in the following years he frequently put forward his opinion, in interviews and so on, about the high, perhaps even superior, intelligence of these animals. In 1960, his ideas hit the front page of the *New York Times* (21 June). The full impact of his views, however, was only felt a year later with the publication of his book, *Man and Dolphin*, an event which was heralded by the extremely influential *Life* magazine in a widely read feature (28 July 1961). From then on, intellectually conversant porpoises with skyrocketing IQs became part of the public imagination. No matter how hard many scientists tried to uproot these annoyingly unscientific beliefs, the myth lived on. Decades later, two despairing dolphin researchers, Louis M. Herman and William Tavolga, summed up the situation as follows:

> Over the years, the hypothesis of a natural language in dolphins, vigorously promoted by Lilly, has failed to receive analytic, experimental, or conceptual support. Lilly's pronouncements are largely behind the popular myth of 'talking' dolphins. Partly through uncritical publicity, partly through public gullibility, and partly through poor science, the myth persists today despite many attempts to lay the ghost to rest. (Herman 1980: 176–7)[5]

Having so often been fooled by real science, the gullible public preferred to side with Doctor Lilly, the ventriloquist who could restore the broken bond to nature as well as to friendly non-human species.

Lilly had fostered the idea of actually speaking with alien species while working at the Laboratory of Neurophysiology of the US National Institute of Mental Health, where he eventually became chief of the Section on Cortical Integration. Having had no success in communicating with monkeys, chimpanzees, dogs or cats, whose brains were found to be ridiculously small, his attention was directed by a whale expert to some other brains really worthy of research. In contrast to the animals mentioned, the whale family seemed to possess 'a brain equal to and larger than the human, and presumably equally complicated' (Lilly 1962: 45). (At that time, I might add, the capacity of computers, all of them very large, grew with their size. They were often called electronic brains.)

Between 1955 and 1957, Lilly conducted his research on the dolphin brain in the laboratory of the Florida Marine Studios. His anatomical as well as electrical investigations into this *terra incognita* confirmed that the animal was, indeed, not only an excellent, but probably the only existing, example of a highly developed non-human intelligence on Earth. The dolphin brain, Lilly claimed, was as complex as ours, and its size and weight even larger (1,700 grammes to Universal Dolphin versus only 1,450 grammes to Universal Man).

While mapping, as he called it, the brain of test animal Number 6 of the series, Lilly suddenly made an astonishing discovery, which prompted him to give up his governmental job at the Institute of Mental Health and open his communication centre in the Virgin Islands, so suitably named for the task of exploration. From Number 6 he had learned that dolphins could be taught to speak English.

Evidently, the doctor's expectations of such interspecies communication were numerous. I shall mention only three of them. First, a dialogue with dolphins would prepare mankind for the encounter with extraterrestrials in space, a topic which, as previously mentioned, was very much on the agenda at that time. Second, the establishment of a dialogue with these animals might also lead to a much-needed improvement of the communication between man and woman. This advance, which was added half-jokingly to the list, revealed Lilly's suspicion that dolphins connoted femininity. Third, the intelligible voice of the dolphin would severely shatter, if not destroy forever, anthropocentrism. No longer would man be the exclusive top of the evolutionary ladder. (Translated into the language of feminism: the position of Universal Man might be changed by the subversive role of a speaking, and especially an English-speaking, dolphin.)

In all its ghastliness, the story of Lilly's expedition inside the dolphin's skull deserves to be retold. Having lost five animals using full anaesthesia, the doctor chose a different approach to Number 6. After restraining the animal by inserting its beak into a hole in a board, so that it could only move 2–3 inches (5–8 centimetres), and after injecting a local anaesthetic into its head, he used a carpenter's hammer to pound a sleeve guide (a kind of hollow needle) about 30 millimetres long into the animal's head. Through this sleeve guide, and through the skin, blubber and muscles, electrodes were placed into the brain and 'the long, slow, and patient examination of this huge brain by electrical stimuli' started. The idea of the electrodes was, in Lilly's clinical discourse, to have 'push-button control of the experience of specific emotion by animals in whose brains we have placed wires in the proper places' (Lilly 1962: 34).

By locating the areas of the brain that responded to the electric current with either positive or negative emotions – that is, with pleasure or pain – the 'human operator' could provoke intense rewarding or intense punishing experiences in the animal, or, for that matter, in humans on whom the method was also used. In Number 6, Lilly was trying to pinpoint the centre of pleasure. If activated, the animal might become so thrilled that it took 'control' and pushed the switch itself. Thus Lilly could not only test his intelligence (Number 6 was a male) but speed up learning processes as well. In this case, the current was the carrot. In the next test, using dolphin Number 7, a female labelled by the doctor a real cry-baby, the method of punishing stimuli was tried. The 'cry-baby' had to operate the switch to shut off the punishment. (Both dolphins quickly learned the trick; both died.)

Let us return to Lilly's experiment and his discovery of the dolphin's linguistic abilities. After the electrodes had been slowly, very slowly, forced down about 60 millimetres into the brain, Number 6 started responding violently. Aside from moving restlessly around in his restraints, he vocalized in 'dolphinese', emitting whistles, buzzings, barks and other noises, the meaning of which the doctor only realized later when he replayed his tape recording. Listening to the tapes, he felt certain that the dolphin, in a Donald Duck quacking way, had been mimicking human laughter as well as some of the technical data he, the doctor, had recited during the experiment. This became especially clear, the scientist claimed, when the tapes were slowed down to half or one-quarter speed.

After this, Lilly felt that he had good reasons to advocate an interspecies communication through what he called an 'education in humanity' of the other. Sponsored by agencies like NASA, the US Navy and the US Air Force, Lilly optimistically continued the project (with and without electrodes) until 1968, when the funding finally stopped and he allegedly came to realize that he had been imprisoning his friends, the dolphins, in a 'concentration camp'. Revolting against the intrusions into their brains, five animals had committed suicide by refusing to eat or breathe. Lilly then set the remaining three free and gave up the research (Lilly 1973: 70).[6] But for a long time, the serious master of science had obviously been controlled by a laughing monster who had carnivalized the very concept of communication.

Displacements nevertheless unsettle this discourse. On the one hand, Lilly's setting is, obviously, deeply embedded in the mechanistic scientific paradigm; nature must reveal her secrets on the doctor's agonizing terms. But on the other, a nature of extraterrestrial origin suddenly discloses a huge brain which, with wires in the proper places, even seems to manifest a desire for communication with scientific Man. In nature's new porpoise consciousness, purpose was surfacing, too.

Properly (re-)constructed by the dolphin scientist, the recorded and slowly replayed voice of the dolphin – that is, of (extra-)terrestrial intelligence – became a representation of a very advanced, highly communicative, non-human species on, as well as beyond, Earth. Paradoxically, it simultaneously represented scientific man himself. Vis-à-vis the divine extraterrestrials, he was but a small child; in the same way that the dolphin, seemingly babbling his first English words, was an infant vis-à-vis the scientist.

BOYS ON A CYBORG DOLPHIN: COMMUNICATIONS WITH COSMOS

In the next narrative strand, our dolphin protagonist moves into yet another context: that of the new cosmology, which science began to advocate in the years following World War II. In order to clarify this new view of cosmos, we shall leave the animals to themselves for a while.

In the first half of this century, the universe was perceived as a dead and barren space by the prevailing astronomic theory. Being the result of a cosmic catastrophe, a chance collision between two stars, our planetary system would have to be unique; the enormous distances between the stars made it highly unlikely that such a fruitful collision could ever recur. Earth (and perhaps a few other planets in our solar system) floated as isolated islands of intelligence in the vast and lifeless cosmic sea. In this universe, man could truly feel supreme.

In accordance with the remappings of Earth and mind after the Second World War, cosmography, trying to reunite the worlds, underwent radical changes during the 1950s. No longer a silent, desert void, the universe was transformed into a kind of supermarket filled with other suns and planets and hence probably with life and intelligence. In early 1962, a Dr Brown suggested this metaphor when he told a US congressional committee, pondering together with some scientists the existence of life in other worlds, that life 'is a very abundant commodity in our universe' (*New York Times*, 23 March 1962). So was superior intelligence. As a huge number of planets had been formed much earlier than Earth, the beings of these ancient worlds would have to be much older and inconceivably much more technologically, morally and intellectually advanced than man. Compared to this superior, extraterrestrial intelligence, man, the offspring of a young generation of planets, appeared as a new-born baby. Confirming what the public, watching UFOs and Sputniks in the sky as well as the alien monsters of the numerous SF films of the 1950s, had suspected all the time, cosmology drew up a new map which clearly indicated that supremacy was changing hands.

A universe with highly intelligent, civilized aliens now became part of scientific imagination too, and from time to time the media reported on the new horizons opening to mankind. 'Tuning In on Other Worlds. If civilized beings exist in space, a project now beginning may permit us to communicate with them', read a headline in the *New York Times* (13 March 1960). Not very surprisingly, the article, written by a chief missiles adviser to the Intelligence Department of the Army, strongly favoured the idea of 'listening for the voices of the "others"'. In undertaking this enterprise, he suggested, we might become the equals of possibly existing astropolitan communities, 'linked together by a wonderful commerce of communication'. The new commodity, well suited to interstellar commerce, was information.

If, as many scientists caught in the rigid concepts of evolution thought, cosmic supercivilizations did exist, the information we might receive from them would, of course, be of profound significance. Professor R.N. Bracewell at Stanford University, California, put forward the idea that an ancient association, consisting of civilizations incredibly more advanced than our own, might already have launched a satellite into orbit around the sun, trying to make contact with us (*New York Times*, 20 June 1960). The report of Bracewell's alien messenger in the sky was published on the front page of the newspaper only the day before it introduced Lilly's intelligent, and perhaps superior, dolphins. The images of divine and helpful supercivilizations and of the friendly, talking dolphins began to merge in both the scientific and public mind. Both involved notions of interspecies communication and of receiving information which could solve nearly all of humanity's problems.

Being the one expert who had actually more or less spoken with an ET, Lilly was invited to the first conference ever held on extraterrestrial intelligence. It opened on 1 November 1961, at the Green Bank Observatory in West Virginia. Less than a dozen scientists participated, some of them very prominent (one, Melvin Calvin, was awarded the Nobel Prize in Chemistry during his stay). Thus all the expertise needed for a thorough scientific discussion on the cosmic connection was assembled. In his presentation, Lilly played the tapes with the 'English'-speaking dolphins and talked about the social attitude of these animals which helped and took care of each other and humans in distress. Since the world, or rather humanity, was deeply in distress because of the threats of red Communism, Lilly did not forget to mention the possible military use of these speedy sea animals. The dolphins could rescue pilots from planes crashed at sea, scout out enemy submarines, serve as detection-proof delivery systems for nuclear warheads to be detonated in foreign harbours and so on. Having learned English, Lilly suggested, the animals might also 'sneak up on an enemy submarine sitting on the bottom of the sea and shout something into the listening gear, as if this were a human communicating with them' (Lilly 1962: 168–9). (Oh boy, would that frighten the bastards!) 'We were all totally enthralled by these reports', the host of the conference, the astronomer Frank Drake, recalls. 'We felt some of the excitement in store for us when we encounter nonhuman intelligence of extraterrestrial origin' (Drake and Sobel 1992: 58).

So captivated and thrilled were the participants by this representation of the dolphin that they formed a kind of brotherhood or lodge at the termination of the conference and christened it The Order of the Dolphin. In the following years, a few other prominent scientists involved in the search for extraterrestrial intelligence were admitted (among others, the Soviet Russian astrophycisist I.S. Shklovsky). From the new Nobel laureate, Calvin, each of the human dolphins got a silver tie pin as an emblem of membership; it was a reproduction of an old Greek coin showing a boy on a dolphin. What does the emblem signify? (1) The picture of the boy on the dolphin identified the Man of Science, searching for intelligence, with the ancient dolphin boy, Apollo, whose transformation into a dolphin or whose ride on the back of the animal is, as mentioned above, culturally associated with both the founding of Delphi and with the rise of the sun – a new bright civilization being born from the womb of the sea. (2) It also connected scientific man on a dolphin with the gigantic space programme, the Apollo project, which President Kennedy had launched less than six months earlier (25 May) in order to beat the Soviets to the moon and re-establish the techno-scientific image of the USA so badly hurt by Gagarin's recent flight. (3) Behind the Apollo(s) on the profit-promising coin, the dolphin lures as a carrier of displacements, of shifting significances, in the cargo of which the parallel formation of a grim and beastly rocket state and a mythic, smiling and humane dolphin state mixes with the images of divinely intelligent extraterrestrial aliens beaming data of wisdom down to a globe in distress. Like the oracular utterances of the Delphian dolphin Pythia, this information would be obscure until decoded. But was that not what Lilly had been doing when he slowed down the tapes and suddenly caught the message of test animal Number 6? The decoding would hardly offer any problem. If so, the cosmic aliens might perhaps teach us the equivalent of dolphinese: 'There might be an attention-getting signal', Morrison said, according to the *New York Times*, 'followed by a "language lesson" and then the equivalent of one volume of an encyclopaedia. This would be followed by further calling, a further lesson, and another volume, and so forth' (4 February 1962).

BETWEEN MOTHER GODDESSES AND MONSTERS: COHABITATION IN A FLOODED HOUSE

Acting as a substitute for both technological man/the man of science and technological superman/extraterrestrial intelligence, our dolphin has now gone through several displacements. Nevertheless, an excess of representation lingered on because of the boundary function of the signifier. Something did not fit; something continuously destabilized the displacements. The dolphin did not properly mirror the Man of Science, however small and primitive he might be compared with a godlike, alien scientist; nor did she merge completely into the fatherly Great Other. On the contrary, an unpleasant question kept popping up in the minds of our technology-fixated scientists: how could the dolphin, lacking manipulative hands and, consequently, tools, represent a technological civilization, not to mention a cosmic supercivilization? With nothing but flippers, the animal was clearly unable to build even the radio telescopes necessary for either listening to or transmitting signals through space. Moreover, it seemed unlikely that the 'superior intelligence' of the dolphins had developed in the primordial waters. In its feature on the Green Bank conference, the *New York Times* summarized the problem in the following way: 'It is possible that their superior intelligence is a heritage of their life ashore. Hence it may be that such intelligence would not arise on a completely oceanic planet' (4 February 1962).

Some scientists tried to bypass the problem by suggesting that the dolphins might develop 'a technological society if given sufficient time' (Cameron 1963: 312). Evidently, such a far-reaching perspective could not save the day for the dolphin fans: her lack, her missing link, was too obvious, too present, too disturbing. Nonetheless, though fading from the scripts of hard science, the dolphin representation of aliens from outer space never quite disappeared. In 1987, at an international symposium on bioastronomy in Hungary, a woman researcher from a US oceanarium used an experiment in which she had taught dolphins sign language as an argument for the possibility of reaching a mutual understanding with the 'real' extraterrestrials (Strelnickij 1988: 60–61).[7]

The dolphins, however, did not quite fit into the patterns surrounding the almighty Father. Consequently, another narrative strand came to the fore, one which had already been suggested by the words about civilizing the dolphins, the education in humanity, which Lilly had used when writing his first book. In this narrative the discourses of ethnicity, gender and childishness dominate, reversing the dolphin's representation of the Man of Science and his Great omnipotent Other, and of the utopian future as well. Instead, she becomes a figure of a nostalgic past from which modern, scientific man had been literally split off. Thus the theme of splits in more than one sense dominates the following quotation:

> [M]an is said to be the most intelligent species because of what he does with his huge brain. May there not be other paths for large brains to take, especially if they live immersed in some other element than air?
>
> In the case of the Cetacea which are without the benefit of hands or outside constructions of any sort [sic!], they may have taken the path of legends and verbal traditions rather than that of written records. (Lilly 1962: 95)[8]

Forgetting the flippers, Lilly focuses instead on the dolphin's strange bodily split(s), which I mentioned earlier, and which here represent(s) the obviously missing genital organ as well as the smiling but toothed mouth. Having been transformed into woman, child and ethnic other, the dolphin vocalizes not only its own lack of technological tools but also the non-technological paradise lost by scientific man. Here, legends and dreamtime, rather than technology, were thought to define existence.

Since the electronic devices (that is, the electrodes) with which the doctor had tried to erase the split between his world and the lost world of legends of innocence did not result in establishing the much-wanted connection between the species, Lilly decided to abandon the quasi-divine model of communication, featuring man of science vis-à-vis the superintelligent extraterrestrial father. Instead, he substituted a human 'mother–child' model of teaching and learning. The dolphin was positioned as the infant, while the scientist was represented by a nurturing virgin-mother. Day and night, for a long period, the human mother and the dolphin child were to live together in a home which, neither terrestrial nor extraterrestrial, transgressed the normal boundaries

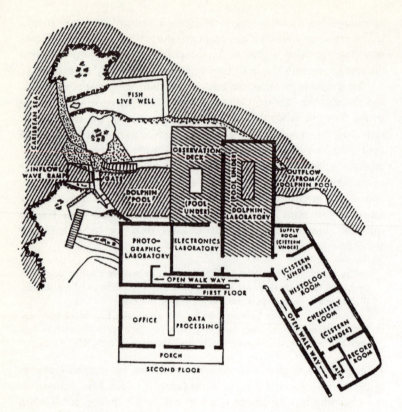

FIGURE 3.2 The plan of the Virgin Islands institute for the experiment in wet live-in. (Lilly 1967a: 226)

between land and sea. Part of the building of The Communication Research Institute in the Virgin Islands was consequently flooded with sea water about 22 inches (56 centimetres) deep in order to carry out an experiment in 'wet live-in'.

After various introductory experiments of interspecies cohabitation, the definitive flooded-house programme started in the summer of 1965 and lasted for two and a half months. The plan was to continue it by means of a more permanent 'man–dolphin' habitat, where the dolphin would be able to come and 'go' as a genuine member of a human family. Figure 3.2 shows Lilly's plan of the Virgin Islands institute, which represents the relations between the sea (nature), the flooded areas (the encounter zone), and the non-flooded offices, and so on (culture) in this living-in experiment.

The plan clearly shows that the flooded area, the observatory deck and the dolphin laboratory are hatched in a way similar to the hatching that indicates the Carribean Sea. However, the lines have been reversed, indicating the special function of this ambiguous encounter zone. Here, nature's and culture's separated bodies were rearranged, reassembled and (re-)united into a new bodyscape.

Metaphorically, the heavily framed, white culture areas form a fragmented yet interconnected body with the physiological processes designated by the rooms of histology and chemistry at the right, and the brain, the head, processing data, in the middle. The 'fish live well' (!), which, although white, is not framed in black, may indicate the displaced location of food and desire, the stomach, the lower part of the body. In the flooded zone, however, white, non-coloured culture, digesting and processing the data, elsewhere represented by the large white squares, has shrunk to a tiny white square, placed on the *outside*, on the observatory deck, while the waves of the food-processing sea, represented by the hatched areas, reappear on the *inside*, in the dolphin laboratory, which also serves as the combined living and bedroom area of mother (woman) and nature (dolphin).

Traditional dichotomies set up by separating culture's white enclosures from the hatched areas of nature fall apart. (In reality, the so-called 'pool under' in the flooded zone designates one and the same thing – the dolphin pool below.) Copulating in nets of displacements, white culture and coloured, hatching nature, inside and outside, brain and stomach, thinking and eating, start proliferating hybrids.

Evidently the respective agents of nature and culture were chosen because of their displaced representations: the dolphin for its brains, not normally ascribed to mother nature, and the woman for her soft and oceanic nature, definitely not part of the image of scientific man. But that which set them apart from their parental environment was, of course, precisely what united them in the encounter zone of their flooded home.

Embodying the location of innocence, the Virgin Islands, a floating, young and virginal mermaid, Margaret Howe, played the part of the (single) mother, educating the dolphin-infant and vacuum-cleaning the house while wading in sea water to her knees. Lilly's role was that of the very distant father. Spending most of his time hallucinating on

LSD in a self-constructed water tank (as if playing a dolphin himself), he rarely visited the project. Thus nobody would intervene in the dyad between Peter Dolphin and Margaret Mermaid.

For a time Margaret had wavered about whom to choose for the baby part, the young and vigorous Peter or the reserved Pamela with the good pronunciation. The pronunciation was important, for Margaret had solemnly pledged that 'no matter how long it takes, no matter how much work, *this dolphin is going to learn to speak English!*' (Lilly 1967a: 218). But as Pam was very shy with humans, having been previously speared several times by a diver in the second *Flipper* movie,[9] Margaret finally settled for the very outgoing Peter, a choice that she came to regret when she discovered the implications.

Apart from the fact that his pronunciation never reached Pam's level, Margaret suddenly found out that she had become the other dolphin in Peter's life – that is, the object of his sexual desires. As he began to open his slits, his mouth with the 88 very sharp teeth, 'still capable', she wrote, 'of drawing blood', and the genital slit with his erected penis, the spell of innocent interconnectedness was somewhat broken. Though she was terrified at first, she realized that Peter's education in humanity must be paralleled by her education in dolphinity, and therefore succumbed to 'lusty little Peter' and his clever tricks of wooing. In Margaret's account, the dolphin gradually and intelligently changes from a wild animal, who tried to rape her, to a seductive gentleman, who gently ran his full set of teeth up and down her legs in order to arouse her. 'Peter led the way', she claims, and she satisfied his sexual desires by masturbating him. As she became his dolphin, he became her man/husband.

After the experiment, Lilly informs us, Margaret, 'like the woman with the chimpanzees in Africa, married her photographer' (an epidemic?) and started a (new) family. The role model referred to was Jane Goodall, who had just become famous for her research on non-human primates in 'the wilds of Tanzania' (Haraway 1989: 136). But unlike Goodall, who began graduate work at Cambridge early in her field studies and eventually took a doctorate, Margaret Howe held on to her intellectual innocence during the entire experiment in wet live-in. While working as a hostess at a remote mountain-top restaurant in the Virgin Islands, she by chance entered into a conversation with one of the guests, Carl Sagan, the astronomer and ardent hunter for extraterrestrial intelligence, who was visiting the laboratory. As she complained of her uneventful and uninteresting days (she was hostess only at night), Sagan introduced her to the multi-scientist Gregory Bateson, who at that time was in charge of Lilly's laboratory, and 'soon Margaret was

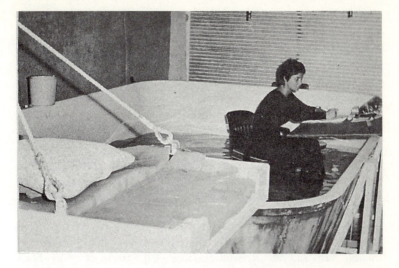

PLATE 3.1 The dolphin mother, Margaret Howe, at the setup for one of her preliminary experiments in wet live-in. The tank contains 18 inches (46 cm) of water. To the left is Margaret's bed. The dolphin infant, Pam, is in the tank, but is not seen in the picture. (Lilly 1967a: Plate 12)

PLATE 3.2 Margaret Mermaid and Peter Dolphin in a three-way telephone conversation during the cohabitation. (Lilly 1967a: Plate 27)

working with dolphins' (Sagan 1975: 174). That was in early 1964, sixteen months before she became director of the laboratory herself and entered into the mothering–marrying arrangement with Peter D. Up to that time, 'she had seen dolphins once briefly in a Florida dolphin circus' (Lilly 1967a: 227). As Bateson soon left and Lilly was busy hallucinating in his isolation tank, the realization of the ambitious flooded-house programme came to depend almost exclusively on her.

Without the intellectual 'burdens' of a scientific education, Margaret Howe was actually better suited than Jane Goodall for the precast role of mediating link between the man of science and his 'naive', non-human other.

PARADOXES OF A DOLPHIN STATE

Margaret and Peter did not act exclusively as characters in the story of scientific man and his successful unveiling of the truths of nature. They also forecast the dolphin narrative of the following decades. Thus the forming of an encounter zone between the two worlds of culture/science and nature already anticipates and mediates a new dolphin icon: the dolphin of the counterculture, of environmental movements like Greenpeace and of New Age ideology. In these discourses the 'lack' of the dolphin, its inability to manipulate nature through technology, becomes a virtue. This may be illustrated by reference to the images contrasting the human with a thumb and the dolphin without thumb that were used by an astrology-oriented psychoanalyst and New Age scholar, Ralph Metzner, whom I interviewed in San Francisco in 1994. Having been very prominent in the consciousness-raising counterculture of the 1960s, Metzner is today deeply occupied with developing an ecological consciousness.[10] Whales and dolphins have bigger brains than humans, he argues, yet these mammals are beautifully adapted to their natural environment. The trouble of humankind, therefore, originates in the combination of brain and opposable thumb: 'Because with the opposable thumb you can make stuff. You can make tools, weapons, and manipulate your environment, and the whales and dolphins don't do that.'

Furthermore, the mysterious split(s) came to signify the healing and wholeness of the two sexes in the formation of a borderline sex, strong womanhood and soft manhood united into a uni-sex, which might not only swing both ways in sexual preferences but also represent the ideals and high morals of simultaneous power and impotence, of non-aggressive, phallic–non-phallic empowerment. Embodying the alternative to patriarchal and hierarchal Western dualism, the dolphin of the countercultures incorporates a reunion of body and mind, of (hu)man and nature, of society and natural law. Why? Because the cetacean, partly due to Lilly, had become the very image of a monstrous paradox: soft and watery nature, endowed with intelligence, language and ethics.[11]

Numerous examples of this can be found in the anthology *Mind in the Waters*, edited in 1974 by Joan McIntyre, president of Project Jonah, a Californian Save the Whales organization. Here the key theme is the reinvention of a mythic dolphin whose non-manipulative intelligence is oriented solely towards warm interpersonal relationships, collectivity, culture, 'humor, empathy, self-control', joyful sexual play and so on. While sharing and mutual assistance have high priority, the delphinic adherents of a socialism with 'a human face' nonetheless know and respect the difference between yours and mine. Obviously, this dolphin state does not involve abolishment of private ownership.

Parallel to the codex of an ideal community worth imitating, the magnificent animal, herself evidently influenced by the upcoming bohemian colonies and expanding personal-growth centres,[12] could also show humans the way back to the (re)birth of a holistic consciousness. McIntyre explains:

> The water is the cradle of Cetacean consciousness. And there, in the strength and power of the sea, is the place to explore the mind. When a human enters the water, what becomes apparent is the integral connection between mind and body that the sea forces on her creatures. Without the alienating presence of objects and equipment, with only the naked body encasing the floating mind, the two, split by technological culture, are one again. The mind enters a different modality, where time, weight, and one's self are experienced holistically. (McIntyre 1974: 94)

This dolphin becomes the emblem of non-technological innocence and exotic beauty and harmony, of the romanticized aesthetics into which both the East and femininity are once more embedded.

However, it would be a belittlement of our subject to let go with this statement. As a fluid signifier, a true boundary figure, the dolphin represents more. In her own way, her paradoxicality also mirrors the brainy mother who mattered so much to so many of us, Western feminism itself.

CONCLUSION

The dramatic remappings of geographic and cosmographic political and mental borderlines that followed in the wake of the Second World War entailed new boundary figures. Few animals, if any, were better suited than the dolphin for the roles of translating and mediating in a world on the threshold of an age of communication and information. Beeping as mysteriously as a Sputnik satellite and floating as rapidly through space as the new commodities, brains, this marine mammal incarnated an upcoming postmodernity.

A 'creature of the interface', the porpoise watcher, Ken Norris, once aptly called it (Pryor 1975: 17). Living where air and water join, the animal meets the period's strong and still continuing quest for hybridizations, for the binding together and rematching of what used to be very odd and incompatible worlds. The worlds of communism and capitalism, rearmament and peace, science and spirituality, immortal aliens from outer space and mortal earthlings, masculinity and femininity, *yin* and *yang*, whites and non-whites, nature and intelligence, animals and humans and technology – embarking on ships of new metamorphoses, all these categories break out of the old order of things and interface in the strange smile of the dolphin.

NOTES

1. Cf. Haraway's study of the boundary function of primates (Haraway 1989). The dolphin may be seen as the oceanic or cosmic Doppelgänger of jungle-bred primates.

2. 'Sonar' is an acronym for SOund NAvigation and Ranging. Originally it referred to man-made equipment designed to detect submarines or mines by emitting pulses of sound which returned as echoes. The words 'echolation' and 'echoranging' are derived from the echoing which indicates where the object is located and how far away it is.

3. Marine Studios, Florida, built in 1938, reopened in a new form after the war. Here, the first 'educated' dolphin, Flippy, made its public appearance in the early 1950s, after a couple of years of training. Until this time, most people had assumed that, of the marine animals, only sea lions could be taught tricks (Jacobs 1960: 144). In 1954, a gigantic Marineland opened in California. Twenty years later, the USA had fifteen oceanaria/marinelands and at least as many laboratories and dolphin research centres (Cousteau and Diolé 1975: 278–9).

4. In 1957, the US movie *Boy on a Dolphin*, filmed in Greece and starring, respectively, Alan Ladd and Sophia Loren as the good, blond doctor and the innocent, alien sea diver/dolphin, reintroduced the boy-on-a-dolphin theme in an Americanized, secular setting.

5. See also Bryden and Harrison 1986: 59 and 163.

6. Lilly, the dolphin man, transgressed cultural boundaries himself. Born in 1915, he transformed from a rather traditional scientist into a guru of the counterculture during the late 1960s and early 1970s. (I am indebted to Susan Leigh Star for the information on Lilly's great significance in the counterculture.) High on psychedelic drugs, for several years he considered himself the medium

and emissary of a cosmic supercivilization which allegedly used him for their channelings. During the 1970s he resumed his research and formed a Human/ Dolphin Foundation in California to help in the efforts to communicate with dolphins. Due not least to his own statements on the superiority of dolphins, time had seen attitudes change towards a demand for protection of these mammals, a view which he now strongly supported. Lilly's function as a scientist of the New Age has not yet ended. In 1995, he was invited as a delegate to the annual Celebration of the Whales conference, held by the Hawaii-based environmental organization Whales Alive (*Ocean Alert*, Winter/Spring 1995: 13).

7. The title of the Russian article referred to here means 'Where are you, brothers in intelligence?' (a very good question indeed!). In *Mind in the Waters*, the cetaceans still figure as 'the most likely candidates for the intelligent non-human life that we occasionally seek to communicate with in space projects' (McIntyre 1974: 53). This anthology, however, sides not with science but with nature.

8. In a chapter entitled 'Some of My Best Friends Are Dolphins', the astronomer Carl Sagan repeats the view of whales and dolphins as possible 'human Homers before the invention of writing' (Sagan 1975: 178; see also Sagan 1973: 128). The image of the intellectual, floating, singing and story-telling cetacean became part of the new textuality with which the counterculture reconstructed the animal.

9. In May 1965, Lilly told a conference of drug-positive psychiatrists and therapists that he had successfully treated the traumatized Pam (as well as other, non-traumatized dolphins) with LSD and with 'tender loving care', provided by what he called 'an "ideal" mother', Margaret Howe (Abramson 1967: 48–9).

10. R. Metzner is president of the Green Earth Foundation and teaches at the California Institute of Integral Studies. In the 1960s, he did psychedelic research at Harvard with the well-known countercultural figures, Timothy Leary and Richard Alpert (alias Baba Ram Dass), and issued the book *Maps of Consciousness*. He has recently contributed to the anthology *Ecopsychology* (1995), edited by T. Roszak, M. Gomes and A. Kanner (Sierra Club Books, San Francisco).

11. The image seems to have played an important role in the reticence of US scientists to undertake invasive research on the dolphin brain. Instead, they preferred to enter into the skull of the ape. Two cetacean scientists state that in the USA, 'it is less acceptable to undertake invasive research upon dolphins than upon apes, although the former are, in general, far less threatened and their mental faculties are not known to be more advanced'. Not inhibited by such social taboos, Soviet scientists got 'virtual monopoly on the physiology of the dolphin brain' (Bullock and Gurevich 1979: 51). The sudden explosion of Soviet research on dolphins, resulting in a flow of publications in the late 1960s and in the forming of a veritable army of investigators, may be traced back to the translation into Russian of Lilly's *Man and Dolphin* in 1965. The following year the Minister of Fisheries issued a decree forbidding the killing and capturing of dolphins for non-scientific (read: non-military) purposes in the Black Sea and in the Sea of Azov. Cf. *Izvestija*, 13 March 1966, where Lilly is also mentioned as a great dolphin specialist, who has shown that the brain size and so on of this mammal is 'strikingly close to our own'.

12. As, for example, Esalen in California; cf. Alexander 1992. See also Lilly's description of his workshop at the Esalen Institute, where he taught the enthusiastic participants how to be dolphins (Lilly 1973: 108–11).

REFERENCES

Abramson, H., ed. (1967) *The Use of LSD in Psychotherapy and Alcoholism*, The Bobbs-Merill Company, Indianapolis, New York and Kansas City.

Alexander, K. (1992) 'Roots of the New Age', in J. Lewis and J. Melton, eds, *Perspectives on the New Age*, State University of New York Press, New York.

Bryden, M. and R. Harrison, eds (1986) *Research on Dolphins*, Clarendon Press, Oxford.

Bullock, T. and V. Gurevich (1979) 'Soviet Literature on the Nervous System and Psychobiology of Cetacea', *International Review of Neurobiology*, 21, pp. 47–127.

Cameron, A., ed. (1963) *Interstellar Communication*, Institute for Space Studies NASA, New York and Amsterdam.

Cocconi, G. and P. Morrison (1959) 'Searching for Interstellar Communications', *Nature* 184, p. 844. Reproduced in D. Goldsmith, ed., *The Quest for Extraterrestrial Life: A Book Of Readings*, University Science Books, Mill Valley, Calif., 1980, pp. 102–4.

Cousteau, J.-Y. and P. Diolé (1975) *Dolphins*, Doubleday & Co., New York.

Doria, C. (1974) 'The Dolphin Rider', in J. McIntyre, ed., *Mind in the Waters: A Book to Celebrate the Consciousness of Whales and Dolphins*, Sierra Club Books, San Francisco, pp. 33–51.

Drake, F. and D. Sobel (1992) *Is Anyone Out There? The Scientific Search for Extraterrestrial Intelligence*, Delacorte Press, New York.

Glueck, N. (1966) *Deities and Dolphins: The Story of the Nebataeans*, Cassell, London.

Haraway, D. (1989) *Primate Visions: Gender, Race, and Nature in the World of Modern Science*, Routledge, New York.

Herman, L., ed. (1980) *Cetacean Behavior: Mechanisms and Functions*, John Wiley & Sons, New York and Toronto.

Irigaray, L. (1985) *This Sex which Is Not One*, Cornell University Press, Ithaca, N.Y.

Jacobs, J. (1960) *Marineland Diver*, Dodd, Mead & Co, New York.

Jeffrey, F. and J.C. Lilly (1990) *John Lilly, so far…*, Jeremy P. Tarcher, Inc., Los Angeles.

Lilly, J.C (1962) *Man and Dolphin*, Victor Gollancz, London (1st edn, New York, 1961).

——— (1967a) *The Mind of the Dolphin: A Nonhuman Intelligence*, Doubleday & Co, New York.

——— (1967b) 'Dolphin-Human Relation and LSD 25', in H. Abramson, ed., *The Use of LSD in Psychotherapy and Alcoholism*, The Bobbs-Merill Company, Indianapolis, New York and Kansas City, pp. 47–52.

———— (1973) *The Centre of the Cyclone: An Autobiography of Inner Space*, Calder & Boyars, London (1st edn, New York, 1972).

———— (1975) *Lilly on Dolphins: Humans of the Sea*, Anchor Books, New York.

———— (1978a) *Communication between Man and Dolphin: The Possibilities of Talking to Other Species*, Crown Publishers, New York.

———— (1978b) *The Scientist: A Novel Autobiography*, Bantam Books, Toronto, New York, London and Sydney.

McIntyre, J., ed. (1974) *Mind in the Waters: A Book to Celebrate the Consciousness of Whales and Dolphins*, Sierra Club Books, San Francisco.

Morrison, P. (1962) 'Interstellar Communication', *Bulletin of the Philosophical Society of Washington* 16, p. 58. Reproduced in D. Goldsmith, ed., *The Quest for Extraterrestrial Life: A Book of Readings*, University Science Books, Mill Valley, Calif., 1980, pp. 122–31.

Nye, D. (1994) *American Technological Sublime*, MIT Press, Cambridge, Mass. and London.

Pryor, K. (1975) *Lads before the Wind*, Harper & Row, New York and London.

Russell, P. (1995) *The Global Brain Awakens: Our Next Evolutionary Leap*, Global Brain, Inc., Palo Alto (1st edn, J.P. Tarcher, Los Angeles, 1983).

Sagan, C., ed. (1973) *Communication With Extraterrestrial Intelligence (CETI)*, MIT Press, Cambridge, Mass. and London.

Sagan, C. (1975) *The Cosmic Connection: An Extraterrestrial Perspective*, Dell Books, New York.

Stenuit, R. (1969) *The Dolphin: Cousin to Man*, Penguin Books, Harmondsworth.

Strelnickij, V. (1988) 'Gde vy, brat'ja po razumu?', *Zemlja i Vselennaja* 3, pp. 58–62.

Szilard, L. (1992) *The Voice of the Dolphins and Other Stories*, Stanford University Press, Stanford (1st edn, 1961).

Wood, F. (1973) *Marine Mammals and Man: The Navy's Porpoises and Sea Lions*, Robert B. Luce, Washington, DC and New York.

4

THE TALE OF THE UNIVERSE

FOR OTHERS

Renée Heller

Even at subatomic level nature presents images of itself that
reflect our own imaginings. (Close 1987: 15)

Cosmology is the study of the universe as a whole. It is ambiguous
because it refers to both a part of the science of astrophysics and to the
metaphysical concern with the overall scheme of things. In both senses
cosmology deals with the origins and development of the universe and
man's place in it:[1] a truly human theme, but also one caught up in
discourses as diverse as physics, New Age and feminism. The discursive
interference pattern made up by these different fields can be seen in
popular-science books, particle accelerator laboratories, Star Wars, television science shows or New Age books. The purpose of this chapter is
to examine this cosmological complex from a feminist perspective. The
search for humanity's place in the universe is, after all, everybody's
concern, isn't it?

I will focus on two opposing pictures of the development of the
universe. One of the pictures I want to discuss was presented by CERN,
the European Particle Physics Laboratory, at the world exhibition in
Seville, Spain, in 1992. It was a world exhibition that wanted to 'com-
pose a colourful mosaic of great diversity whose visit will provide overwhelming evidence that, even if the world is unique, humankind is
plural' (León 1992: 45). The other picture is taken from a CERN
brochure, *Back to Creation* (CERN 1991: 6).

The European Particle Physics Laboratory, CERN (Conseil Européen pour la Recherche Nucléaire), is located in Geneva, Switzerland. This laboratory was founded in 1954 as a truly European enterprise. The founding countries wanted to restore Europe's leading role in fundamental science, which had been so evident before the Second World War. CERN's major research facility is a particle collider housed in a 27 kilometre underground ring. The experiments are carried out by large university collaborations, with participants from the European member states and researchers from all over the world.

The pictures in Plates 4.1 and 4.2 are similar in style and colour but differ in a significant way. The picture from the world exhibition is circular and is said to represent the mythical image of the *Oroboros* (Plate 4.1). The picture in *Back to Creation* is more linear (Plate 4.2). I will refer to the two pictures as the 'Oroboros picture' and the 'Back-to-Creation picture'. These images tell tales about the ways in which physics conceptualizes our relation to the universe. They are monstrous and powerful pictures on the boundary between the highly specialized techno-scientific complex of particle physics and a general and hybrid public audience. The opposition between the images is the point of departure in my discussion of the inward and outward movement of cosmology over the fluid boundaries of several techno-scientific, spiritual and political discourses of the postmodern age.

COSMOLOGICAL OTHERING

Metaphors and analogies in science, as in the visualizations of the universe I describe here, are not arbitrary or merely personal as they can be in literature. It is precisely the lack of perceived arbitrariness that makes particular metaphors or analogies acceptable as science, as Nancy Leys Stepan shows in a study of analogies in nineteenth-century science on race and gender (Stepan 1986). Constraints on the choice of a certain metaphor come from the nature of the object studied, the social structure of the scientific community, and the history of the discipline, and not only from their supposed success at describing reality. The basic values of a culture are usually compatible with the metaphorical structure of the fundamental concepts in the culture, so '[n]ot surprisingly, the social groups represented metaphorically as "other" and "inferior" in Western culture were socially disenfranchised in a variety of ways' (Stepan 1986: 265). I want to suggest here that this process is not a one-way street where science dictates the views society holds, but a constant interaction without origin, only a trace of the sign of the times.

PLATE 4.1   Oroboros
(Photo: Sciences et Avenir)

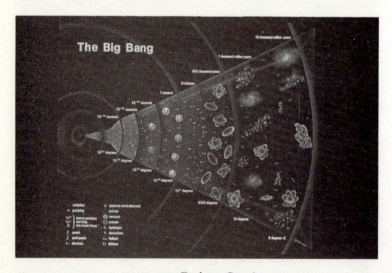

PLATE 4.2   Back to Creation
(Photo: CERN)

In the process of othering that took place during the scientific revolution, Woman, together with Nature, Body, Matter, Native, and so
on, was constructed as objectified other to the subject of science (Lykke
and Bryld 1994; Merchant 1980). The natural sciences still bear the
signs of this move. For instance, physicists are extremely good at taking
things apart but they often forget to put the pieces back together again.
In this process of reducing a whole to its parts, we also forget that this
is only one possible way of thinking about the world. The ideology of
physics is extremely powerful. Feminists have to take a discourse such
as physics seriously, because in our Western, post-capitalist, postmodern,
cybernetic context, it not only rules our material world through household, computer and war technology, but also influences our conception
of the world. This occurs whether we think of ourselves in terms of
clockwork machines as Descartes did, steam engines as Freud did, or
perhaps as a floating point on the grid of cyberspace.

The history of cosmology is in line with the general view of modern
science as a mechanistic discourse which has constructed a range of
objectified others. When we focus on the question of integration or
separation of metaphysical and scientific questions, however, the picture
becomes more complex. The methodological and sociological specialization of science – beginning with the scientific revolution and refined
in the nineteenth century with the professionalization of the sciences –
led to the abandonment of broad and general questions about cosmic
interrelatedness. Before the scientific revolution, cosmologists studied
the tracks of the planets and stars not just for timekeeping. They also
considered them as important conveyers of religious and symbolic meaning, and they speculated about the place of humanity in the cosmos.
With the growth of specialized disciplines, these functions became
separated. Metaphysical questions on 'the Whole' became the 'other' of
science. This is an aspect of the reductionism of modern science. On
the other hand, according to the philosopher Stephen Toulmin, postmodern science makes it possible to review these questions again within
science. In our postmodern times of global crisis, science cannot abandon matters of ecological disaster such as global warming, pollution
and nuclear fall-out. Postmodern science looks at itself as socially and
textually constructed and is conscious of the role of the scientist in the
whole process of knowledge creation; a space for ethical issues is thereby
(re-)opened (Toulmin 1982: 217–74).

The possible danger of this development lies in the monstrous
combination of ethical questions with a reductionist ideology of science.
The reincorporation of metaphysical questions does not on the whole

necessarily entail a fundamental change of scientific ideology. It may instead mean that social, ethical and cultural issues are narrowed down to scientific ones or removed from the agenda altogether, and that reductionism is thus reinstalled at another level. The widespread and authoritarian belief in popular-science stories on cosmology and particle physics endows physics with the power to reframe reductionism in this way.

When we look at the two pictures from the point of view of such considerations, we see that they represent two different visualizations of the place of humanity in the cosmos. How these differences can be interpreted and which ethics are involved will be the subject of the rest of this chapter.

FROM THE BIG TO THE SMALL TO EVERYTHING

The standard theory of scientific cosmology is the Big Bang theory. The two pictures I shall analyse are both representations of this paradigm. The first idea for this creation model came in the 1920s, but it was not until the 1960s that it became accepted. Cosmologists are of the opinion that until 10^{-43} seconds after the Big Bang the universe was so small that quantum-effects must be taken into account. As a result of this, a theory concerning this period should include both the theory of relativity and the theory of quantum mechanics. The general theory of relativity by Einstein describes gravity and the construction of the universe on a large scale; quantum mechanics describes phenomena on a small scale. Attempts to combine these two theories are called Total Unified Theories, Theories of Everything, or Quantum-gravity (Achterberg 1989): symbolic of the arrogance of the physicist who thinks he knows it all.

From the 1980s on, cosmologists used elementary particle physics to study the origin of the universe because

> Atoms are the complex end-products of creation. Their basic constituents were created within the first seconds of the Big Bang. Several thousand years elapsed before these particles combined to make atoms. The cold conditions where atoms exist today are far removed from the intense heat of the Big Bang. So to learn about our origins we have to see within the atoms, and study the seeds of matter. (Close et al. 1987: 7)

So, we look at ourselves when we look at elementary particles. As I have said, this can be very reductionistic. Let me illustrate by an example. Theoretical particle physicist John Ellis from CERN explains how physics can answer metaphysical questions:

Above the blackboard in my office I have a fading picture 'D'où venons nous? Que sommes nous? Où allons nous?' by Paul Gauguin. At the European Laboratory for Particle Physics, CERN, where I work as a theoretical physicist, these are some of the questions that we are trying to answer using particle physics. (Ellis 1991: 43)

Nowadays not only cosmology but also particle physics is related to questions concerning the origin of (hu)mankind. It is a smart strategical and political move to take particle physics and cosmology out of the obscurity of theoretical physics and relate them to the big issue of the origin and destiny of (hu)mankind. The cost of particle accelerators is extremely high, so the issue at stake has to be very important in order to get public funding.

MULTI-DIMENSIONAL SPACE–TIME OF COSMOLOGY

The spatial linearity and circularity of my two pictures constructs different processes of time.

On a first level of analysis, the Back-to-Creation picture represents linear time. It shows a historical universe, starting with the Big Bang 10 to 20 billion years ago, from a singularity in which matter was compressed to extremely high density. Due to the expansion of space during the 'explosion', density, temperature and energy became much lower. Cosmologists think that the expansion was not regular; in the time up till 10^{-43} seconds after the Big Bang a faster expansion, called inflation, took place. Until the beginning of this period the four forces we know now – gravity, strong force (responsible for the formation of the nucleus of atoms), weak force (responsible for radioactivity) and electromagnetic force – were still one. After 10^{-43} seconds gravity separated from the other three forces. When the inflation started, the weak and electromagnetic forces decoupled from the strong force. They disconnected after 10^{-10} seconds. After about three minutes, nucleosynthesis took place, and 300,000 years later light elements were created. The first galaxies were formed after about 1,000 million years. (CERN 1991; Achterberg 1989)

Elements of this development can also be seen in the Oroboros picture, although not with this clear chronology. The circle is composed of the following main sectors: inner space, including particles, nuclei and atoms; living material, including DNA, viruses, cells, the human body and the biosphere; outer space, including the solar system, nearby stars, galaxies and clusters; and finally the cosmic background radiation representing the continuity from the very large to the very small. These structures of the universe are bound by two arrows originating from the human figure and pointing to the background radiation. The Oroboros picture in its round shape suggests a circular concept of time.

During the last twenty years, several feminists have been arguing from sociological, spiritual and psychoanalytical perspectives that male and female time differ in an essential way. Depending on the theory, female/male is used to denote a socio-cultural average woman/man (in sociological theories) or to refer to a symbolic level, understood either as language (as in Lacanian-inspired theories) or more generally as culture (as, for example, with some spiritual feminists). In the theories which I will discuss here, female/male correspond more or less to real biocultural women/men. This is highly problematic from both a post-modern and a feminist point of view, because it equates the ideological level of representations and images of woman (Woman) with 'real life' women. This is what phallogocentric theories do all the time. Further-more, in doing so, differences between and within several layers of our existence get lost. For instance, differences between women and the various ways in which the historical contexts of race, class and sex affect us are not taken into account.

When I analyse the two pictures as cultural representations, the complex relationship between Woman and women is not my first concern. It should, however, be possible to analyse representations of Woman and Man without immediately having to consider the con-straints and possibilities these representations give women and men, as well as discuss what they tell about the culture in which they are created. So, keeping the critique of essentialism and the non-identity between Woman/Man and real life women/men in mind, I will there-fore without further discussion recycle the theories and use them to show how the relations of Woman/Man to time are inscribed in my two pictures.

In the above-mentioned feminist reflections on time, male time is often represented as linear and fragmented, while female time is con-sidered circular and context-related. Some feminists link these time concepts to the development of cosmology and physics. For instance, the spiritual feminists Heide Göttner-Abendroth and Geraldine Hatch Hanon use modern physics to reclaim 'female time' (Göttner-Abendroth 1989; Hatch Hanon 1990). Cyclic time, they say, was, because of the female cycles of menstruation and pregnancy, essentially female. In matriarchal times it was connected to the concept of the goddess. Spiral time, considered as an elaboration of cyclic time, was an expression of the movement of planets and stars and of human history. With the decline of the powerful role of women and matriarchal mythology in early patriarchal societies, the concept of time became linear. Cyclic time became a symbol of that which had to be repressed, woman and nature, but it survived in mythic and religious contexts. With the rise of modernity, time faced another split: between historical and scientific time. With the development of precise clocks, time became a scientific concept which could be defined independent of the stars and planets. Newton's mechanistic, linear, context-independent concept of time became the foundation of all science until, according to Abendroth, Einstein's theory of relativity in a way restored the mystical conception of the continuity between space and time. When the theory of relativity explained time as the fourth dimension in space–time, time could no longer be considered an absolute in itself. Astronomers now chose the speed of light as an absolute unit. The concept of independently forward-moving linear time was discarded completely. When astronomers look through telescopes to the universe they look back in time, according to the theories of new physics. One can see the origin of the universe and all moments later simultaneously. Furthermore, space–time, as defined by Einstein, is curved. For Abendroth, this means that new physics revives the spiral, mythic matriarchal time concept.

In her essay 'Women's Time', Julia Kristeva makes another distinction between concepts of time. She uses the categories of historical, monumental and cyclical time (Kristeva 1986). Historical time is linear, teleological time which is connected to the logical and ontological values of a civilization. Cyclical and monumental time form the discontinuous time of unconscious processes. They are traditionally related to female subjectivity. Everyday life and the cycles of the female body dictate a cyclic time. The eternal or long socio-cultural periods form a monumental time. As far as the discussion on Woman and women is concerned, Kristeva's work is rather obscure; the relation between female subjectivity and the time concepts remain unelaborated. Although her work should be interpreted as dealing with a symbolic level, a certain biologism is hard to deny because she directly relates the female body to subjectivity. For my purpose, however, her categories can be used, if we keep in mind that the relation between female subjectivity and time concepts is not properly unfolded in the theory. So I shall use Kristeva's time concepts in order to highlight the relation between Woman and time on a cultural and symbolic level.

Let us now return to the two pictures. Following the two big arrows in the Oroboros picture, other time dimensions than the linear time of the Back-to-Creation picture become apparent. The arrows start at the human figure and go up to a light spot. This spot suggests an explosion which can be interpreted as the Big Bang, but it is supposed to represent the present background radiation originating from the Big Bang and the origin itself, according to León's comments to CERN's world exhibition pavilion, where the Oroboros picture was presented (León 1992). The difference these two interpretations make regarding the time dimension involved depends on whether we are dealing with a representation of the present universe or looking at a picture of a developing universe. If we interpret it as the present universe, the arrows refer to the scale and relations between the elements of which the universe is built. From small to big: from the Earth to the galaxies, and from big to small: from the cell to the elementary particles. The centre is the human being, the thinker, who generates the whole of the cosmos. This can be taken as a metaphor for science. All this, combined with the fact that it is a non-ironic representation of the place of (hu)mankind in cosmos, creates the impression of a picture meant as an image of eternal truth. If we look from the other perspective and interpret the picture as a representation of the developing universe, the circular concept is lost. Furthermore, time seems to be reversed: Seen from this point of view, the Oroboros picture mirrors the Back-to-Creation picture and its way of representing the thinker looking back at creation.

As we can see in both pictures, modern cosmology can represent the cosmos in both linear and cyclic terms. These representations of modern cosmology are not, as Göttner-Abendroth and Hatch Hanon claim, a restoration of cyclic or spiral female time, but neither are they a celebration of mechanistic, linear male time. The Oroboros picture, in its suggestion of eternity, comes closest to Kristeva's monumental time. In general, the pictures show how our cosmology floats between linear, cyclic and monumental time concepts, depending on the messages to be conveyed.

OROBOROS AS A SYMBOL
FOR THE MULTIPLE FIELD OF NEW AGE,
PHYSICS AND FEMINISM

The Oroboros symbol was used not only as a picture but also in the physical arrangement of the CERN exhibits at the world exhibition. The idea of the Oroboros as a self-explanatory paradigm for the development of the universe came from the theoretical physicist and

Nobel Prize winner Sheldon Glashow at the end of the 1970s. It has been used since then for different audiences (León 1992: 46).

Several old religious and symbolic patterns from mythology can be found in the Oroboros picture. The first is, of course, the Oroboros, the mythical figure of a snake or dragon biting its tail. Several interpretations from different cultural sources make up its symbolic contents. Oroboros is the Greek name for the Hermetic World Serpent encircling the Earth. Another source states that the symbol appears principally among the Gnostics, the anti-Christian sects of the first centuries of the Christian era, and that it was later used by the alchemists (Cirlot 1971: 246). In this figure, some interpretations of much older symbols such as the circle, serpent and the world egg resonate (Walker 1983; Sjöö and Mor 1987). Oroboros suggests cosmic unity, androgyny, *yin–yang*, the self-sufficiency of nature, fertility, the continuity of life, and the dissolution of the body. I will elaborate on some of these symbols and their histories to show how multilayered the choice of Oroboros as techno-scientific, spiritual and political sign of the times seems to be.

The circle gives the Oroboros connotations of completeness in all senses: universality, eternity, unity and wholeness. To lay claim to universality is natural for the sciences. It is at the heart of the definition of what makes a theory scientific. A modest scientist will apply this principle only to his own subject; a cosmologist will apply it to the whole cosmos. As stated earlier, the connotation of eternity discards the concept of forward-moving linear time. Rational Man exists forever in this universe: the dream of eternal life. Paradoxically, it is a concept which is opposed to the paradigm it tries to explain, the Big Bang and the development of the universe. In a certain sense, the notion of eternity, represented in the picture, may be connected to Kristeva's monumental time. Some connotations of the circle are, however, dissonant with this paradigm. Whereas Kristeva's monumental time does not preclude change occurring, the eternity of the circle seems to leave out every possibility of this kind.

The idea of cosmic unity and 'the one is all' is very important in New Age thought. New Age centres around concepts (and practices) such as global awareness, healing, processes of scientific, cultural and spiritual transformation (Lykke and Bryld 1994). New Age philosophy is holistic and, among other things, based on revaluations of pre-mechanistic thought, Eastern religion and mysticism. In this respect, New Age thinking converges with spiritual feminism.[2] Both trends are, for example, against established religion, which they see as based on a split between the world and the divine, rather than on wholeness.

Newtonian science is also criticized, since it is built on parts rather than wholes; furthermore, it denies the transcendent in its materialist character. From this critique, both New Age thinking and spiritual feminism foresee a transformation or paradigmatic change (Bednarowski 1992). According to New Age science journalist Marilyn Ferguson, the shift of paradigm means emergence of new forms of government, politics, business, education, gender roles, science, religion and psychology (Ferguson 1982). The New Age idea of a paradigm shift relies on the terminology of new physics, which, in this context, is often understood as synonymous with quantum mechanics, but which can also refer to chaos theory and thermodynamical theories on self-organizing systems.

Quantum mechanics seems to conceptualize time, space and causality in a manner different from that which we are used to from our experience in the macroscopic world, as described by classical mechanics. Not only New Age thinkers find in quantum mechanics a point of departure from which a new, different scientific ideology – less objectifying, less dualistic, less deterministic, less repressive – can be developed. This applies to several very different thinkers. Among them are, for example, the physicists Fritjof Capra, David Bohm and Paul Davies, as well as feminists like Carolyn Merchant and Zulma Nelly Martinez. Although they differ in their opinions, they have one thing in common: they think that the old world-view which was ruled by objectivity, determinism and reductionism is dethroned by quantum mechanics and other new physics. The old paradigm should be replaced by a new, more holistic one.

But the ideology of physics is powerful; so powerful that it succeeds in letting us all believe that physics does not only give us information about dead matter, but also about how we should perceive the world around us and our place in the universe. In Gramsci's words, it lets us perceive the particular (physics) as the general (a world-view) (van Alphen 1987), one of the powerful functions of ideology. To use Lyotard's terminology, physics functions as a *grand narrative*, or *master narrative*. It has given social legitimation to certain forms of knowledge and certain purposes. It represents an account of reality which we have endowed with so much power and authority that it, on a very extensive basis, can legitimate cultural and scientific truths (Lyotard 1979). Because of these qualities assigned to physics, it seems necessary for us to reassess our world-view with every new physical theory. We tend to forget that world-views based on new physics as well as our previous mechanistic world-view are social constructions. There is no ground on which we can stand and build a new truth; there is no reality we can rely on which we did not create ourselves. To quote Katherine Hayles on the discourse of chaos in literature and science,

> The accommodations, resistances, and convergences that occur between the scientific and literary paradigms indicate how fissured and multilayered the cultural response is to the transvaluation of chaos. Change arrives not as a monolithic unity, but as complex vortices of local turbulence. Not to see that the agitation is general is to miss the fact that there are significant changes in the underlying cultural currents; not to notice that the turbulence follows different dynamics at different sites is to miss the complexities that the new views of chaos both initiate and signify. (Hayles 1989: 321)

FROM WORLD-EGG TO YIN/YANG TO QUANTUM STATE

Let me return to one of the mythical layers of the Oroboros picture, the matriarchal origin myths. The world egg in the matriarchal myths from before 4000 BC symbolized the ancient Great Mother of All Living who gave birth parthenogenetically to herself and the entire cosmos. The two halves of the egg contained all polarities and dualisms. The Great Mother was life and death, and in a symbolic dance her breath created and destroyed the universe. According to the spiritual feminists Monica Sjöö and Barbara Mor in their book *The Great Cosmic Mother* (Sjöö and Mor 1987), the image of the world egg is connected to the *yin/yang* principle. The two halves of the world egg were white and black. It contained, as mentioned, all oppositions, but it represented also the union of opposites. Eastern religion has formalized this principle in the concept of *yin/yang*: *yin*, the dark, negative, earth, female side; and *yang*, the light, sky, male side. Originally, these poles functioned in a complementary, not dualistic manner. Only later, with patriarchy, was the *yin/yang* principle, according to Sjöö and Mor, linked to a hierarchic interpretation.

The Oroboros itself is also often half-light/half-dark. This symbolism can be related to the Eastern *yin/yang* concept (Cirlot 1971). In his popular-science book, *The Dancing Wu-Li Masters*, the physicist Gary Zukav uses the *yin/yang* principle as a metaphor to describe the transformation of the mechanistic world-view into the quantum-world (Zukav 1979). Parts of Zukav's views are based on Fritjof Capra's influential book, *The Tao of Physics*, which compares quantum mechanics and Eastern philosophy (Capra 1977). According to Zukav, important aspects of quantum mechanics make it necessary for us to change our world-view. These are the impossibility of objectivity and knowability in quantum mechanics. These characteristics are very similar to concepts of the connectedness and oneness of reality in Eastern mysticism. Furthermore, both quantum mechanics and Eastern mysticism can be related to the human brain, because 'the new physics was not based on truth, but on us' (Zukav 1979: 74). Other New Age science writers such as Marilyn Ferguson and Fritjof Capra do something similar. They argue that because quantum mechanics integrates both left (*yin*) and right (*yang*) brain thought, society should do the same. The genderization of both science and society is at full play here. Modern science and society are equated with maleness, which can become fully human by integrating its quantum mechanical, female part.

FROM THE REPRODUCTION OF DUALISMS
TO AMBIGUITY

The Oroboros biting its own tail is symbolic of self-reproduction, and thereby it can be associated with the matriarchal myths of the Great Mother of All Living. Oroboros is also the symbol of a self-sufficient nature: nature which continually returns within a cyclic pattern to its own beginning – a representation of cyclic, female time. In this sense there is a relation with the holistic view of nature of spiritual feminism. However, the Oroboros picture shows the rational human as being pregnant with the universe instead of showing the self-sufficiency of nature.

In the ancient myth the Oroboros was also the dissolution of the body. This aspect of the myth is present in the picture: the human body is represented by *The Thinker*, sculpted by the nineteenth-century French artist, Auguste Rodin. *The Thinker* can be interpreted as a portrayal of absolute disembodiment. Although the body, with all its muscles, is very much present, the pose of the male is very unnatural.

What happens in the Oroboros picture would seem to be the following. Human becomes man; that is, rationally thinking, disembodied man in his nineteenth-century image implying an invisible company of objectified others – Woman, Native, Nature, Worker and so on. 'We', humanity, are represented by the specific – a white man – who again is made to represent the general. The suite of objectified others is not represented. The whole phallogocentric dualistic machine is thus set to work in this picture: man–woman; mind–matter; mind–body; culture–nature; rational–irrational; white–black. All this in a fantasy of cosmic unity. As Donna Haraway warns us in her famous 'Cyborg Manifesto':

An origin story in the 'Western', humanist sense depends on the myth of original unity, fullness, bliss and terror, represented by the phallic mother from whom all humans must separate, the task of individual development and of history... (Haraway 1991: 151)

However, while the phallogocentric, dualistic machine is working, ambiguity is at the same time ruling at all levels of the two pictures. In conclusion, let me, therefore, emphasize the simultaneity of a complex web of trends.

In very different ways, both the Back-to-Creation picture and the Oroboros picture displace modern conceptualizations of the time–space of the universe, although in very different ways. First of all, the two pictures exist simultaneously in the same context. At one level they are opposites: linear versus cyclic time, dualisms versus unity, male versus female. On this level, the Back-to-Creation picture is the standard phallogocentric image. The choice of the Oroboros as a visualization of man's place in the cosmos can be viewed as a sign of our postmodern times where there is supposed to be unity on all levels, and female values are revived. However, at another level, the oppositions which can be found between the pictures are all present within each picture. So we have resolved dualisms, blurred boundaries, origins and separation, diversity and plurality at the same instant. Both pictures are monstrous pictures, crossing many formerly fixed boundaries.

But the two pictures do, indeed, also rely heavily on mechanistic dualisms. In my introduction, I spoke about the monstrous mixture of ethics and reductionism found in the big questions cosmology tries to answer. The intention to represent the plurality of humankind at the world exhibition is in sharp contrast with the maleness of the representation of humanity in the two pictures. Neither one of the pictures escapes from the totalizing frame of phallogocentrism. Both are images of Man who has 'emerged from the dust of the stars to contemplate the Universe around him' (CERN 1991: 7).

NOTES

I want to thank Nina Lykke for the inspiring discussions we had on my work.

1. Astrophysics is predominantly a male discourse with 95 per cent male scientists. In philosophy there are more women; but, as feminist critique has shown, this is also a male discourse. Only the cosmological 'other' of both, astrology, is a more mixed discourse (Lykke and Bryld 1994).

2. I focus here on the commonalities; however, there are important aspects on which the movements differ. New Age conceptualizes the sacred in impersonal

terms and hierarchizes it, while spiritual feminism personalizes the sacred. On the level of politics, spiritual feminism discusses alternative kinds of political systems in terms of 'earth-based' global interconnectedness. New Age tries to make connections to other realms of reality and looks at a more universal perspective (Bednarowski 1992).

REFERENCES

Achterberg, B. (1989) *Kosmologie*, unpublished lectures, Rijks Universiteit, Utrecht.

Bednarowski, M. F. (1992) 'The New Age Movement and Feminist Spirituality: Overlapping Conversations at the End of the Century', in J.R. Lewis and J.G. Melton, eds, *Perspectives on the New Age*, State University of New York Press, Albany, pp. 167–78.

Bohm, D. (1980), *Wholeness and the Implicate Order*, Routledge, London.

Capra, F. (1977) *The Tao of Physics: An Exploration of the Parallels between Modern Physics and Eastern Mysticism*, Toronto.

CERN (1991) *Looking Back at Creation*, CERN publications, Geneva.

Cirlot, J.E. (1971) *A Dictionary of Symbols*, Routledge, London.

Close, F., M. Marten, C. Sutton (1987) *The Particle Explosion*, Oxford University Press, Oxford.

Ellis, J. (1991) 'The Universe According to LEP', *New Scientist*, no. 1783.

Ferguson, M. (1982) *The Aquarian Conspiracy: Personal and Social Transformation in Our Times*, Paladin, London.

Göttner-Abendroth, H. (1989) 'Urania – Time and Space of the Stars: The Matriarchal Cosmos through the Lens of Modern Physics', in F. J. Forman, ed., *Taking our Time: Feminist Perspectives on Temporality*, Pergamon Press, Oxford.

Haraway, D. (1991) *Simians, Cyborgs and Women: The Reinvention of Nature*, Free Association Books, London.

Hatch Hanon, G. (1990) 'The Birth of Feminine Time', in *Sacred Space: A Feminist Vision on Astrology*, Firebrand Books, New York.

Hayles, N.K. (1989) 'Chaos as Orderly Disorder: Shifting Ground in Contemporary Literature and Science', *New Literary History*, vol. 20.

Kristeva, J. (1986) 'Women's Time', Toril Moi, ed., *The Kristeva Reader*, Basil Blackwell, Oxford.

León, J. (1992) 'The Pavilion of the Universe in the Universal Exposition Seville 1992', *Particle World*, no. 2.

Lykke, N. and M. Bryld (1994) 'Between Terraforming and Fortune Telling', in W. Harcourt, ed., *Feminist Perspectives on Sustainable Development*, Zed Books, London.

Lyotard, J.-F. (1979) *La Condition Postmoderne*, Minuit, Paris.

Martinez, Z.N. (1994) 'Rituals of Celebration: Women and Language within the Emerging Paradigm', Gender–Nature–Culture: Feminist Research Network Working Paper, no. 4, Department of Feminist Studies, Odense University.

Merchant, C. (1980) *The Death of Nature: Women, Ecology and the Scientific Revolution*, Harper & Row, San Francisco.

Sjöö, M. and B. Mor (1987) *The Great Cosmic Mother: Rediscovering the Religion of the Earth*, Harper & Row, San Francisco.

Stepan, N. Leys (1986) 'Race and Gender: The Role of Analogy in Science', *ISIS* 77.

Toulmin, S. (1982) *The Return to Cosmology*, University of California Press, Berkeley.

van Alphen, E. (1987) *Bang voor schennis? Inleiding in de ideologiekritiek*, HES, Utrecht.

Walker, B.G. (1983) *The Women's Encyclopedia of Myths and Secrets*, Harper & Row, New York.

Zukav, G. (1979) *The Dancing Wu-Li Masters. An Overview of Modern Physics*, William Morrow, New York.

5

OBJECTIVITY IN THE DESCRIPTION OF NATURE: BETWEEN SOCIAL CONSTRUCTION AND ESSENTIALISM

Kirsten Gram-Hanssen

This chapter will continue and develop a discussion begun at a conference with Belgian philosopher of science Isabelle Stengers.[1] Ineke van Wingerden (author of Chapter 11 of this volume) and I were invited to respond to two lectures about scientific objectivity and feminism given by Isabelle Stengers (Stengers 1994; van Wingerden 1994; Gram-Hanssen 1994). As an introduction to this chapter, I want to quote from memory what Isabelle Stengers said after having heard our responses: 'One of you tells me that I have to see science as a totally socially constructed enterprise, and the other tells me that I have the possibility of understanding nature, because I am a part of it. So what am I going to believe?'

The question I am going to ask here is whether it is possible to believe both of us. Social constructivism is one of the important elements in recent feminist criticism of science and technology. In this chapter I intend to confront the ideas of the social constructivists with the problems that are posed by the dualistic split between humans and nature in modern Western thought.

Feminist science critics have often pointed out how the development of modern thought and science is interwoven with the process of 'othering'.[2] In my work, the focus is on the othering of nature and matter and on the problems that confront us today as a consequence of this process. These are environmental problems, and the problems we recognize in relation to our inner nature. I see these as interconnected, although the main focus in my work is on the environmental problems.

The first part of the chapter discusses some of the limits of social constructivism. I argue that, in the understanding of social relations in this movement, the human sphere is still seen as something which can be perceived as totally separated from nature; the intense focus on social conditions leaves nature itself completely undescribed.

I agree, however, that every description of nature is in some way socially constructed. My aim is to develop an understanding of nature which goes beyond the human–nature dichotomy, and which at the same time is based on the fundamental insight that every view of nature is seen from a specific point and that every time we express nature in words we do so in a human and, consequently, socially constructed language. The idea of situated knowledges put forward by Donna Haraway is presented as an interesting contribution to this discussion, but I find the notion of objectivity in Haraway's writing loose and unsatisfactory. I maintain that a closer look at the subject–object relation is needed to elaborate further the notion of objectivity.

In the second part of the chapter, I describe phenomenology as developed by the French philosopher Merleau-Ponty. It is a philosophy that in its very essence demolishes the subject–object dichotomy. On this basis I discuss the possibility of gaining objective knowledge of nature.

SOCIAL CONSTRUCTIVISM AND NATURE

French philosopher of science Bruno Latour has had a lot of influence on the development of the social constructivist approach to science discourse. In his analysis of science, Latour takes a close look at what goes on in the laboratories. He and his colleagues conclude that nothing extraordinary or 'scientific' takes place within the secret walls of these temples (Latour 1983). What, then, is all this science about? Why does society support it financially? The answer is, according to Latour, that scientists convince society that their work concerns interesting, relevant and necessary knowledge. The successful scientist is one who has the capacity for social networking. To summarize the viewpoint of the social constructivists, let me cite Ineke van Wingerden:

> Scientific knowledge is not a 'reflection' of reality, but this knowledge is 'made' in accordance with norms, values, visions of the world, social conditions and so forth and hence has to be understood as a social construction. (van Wingerden 1994: 11)

What I, and many others, see in the social construction of science is, first of all, a strong position from which to question the objectivity of modern science. However, at the same time social constructivism leaves us in a vacuum, out of touch with nature. The above quotation from van Wingerden causes me to pose some questions to this kind of thought. First of all: Is scientific knowledge *in no way* a reflection of reality? And, if so, does that mean that reality is not there at all; or does it mean that human beings are unable to reflect nature; or does it mean that nature is something to be moulded in the hands of the scientist? These are questions related to the notion of nature. Another fundamental question is related to the notion of culture: it is said that scientific knowledge has to be understood as a social construction. My question is whether it is possible to understand the social sphere as something that is completely separated from nature. To summarize my questions: Does social constructivism at any point abandon the human–nature, mind–matter, culture–nature dichotomies?

Keeping in mind the writings of Latour in the 1980s and the work of those who call themselves social constructivists, I believe that all these dichotomies are still present. The focus in their work is exclusively on human–human interaction. The interaction between human beings and nature, the subject and the object, is not considered at all.

In his newest book, *We Have Never Been Modern* (1993), Latour actually distances himself from the above version of the social construction of science discourse. He writes that when he and his colleagues showed how the social sphere was interfering totally with the production of modern science and technology, they simultaneously destroyed the basis of their own social sciences. Latour states that modern society and modern social sciences rest on the dual conception that nature and society as well as nature and subject are totally separated. Yet modern society, to a greater extent than any other society, keeps on producing hybrids. By hybrids, or quasi-objects, Latour refers to all things that are neither totally human nor totally nature, and by that he does not mean only monsters; he means all the things we have produced and are surrounded by. Take a look in the newspaper and see what is in the headlines: the hole in the ozone layer, the AIDS virus, computers, and so on. None of these things is described as, or indeed is, pure nature or pure culture. The only way to understand them, according to Latour, is as a network consisting of human beings and things/nature.

As a consequence of departing from the dual understanding of society and nature, Latour argues for 'The Parliament of Things'. Just as different human groups have people to represent them in different political decision-making processes, Latour argues that scientists and engineers are representatives of nature and things. Actually The Parliament of Things only brings to light what is already happening. 'We have never been modern', Latour writes, and by that he means that our world is less than ever populated with pure natural objects and pure human subjects or pure social relations. He wants us to admit this, thus making it more possible to discuss which of the hybrids/quasi-objects we want to live with.

In his book, Latour has taken a big step forward, leaving the most problematic aspects of social constructivism behind: Nature *does* exist, and it is *not* possible to understand the social sphere as totally separated from nature. But there still remain unanswered questions about the dualistic split between human beings and nature. Latour does not answer any questions about objectivity in modern science. All he does is change the focus, saying that we need modern science, not because of its objectivity but because of its fantastic capacity for making networks between humans and non-humans. If, however, Latour wants to speak of The Parliament of Things, it is most important that the discussion should focus on the ontological possibilities that human beings have of revealing some kind of truth about nature. This is the only way to argue that his Parliament is actually some kind of a democracy. To put the point another way, Latour has overcome the human–nature and the culture–nature dichotomies; what still remains to be discussed is the mind–matter dichotomy.

One aspect of this is the relation of domination between human beings and nature. Karen Warren is an American philosopher and ecofeminist who has written about the connection between feminism and ecology. She describes the different views ecofeminists have on the relationship between woman and nature (Warren 1990). These views cover a broad spectrum ranging from spiritual ecofeminists, who argue that woman and nature are closely related for essential reasons, to those who see a historical correlation between the domination of woman and the domination of nature. Irrespective of their views, Warren argues that feminists who are fighting to abolish the masculine domination of women can hardly overlook other kinds of oppression, such as the human domination of nature.

My point is that if feminists and others want to react to the human domination of nature, then any analysis that questions the objectivity of modern science is a step in the right direction. However, I think that any theoretical understanding that rejects, or does not discuss, the capability of human beings to reveal some kind of truth about nature leaves us in a vacuum, a position from which it is impossible to seek alternatives to the oppression of nature.

Donna Haraway sets herself in the complex between being a social constructivist, a feminist who takes account of body and nature, and a biologist, who believes that science reveals some kind of truth about nature. The 'answer' to these three poles in the discussion of objectivity in science is, according to Haraway, the notion of 'situated knowledges' (Haraway 1988). Donna Haraway describes the meaning of situated knowledges by a discussion of the persistence of vision. My under-standing is that she uses 'vision' as a metaphor for the sciences and, at the same time, as part of our sensory system in a more material sense.

First of all, situated knowledges are knowledges related to a body. The seeing is always seeing from somewhere. Haraway insists on the embodied nature of all vision. This is in contrast to the 'scientific eye', which is a conquering gaze from nowhere and which 'claims the power to see, and not be seen, to represent while escaping representation' (Haraway 1988: 581). In Haraway's understanding of knowledge, the embodied nature of seeing is intimately linked with the power relation. Like most critical feminists, when describing the power relation she thinks not only of the power relation between sexes but also of that between races, classes, and so on.

Seeing is always seeing from somewhere. The question that the social constructivist refuses to answer is whether some of the visions are to be preferred. Haraway does not hesitate to answer this question: 'Subjugated standpoints are preferred because they seem to promise more adequate, sustained, objective, transforming accounts of the world.' (Haraway 1988: 584). When Haraway uses the word 'objective', it is obviously not in the positivistic sense of the word. She writes:

> I want to argue for a doctrine and practice of objectivity that privileges contestation, deconstruction, passionate construction, webbed connections, and hope for transformation of systems of knowledge and ways of seeing. But not just any partial perspective will do; we must be hostile to easy relativisms and holisms built out of summing and subsuming parts. (Haraway 1988: 584)

When Haraway insists on using the word 'objectivity', it must be be-cause she wants to get away from the social constructivist thought that 'anything goes'. On the other hand, what is the basis from which she judges which partial perspective *will* do? As mentioned, one of her criteria is that the subjugated perspective is preferred. This is a crite-rion reflecting solidarity with the subjugated groups of human beings, with 'the Essentialized Third World Woman'[3] (Haraway 1988: 586). As I see it, however, this is not a criterion that brings about any change in the human domination of nature. Some feminists (see, for instance, Shiva 1988) would argue that changing the perspective to that of the Essentialized Third World Woman would ensure a change in the view of nature. However, this is probably not an argument with which Haraway would agree. What I find wanting are Haraway's criteria for deciding what perspective will do. What perspective is objective, in her sense of the word, in relation to nature? This is not because Haraway is unaware of the problems with nature and with the subject–object relation between human beings and nature. Actually she is very much aware of it, and she has some interesting reflections on it.

Nature, according to Haraway, does not speak for itself; nor does it totally disappear through human theorizing. In the preferred knowing process, a dialogue between subject and object takes place,[4] although 'no particular doctrine of representation or decoding or discovery guarantees anything' (Haraway 1988: 593). She goes on to speak of nature as a trickster which, through the process of knowing, will try to hoodwink the scientist. This is nature as a witty agent.

In the article in question Haraway argues that we should not rely on just any perspective. On the other hand, she leaves us without any tools to decide which perspective is objective in her sense of the word in relation to nature. In Haraway's terminology, there are some 'bad words'; these are 'essentialism', 'naturalizing' and 'universalizing' (Asdal et al. 1993). Her distaste for these words is, of course, closely related to her understanding of the power–knowledge relation. As I interpret it, this is the reason why Haraway does not give the reader a lead in deciding which perspective on nature to rely on. From the fear of building new authoritative knowledge castles, Haraway does not offer us the smallest island to serve as safe ground in troubled waters.

In the following section I want to look for such islands of possible safe ground. I will do this without abandoning either the perspective that there are many kinds of situated knowledge or the perspective that all knowledge is socially constructed.

PHENOMENOLOGY AND PERCEPTION

Objectivity in the process of knowing nature and the demolition of the subject–object dichotomy form the focus of this chapter. In Haraway's work I found some points of great interest to this discussion. They are concentrated in the notion of situated knowledges. The promise of this notion is that the subject–object dichotomy is abandoned and that the notion of objectivity has a meaning. Nevertheless, what I miss in Haraway's work is close examination of the subject–object relation in the knowing process. By knowing process I am not thinking exclusively of the scientific knowing process, in the sense used by modern science. If one wants to go beyond the social constructivist approach, examination of the subject–object relation is essential in the discussion of objectivity, in my opinion.

To help further elaborate this discussion, I have found the work of French philosopher Merleau-Ponty especially inspiring. His is a phenomenological philosophy that, at the same time, has the ambition of granting the naive and immediate experience of the world a status through philosophical argumentation, taking into account our linguistic, historical and social life. At the very centre of Merleau-Ponty's work is the demolition of the subject–object dichotomy.

The phenomenological tradition originates with the German philosopher Husserl. In reaction to the scepticism revealed by both the positivistic and the empirical traditions, Husserl was looking for a bedrock on which to found his philosophy. As a short introduction to Husserl's phenomenology, giving Husserl's response to this scepticism, I will describe some aspects of phenomenological methodology (Bengtsson 1988; Tranøy and Hellesnes 1970). The phenomenological method is about 'bracketing' all assumptions, forgetting the theory and thinking behind one's own interest in the object. It is a contemplation without any preconditions. It is about describing, not analysing or explaining.

In his early work, Husserl was engaged in the study of mathematics and logic. The goal of his work was to enlarge the notion of experience. In the positivistic and empirical tradition, which he opposed, the sensory experience[5] was seen as the only way to gain scientific knowledge. Husserl wanted to enlarge the notion of experience to include the kind of experience which reveals mathematical and logical knowledge. Indeed, he saw mathematical and logical knowledge as the foundation of all meaningful sensory experiences and thus of all empirical science. It was to gain this kind of knowledge that he developed the phenomenological method. In the world of mathematics and logic, one might say that the phenomenological method only clarifies and develops what all philosophers have always done. However, Husserl wanted to use this method in the whole area of philosophy.

Husserl distinguished between eidetic and empirical sciences. The empirical sciences include psychology, physics, biology, and so forth. They are based on sensory experiences, in the Cartesian sense, and are concerned with causal regularity; their results can never be absolute truth. In this view Husserl was in accordance with both the empiricist and the positivist traditions.[6] In contrast to the empirical sciences, the eidetic sciences – for instance, logic – concern absolute truth, according to Husserl. Therefore eidetic sciences cannot be based on the same kind of sensory experience. The eidetic sciences are built on intellectual contemplation or intuition, which is cultivated in the phenomenological method.

According to Husserl's philosophy, it is possible to gain knowledge through different acts of consciousness. These include, for instance, the act of imagination, the act of recall or remembering, and the act of perception. Through a variation of these acts and with the help of fantasy, which makes transcending these acts possible, one may reach the essence of phenomena. It is in this process that all assumptions one has about the object are to be bracketed. This means that one has to set aside all theory and all interest one might have about the object in a systematic and conscious way in order to meet the object unconditioned. This is called the eidetic reduction.

What is the status of the object in the phenomenological method? It cannot be the same as that of the objects of the empirical sciences. Husserl's answer was that the objects are spontaneously given to the human consciousness. The next question might be: Is this object then totally subjective, something that only exists in the individual subject? To counter this idea, Husserl developed the notion of intentionality: consciousness is always about something. The act of knowing is to some extent subjective, though the object of the process is not. Still one might ask: What is the ontological status of the object? Does it exist in itself, independent of our consciousness of it? Husserl never really gave an answer to this question, although he was aware of the problem; this question might therefore indicate one of the problems in his philosophy.

In contrast to Husserl, Merleau-Ponty insists that the world exists before any analysis we might make. Merleau-Ponty breaks with Husserl's idealist tradition, although the world that exists is not the world that sciences describe. One might say that it is both a pre-objective and a pre-subjective world (Kemp 1970). The world is there before subject becomes subject and object becomes object. Merleau-Ponty writes:

> To return to things themselves is to return to that world which precedes knowledge, of which knowledge always *speaks*, and in relation to which every scientific schematization is an abstract and derivative sign-language, as is

geography in relation to the countryside in which we have learnt beforehand what a forest, a prairie or a river is. (Merleau-Ponty 1962: ix)

At the very centre of Merleau-Ponty's work is the demolition of the subject–object and the mind–matter dichotomy. I will show this by describing the relation between body and language and the way painters see the world.

In the description of language, Merleau-Ponty opposes both mechanistic thought and 'intellectual psychology' (Merleau-Ponty 1962). He states that the word is neither an empty cover for thought nor a mechanical sound picture. Word, thought and reality cannot be separated. The meaning of words has a connection to reality, and thought cannot possibly exist independent of words. The word is the body of the thought. To illustrate this, he describes some investigations into colour-name aphasia, which is a linguistic disturbance of the capacity to name colours. Merleau-Ponty argues that it is not only the capacity to use the names of colours that is disturbed but, first of all, the experience of colours. If the patient is asked to group some ribbons according to colour (for instance, to put the red ribbons in one group, and so on), the patient becomes very confused. He may take two ribbons that are alike according to colour, but the next ribbon he takes might be similar according to lightness or darkness. Merleau-Ponty maintains that the patient has not lost his intellectual understanding of the principle of colours; instead, he has lost the spontaneous grasp of the sensory world. The patient has lost the capacity to see the eidos of colours, which in essence makes the blue ribbon blue, however light or dark it is. Through this and other examples, Merleau-Ponty illustrates how word, meaning and the perceived world are interrelated.

In another example, following the development of words from gesture, Merleau-Ponty shows how word, meaning and body are intimately interconnected. The body has to be identical with the intention if it is to express the intention. The body is what speaks.

The essay L'oeil et l'esprit (The Eye and the Spirit), which is Merleau-Ponty's last work, written a year before his death, is one long homage to painters and the way they see the world (Merleau-Ponty 1964). At the same time, it attacks the limited understanding of our sensory experiences on the part of the sciences. The basic element in this work is again the body, which at the same time sees and is seen. To see is to be at a distance, and what the painter expresses is but the mystery of vision. The role of the painter is to paint what seeing is to him. Merleau-Ponty writes that inspiration should be taken literally. It is like a breath with the inspiration and expiration of being; a breath which erases the barrier between who is painting and what is being painted.

I regard this essay as a strong plea for the possibility of actually seeing the world, not in a simplistic, naturalistic way, but as a process or a dialogue where the world is born through the process of seeing. There are many points in Merleau-Ponty's essay which seem close to Goethe's thoughts in his theory of colours. Elsewhere (Gram-Hanssen 1994), I have described in more detail the view of nature that underlies Goethe's theory of colours and have discussed the consequences this might have for an ethic concerning nature.[7]

Merleau-Ponty's work is especially interesting because it captures the interconnection between the subject and the object, and at the same time expresses a historical and cultural understanding of perception. To describe this, I shall stay in the field of painting, more precisely the perspective of painting, and will use the work of the American philosopher, Don Ihde, including his writing on Merleau-Ponty.

I would like to introduce two pairs of words concerning perception from Don Ihde's work (Ihde 1986). The first pair is 'multidimensionality' and 'multistability'. Multidimensionality as a paradigm for perception is, according to Ihde, the inheritance from Husserl. In contrast to the modern tradition, Husserl enlarges the notion of the sense of the object by including within perception itself both what is manifest and what is latent, the 'given' and the 'meant'. Husserl adds more dimensions to the notion of perception. What Merleau-Ponty does is to add the notion of multistability, which means that each dimension is stable in itself, while at the same time excluding the perception of other dimensions. Don Ihde uses a simple drawing to illustrate this:

There are at least three ways of seeing this drawing. Two of them present it as a perspective drawing – either as a topless pyramid or as a room with three walls and a floor. The third way of seeing it is as a 'flat' drawing without any perspective; here it might look like a robot with two arms, two legs and a body without a head. This example illustrates the principle of multistability. There are at least three equally right ways of seeing the drawing; however, each of them simultaneously excludes the other ways of seeing. It is not possible, at the same time, to see the drawing as a topless pyramid *and* a room, for example.

The other pair of words, 'microperception' and 'macroperception', introduce the historical and cultural aspects of these phenomena. Microperception is perception in the more strict meaning of sense perception, as understood by Husserl. Macroperception includes two aspects. First, it includes the way our interpretative understanding is clearly culturally-historically sedimented – as, for instance, the French deconstructivists have shown. Second, it includes the way different views or perspectives reveal different worlds.

What Merleau-Ponty does is to unite these two aspects of perception (micro- and macroperception), stating that perception is always simultaneously sensory *and* cultural. This is how the notion of multistability gets its cultural, historical dimension. The Renaissance perspective is a cultural fact that influences the way the painter sees the world. However, the Renaissance perspective is not only culture. If perspective becomes Euclidian, as with the Renaissance perspective, it is because perception allowed itself to be oriented by this system. When the painter sees, he sees the world, and he sees the perspective. This is why Merleau-Ponty states that *culture is perceived*.

Finally, let me summarize the kind of objectivity that I find from reading Merleau-Ponty's philosophy. The phenomenological method 'is the exploration of variation in order to discover invariants or structures' (Ihde 1986: 31). The essence of perception is not truth, it is our access to truth; or, in other words, the phenomenological philosophy is not a reflection of truth, it is a realization of truth.

FEMINISM, OBJECTIVITY AND PHENOMENOLOGY

What about the feminist perspective in relation to these phenomenological answers to the question of objectivity? This question will be answered in two ways, which will, nevertheless, lead to similar positions. The first way will concentrate on my own history; how I came to work with these subject-matters.

I was educated as an engineer, specializing in environmental problems. Being interested in feminist issues in other parts of my life, it was quite obvious to me that the technical world is influenced and dominated by a masculine way of thinking. However, it was not immediately obvious then, or now, how deeply this thinking has influenced technical knowledge itself. This question – whether knowledge

of nature and technology is itself influenced by masculine dominance –
together with an interest in environmental problems made me ask the
questions: Are there ways of describing nature other than the one
modern science presents? What kind of technology would these other
descriptions go with? How would they influence our environment?
These are the overall questions that guide my research. They are partly
feminist questions, though the answers I seek to them are not especially feminist answers.

Some ecofeminists would argue that the ecological and the feminist
questions need the same solutions. To agree on this point would be to
agree with the construction that defines both woman and nature as
others. On the contrary, what is interesting is to break down this
definition. One way of doing this is to keep on asking feminist questions
about our concepts of nature.

This leads to the other way of answering the question as to how the
phenomenological answer to the question of objectivity relates to a
feminist perspective. Seeing is always seeing from somewhere, from a
specific body, history and culture. Seen in this context, what does it
mean that the bodily subject has a sex? Corresponding to the overall
positions presented in this chapter, gender differences can be regarded
either as a social construction or as an essential biological difference, in
a broader sense than the scientific one. In my opinion, there *are* differences in the knowing of nature which stem from the essential sexual
biology, though they are very difficult to separate from the socially
constructed differences. Here we get closer to Haraway again. To me,
being a feminist eco-subject means being aware of, and trying to
change, oppression in all its forms, not least in our production of knowledge of nature. This again means that feminism is one position from
which it is possible to keep on asking new questions about dualism,
othering and domination. One way of doing this is to get inspiration
from what the masculine system defines as the feminine position –
taking care of, relating in an empathetic way, being sensitive to, and so
on – not because these are feminist issues, but because they might
point to interesting alternatives to modern science inasmuch as they
have been so deeply separated from it.

What I find in phenomenology is not a feminist answer to the
question of objectivity in science, though phenomenology points to
fundamentally different and non-dualistic ways of perceiving nature,
and, as such, is an answer to a question that is partly feminist.

CONCLUSION

The question that I posed at the start of this chapter was whether it is possible to see science as a social construction and, simultaneously, to say that human beings have the possibility of understanding nature given that we are part of nature ourselves. My reason for asking this question is that I see a connection between the view of nature that is expressed in modern science and our environmental crises. The reason I find this question interesting is that I see social constructivism as a strong position from which to pose a question about the objectivity of modern science, and thereby open up to alternative views of nature. At the same time, however, I find the constructivist approach very problematic because it is in no way open to abandoning either the subject–object or the human–nature dichotomy.   *(puts a taboo on "nature," "biology*

It is interesting to see that one of the founding fathers of social constructivism, Bruno Latour, in his recent work distances himself from reductionist versions of social constructivism which do not take the human–nature dichotomy into account. Yet I find no abandonment of the subject–object dichotomy in his work. In this respect, Donna Haraway's work is particularly interesting, because she takes a constructivist point of departure and discusses the subject–object and human–nature dichotomies. In my opinion, however, her definition of objectivity in relation to nature is wanting.

What I find in Merleau-Ponty's work is obviously not a constructivist approach, although it prefigures many of the insights of Haraway with which I agree – such as that seeing is always seeing from a certain point of view, which is based on body, history and culture, and that the starting point is the demolition of the subject–object and the human–nature dichotomies. What I find in Merleau-Ponty, and not in Haraway, is an enlargement of the notion of our capacity to sense our environment. As Don Ihde states, Merleau-Ponty includes within perception itself both what is manifest and what is latent, what is 'given' and what is 'meant'. The social constructivist approach maintains that science is not a reflection of reality. Merleau-Ponty holds that the phenomenological method is not a reflection of truth; it is a realization of truth.

NOTES

1. Isabelle Stengers, together with the Belgian physicist and Nobel Prize winner in chemistry, Ilya Prigogine, has written one of the very important books on shifts of paradigms in science, *Order Out of Chaos* (Stengers and Prigogine 1984). The conference referred to in the opening paragraph of this chapter,

'Metamorphoses of Science. Feminism and Shifts of Paradigms', was organized by the feminist research network Gender–Nature–Culture, at Odense University, Denmark, 1 October 1993. Isabelle Stengers was the keynote speaker.

2. The process of 'othering' refers here to the construction of 'Nature, Matter, Body, Woman, Native, and so on ... as objectified others, objects of study for the knower, critically identified as the enlightened, white-skinned, bourgeois "man of science"' (from Nina Lykke's Introduction to this book).

3. With this expression, Haraway refers to Chandra Mohanty's 'Under Western Eyes' (1984), which describes how Western feminist literature has constructed an Essentialized Third World Woman.

4. This seems similar to the subject–object relation that Evelyn Fox Keller describes (Keller 1985).

5. Sensory experience is here intended in the Cartesian sense, in contrast to Merleau-Ponty's understanding, which is described later in this chapter.

6. It is to be noted that the possibility of gaining absolute truth is here rejected on the grounds of arguments that are completely different from the social constructivist ones.

7. I am not aware whether there are any direct connections between Goethe's work and the work of Husserl and Merleau-Ponty. An indirect connection between Merleau-Ponty and Goethe might be found through some of the painters Merleau-Ponty refers to, since many painters worked with Goethe's theory of colours.

REFERENCES

Asdal, K., B. Brenna, and E. Gulbrandsen, I. Moser and N. Refseth (1993) 'Donna Haraway om natur og vitenskap', *Nytt om Kvinneforskning. Natur, vitenskap, naturvitenskap*, no. 5, Norges forskningsråd.

Bengtsson, J. (1988) *Sammenflätner. Fenomenlogi från Husserl till Merleau-Ponty*, Bökforlaget Daidalos, Göteborg.

Gram-Hanssen, K. (1994a) 'Breaking the Monopoly of Modern Science – A Reply to Isabelle Stengers', *Newsletter*, no. 3, Feminist Research Network Gender–Nature–Culture, Odense University, Denmark.

———— (1994b) 'Towards an Expanded Concept of Ethics', in E. Gunnarsson and L. Trojer, eds, *Feminist Voices on Gender, Technology and Ethics*, Luleå University of Technology.

Haraway, D. (1988) 'Situated Knowledges: The Science Question in Feminism and the Privilege of Partial Perspective', *Feminist Studies*, vol. 14, no. 3, pp. 575–99.

Ihde, D. (1986) *Consequences of Phenomenology*, State University of New York Press, Albany.

Keller, E. Fox (1985) *Reflections on Gender and Science*, Yale University Press, New Haven, Conn.

Kemp, P. (1970) Foreword to the Danish translation of Merleau-Ponty, *L'oeil et l'esprit*, in *Maleren og filosoffen*, Vintens bogforlag, Copenhagen.

Latour, B. (1983) 'Give Me a Laboratory and I Will Raise the World', in K.

Knorr-Cetina and M. Mulkay, eds, *Science Observed: Perspectives on the Social Study of Science*, Sage, London.

——— (1993) *We Have Never Been Modern*, Harvester Wheatsheaf, London and New York.

Merleau-Ponty, M. (1962) *Phenomenology of Perception*, Routledge & Kegan Paul, New York.

——— (1964) *L'oeil et l'esprit*, Gallimard, Paris.

Mohanty, C.T. (1984) 'Under Western Eyes: Feminist Scholarship and Colonial Discourses', *Boundary* 2.

Shiva, V. (1988) *Staying Alive – Women, Ecology and Development*, Zed Books, London.

Stengers, I. (1994) *From Describing Falling Bodies to Understanding People: What is Scientific Objectivity? Metamorphoses of Science: Feminism and Shifts of Paradigms*, Working Paper No. 7, Feminist Research Network Gender–Nature–Culture, Odense University, Denmark.

Stengers, I. and I. Prigogine (1984) *Order Out of Chaos*, Heinemann, London.

Tranøy, K.E. and Hellesnes (1970) *Filosofi i vor tid*, Stjernebøgernes Kulturbibliotek, Vintens bogforlag, Copenhagen.

Warren, K. (1990) 'The Power and the Promise of Ecological Feminism', *Environmental Ethics*, vol. 12, no. 2.

van Wingerden, I. (1994) 'From Discovering Falling Bodies to the Construction of the Female Body – A Response to Isabelle Stengers', *Newsletter*, no. 3, Feminist Research Network Gender–Nature–Culture, Odense University. Denmark.

ON HEALING SELF / NATURE

Julia Martin

Science, technology, health care, objectivity, othering, truth: these words, which we hear again and again in this book, remind me of my father in a coma after an accident. The hospital was doing everything it could for him: machines that breathed, drips that fed, monitors for brain, heart and blood, intensive care. But the doctor standing over his bed warned us not to be optimistic. So, when my mother and I started talking to him, singing, holding his feet, breathing with him, visualizing healing colours, the doctor said, 'What you're doing is all right, but we have to inject a note of reality into all this.' Reality? Who knows what that is? What's going on here? I felt angry and upset. I'm sure we all wanted to care for my father, to relieve suffering. But we each found the discourse of the other inaccessible. Responding to what seemed like the hard, mechanistic, atomizing, objectifying science of the hospital, my mother and I began to express its polar opposite. Speaking in our own voices, trying to heal, we began to articulate something of the intuitive, imaginative, non-analytic approach which has tended to be associated with 'the feminine'. At the time this seemed necessary, the only way. But how did we find ourselves in this binary, almost oppositional, relation to the undeniably efficient machinery of medical science? In retrospect I wonder how it could have been different.

Some time after my father left hospital I was present at a discussion of Capra's film *Mindwalk*. A woman who identified herself as a systems theorist made a comment which clarified for me what seemed to be missing from the doctors' approach. She said that the dominant medical paradigm works by an atomizing focus on disease and illness, but it has no full understanding of *health*. For this, one needs a holistic, systems approach. Perhaps there is an analogy here in the tendency of contemporary theory to analyse and identify problems, silences or contradictions – the problem of dualistic epistemology for example – with little sense of an alternative vision or a practical method for realizing it. But for feminists and other social or environmental activists this is not enough. Acknowledging the extraordinary suffering of our world, we are committed to transforming it. So if the feminist critique of phallocentric discourse is to empower people with real alternatives, we need to go beyond the oppositional relations by which it functions, neither allowing ourselves to be defined as 'other', nor seeing our fellow beings as such. Both in theory and in practice there are many ways to approach such a perspective. What follows are hopes and guesses, provisional propositions and ideas for practical experiment. If liberation into a non-exploitative, non-dualistic, whole, healthy, compassionate world seems unattainably utopian, we can always start small, act and organize locally, liberating at least some space for creative engagement.

Let me begin this discussion by identifying where my point of view is coming from. For those of us working with contemporary theory, the idea that anyone can claim an absolute vantage point for 'truth' is, of course, an illusion. From postmodern critiques of totalizing systems, from feminist analyses of the politics of 'objectivity', from the deconstructive strategies of Madhyamika Buddhism, from Gödel's and Church's Theorems – we know that no theoretical system is transcendent or complete. So we try to identify the assumptions and experiences which condition our approach, recognizing that to avoid doing so is potentially oppressive. Growing up in a liberal family, classified 'white' in apartheid South Africa, I soon learnt that the dominant system was dangerous and cruel. But living in a country in which hierarchic dualism was not only foregrounded but even formally legislated also gave me a sense that oppressive mastery cannot be eradicated merely by reversing the existing hierarchy of values. We need a different approach altogether. In South Africa, progressive people's vision of the just society we are working to materialize cannot, in the end, be 'black consciousness' or even 'multi-racial'. We want *non*-racism, *non*-sexism. Similarly, then, in participating in feminist debates, I am interested, of course, in women's empowerment or voicing women's lives, but this is part of a longer-term concern with approaches to *non*-dualism.

The work I do also shapes this way of seeing. I teach English at a progressive university where most of the students come from economically and educationally disadvantaged (that is, 'Coloured' or 'black') communities. Much of our work involves teaching what may be called cultural and critical literacy. I am also involved in an eco-political organization engaged in dialogue and actions with people in community organizations, identifying correspondences between environmental degradation and social inequality. These involvements inform one another and are also shaped by a practical and research-related interest in Buddhism.[1] This means that, in addition to the focus on non-dualism, the priorities I bring to this inquiry into healing alternatives to systems of 'othering' lead to questions such as: How can this approach be related to the South African situation? How would my students respond to it? What elements could be appropriate for grass-roots media? How does it accommodate the 'spiritual' aspects of experience? In all this, at whatever level, my attention keeps returning to some very simple ideas:

• that suffering and exploitation are facts of our experience which demand a response;

• that a mistaken conception of what is called the 'self', and a mis-understanding of its relation to 'nature', are an important aspect of what goes wrong;

• that for this eco-social-spiritual illness to be cured we need not only analysis of the disease but also an experiential understanding of health;

• that transformation cannot take place in the realm of theory – we need practical engagement as well.

With reference to these ideas, I will comment briefly on two current forms of critical response to phallocentric science and technological power structures, referred to in the title of this book by the terms 'goddess' and 'cyborg'. Then I will suggest in more detail what the teachings of non-dualism in some contemporary interpretations of Buddhism might contribute in theory and practice to curing the disease that feminists and ecologists are concerned with. I am hesitant to do this because my understanding of these powerful, complex teachings is very limited, and it keeps changing. But the Buddhist approach is potentially so valuable that it seems necessary to make the attempt, in the hope of provoking readers to find out more about it elsewhere.

ARE THE MOTHER GODDESS AND CYBORG
APPROPRIATE METAPHORS?

First, I shall consider the metaphor of the healing Mother Goddess, or Mother Nature, as a response to the simultaneous exploitation/othering/ marginalization (etc.) of women and the natural environment. My workroom is full of images of the goddess, and there are more in my ceramic studio downstairs. I love her earth/water power; her mythic connectedness with living systems; her reminder of a forgotten, buried, hoped-for space before patriarchy, of oneness before the fall into division and language, of Mother in the beginning. She offers, certainly, a powerful counter to the phallus, and, in her form as Mother Gaia, has been promoted as the image of the Earth as nurturing biosphere.[2] And yet, although these metaphors may be productive in some contexts, they can also be problematic – for women, for men and for ecological politics.

The discourse of the Mother Goddess which is prominent in some forms of ecofeminism promotes the image of the mother as being inherently appropriate for ecological healing. Women are said to be closer to nature than are men because of their experiences of the fertility cycle, childbirth, motherhood, and so on. Aside from what it could mean for men, where does this 'fact of life' (Salleh 1984: 340) leave women who are not mothers? And who are these universal women, anyway? As Bina Agarwal argues in some detail, the recent ecofeminist focus on constructs of woman and nature avoids giving attention to the diverse and particular social, economic and political structures in which these constructs are produced and transformed (Agarwal 1992: 216–18). This makes for, among other things, a First World bias which renders this material less accessible to people living in another context.[3] Unable to recognize herself in the stories of 'woman' and the Goddess we were studying in a postgraduate module on Northern ecofeminism, one of my students asked, 'But how does this relate to *my life* as a black South African woman?'

So, instead of radically challenging the essentialist categories of 'woman' and 'nature' inherited from patriarchal discourse, such approaches tend to retain them.[4] Instead of eradicating the 'disease', essentialisms of this kind tend to keep it going, and to let a simple and fundamental epistemological mistake go unquestioned. As Catherine Roach puts it, 'None of us can be [closer to or] "farther away" from nature for there is nowhere we can go, nothing we can do to get away from this implication in the environment' (Roach 1991: 53). Thus, by gendering the planet as feminine, as a projection of human ideas about motherhood, as a goddess instead of a sky-god, feminists and environmentalists may well be working against their own ostensible agendas for health and liberation.[5] The binary hierarchies that are at the root of the illness are at best inverted, not subverted, or, as Roach would prefer, 'biodegraded' (Roach 1991: 54).[6]

Challenge and subversion of this kind are, of course, characteristically postmodern, and so is my second example. Since its appearance in Donna Haraway's 'Manifesto for Cyborgs: Science, Technology and Socialist Feminism' (1985), the image of the playful, blasphemous cyborg which inhabits the networks of high-tech culture has provoked some important discussions among feminists.[7] Haraway suggests that the hierarchical dualisms and dichotomies which have persistently characterized the discourse of the West, and sanctioned its systems of othering, are now being significantly challenged by the polymorphous world of information systems. The figure of the cyborg is of one who moves playfully, ironically, non-innocently beyond the old identities of human, animal or machine, deconstructing the phallocentric definitions of 'selfhood', 'woman' or 'nature' among many others. It is a fascinating approach, useful not only for its affirmation that feminists cannot afford to create 'science' as an enemy, but also for the way it enables us to shift perspective on received boundaries and see our contemporary practice as feminist researchers: fax, computer, photocopier, car, telephone, aeroplane have all contributed to writing this paper – where is the 'me' that is separate? Although obviously deconstructive, the cyborg does what postmodernism generally avoids. It represents (if ironically) a kind of affirmation – not of solid, inherent 'identity', a 'self' in opposition to 'nature', but of a networking life that is polymorphous, changing and so potentially more liberated.

This is an exciting approach, but who in fact profits from it? And who, or what, bears the cost? Not far from our apartment in Cape Town, people are living without electricity or adequate sanitation, collecting firewood for the evening meal, living without books, without the written word. From such a perspective, which is shared by people throughout the Two-Third's World, the position from which Haraway publishes must surely appear so remote and privileged that the deconstructions it proposes can make no sense. In recent decades, the lives and environments of such people have been steadily impoverished by the business/money/power relations of Northern-style development which make computers, laser games and biotechnology possible. Silicon Valley, transnational corporations, cheap labour from the South, the military-industrial complex – the deconstructive (liberated?) play of the high-tech cyborg is inextricably networked into global systems of control and exploitation more powerful and coercive than anything we have known before.

But perhaps this criticism seems inappropriate. After all, the cyber-space that feminists are investigating is precisely not an ethical domain. Ironic and postmodern, the cyborg is constituted wholly within the networks of text and language, offering no ground of place or value beyond these signs. Postmodern theory would say this is all we can ever expect. But is it really? If the disease we are concerned with manifests itself as enormous personal/global suffering and exploitation, then our task as health care workers demands that we recognize the possibility of something more.[8]

BUDDHIST APPROACHES AS PATHS TO NON-DUALISM

I would now like to discuss some approaches derived from an interpre-tation of Buddhism, in particular those teachings which are presented as a Middle Way between absolutism and nihilism. The traditional response to the problem of suffering is to identify its cause in desire and attachment, and to propose a practical path of liberation which seeks to remove this suffering by eradicating or transforming the cause. Like much of postmodernism, this perspective sees the imaginary con-struction of the 'self' as an entity in opposition to a world of others as being at the root of people's social/psychological/spiritual malaise. Motivated by the desire to establish our solidity as a separate 'I', we are bound as 'subjects' into patterns of clinging to 'objects' or pushing them away. Like Lacanian theory, Buddhism recognizes selfhood's desire as being insatiable. But instead of seeing the suffering it involves as being without remedy, the whole purpose of the teaching is healing, liberation. 'Health' in this context means waking up from the dream of separateness into an awareness that the nature of mind (including all phenomena) is non-dual. This is why Buddhism can be valuable for feminists and others who find postmodernism useful as a critique but disturbingly lacking as a basis for transformation.[9]

The teachings frequently refer to the concept of *pratityasamutpada* as a remedy for curing the habitual attachment to an illusory world of subjects and objects. Translated as 'dependent co-arising' the term refers to the insight that all mental and physical phenomena are interdependent, taking shape in interaction with one another. In Mahayana tradition, this concept of dependent co-arising is equated with emptiness, devoidness, *sunyata*. Manifesting only in relationships, all 'things', including the 'self', are devoid of essence, empty of self-existence:

> When this is, that is;
> This arising, that arises;
> When this is not, that is not;
> This ceasing, that ceases.[10]

This way of seeing was given complex philosophical attention in the work of Nagarjuna, second-century founder of the Madhyamika school of Buddhism, the 'Middle Way'. For the Madhyamika, 'emptiness' is not an ontological concept, a 'void'. It is neither a something nor a nothing; rather, it is a negation of the extremes of both absolutism and nihilism. The point here is not that 'nothing exists'. For most everyday purposes, everyone is committed to the linguistic and other conventions in which we relate to objects of knowledge as being 'real' – fixed, solid and self-existing. This is the perspective of what is called conventional truth (*samvrtisatya*). But it is also possible – even at the same time – to perceive the same world without attachment either to objects as entities, or to the discursive thinking which defines them as such. This way of seeing, that of *paramarathasatya,* or ultimate truth, recognizes the emptiness of phenomena and gives up discursive thinking in place of *prajna*, wise non-dual awareness.[11] Nagarjuna's method involved deconstructing the philosophical assertions of his contemporaries, without making any assertions of his own. Demonstrating repeatedly that nothing has a stable essence, that all things arise dependently, his approach used exhaustive theoretical analysis to turn theory against itself. The aim of this was to eliminate attachment to the conceptual way of thinking, the clinging to any linguistic proposition of 'truth' as absolute, and to awaken the questioner to another way of knowing. In Madhyamika texts, the teaching of emptiness is therefore described as being a medicine, or like water, a 'soteriological device to expunge the disease or fire [of attachment] so that human beings are released from their misery' (Cheng 1991: 49).

There are clear similarities between this approach and aspects of contemporary deconstruction. But again, because of its emphasis on cure and healing, Buddhism is only concerned with theoretical analysis to the extent that it works to relieve the suffering of selfhood's desire. Where postmodernism denies that this is possible, the purpose of this deconstruction is precisely to enable the practitioner to step beyond the texts of subject and object, to realize the unconditioned (non-dual) potentiality in which all things, all causes and conditions arise. The Nyingma teacher Thinley Norbu puts it like this:

> From the beginningless beginning, the essence of non-dualistic wisdom mind is pure and stainless like a mirror. All measureless phenomena can arise through this unobstructed, mirror-like quality without causing division between subject and object. Without division between subject and object, there is no grasping or clinging and there are no temporary circumstances, so all manifestation is wisdom display. (Norbu 1992: 3)

In Mahayana Buddhism, practitioners commit themselves to realizing the wisdom of emptiness in order to liberate all sentient beings from their suffering and confusion.[12] Thus wisdom is inseparable from compassion; theory can only be realized in practice.

THE EXPERIENCE AND PRACTICE OF NON-DUALISM

Since Buddhism avoids the dichotomy between theory and practice, I will now refer to some examples from contemporary interpreters of the teaching which attempt to give the practitioner an *experience* of nondualism, emptiness/interdependence, rather than just a theoretical idea. Of course academic texts don't usually do this, but I am engaging in a slightly transgressive experiment here because theory is so often disconnected from practical experience, and I see this as a problem. Feminist readings and writings of 'the body', for example (and to a lesser extent 'the environment'), are now part of the discourse of critical theory, yet this material so often shows little relation to (or acknowledgement of) non-academic activities like the 'bodywork' being done in alternative health care, or programmes of ecological activism. So often in universities I find that I am sitting in seminar rooms of talking heads, as alienated as ever from the pain and joy of living bodies, the myriad interrelationships of things. It doesn't have to be like this, but what is to be done? For the chronically 'head-bound' postures of academic theory-making to shift and realign, we will need to experiment. So here are some ideas for discovering in practice a healing deconstruction of body/mind, self/nature dualisms.

First, a comment about terminology. Alternatives to dualism are sometimes described as a 'union' of body and mind, self and nature, self and other, perhaps even a 'mystic union'. But here, in the words of Seng Ts'an, the Third Zen Patriarch, is a different way of putting it:

> In this world of Suchness
> there is neither self nor other-than-self.
> To come directly into harmony with this reality
> *just simply say when doubts arise, 'Not two.'*
> In this 'not two' nothing is separate,
> nothing is excluded.
>
> (my emphasis – JM)

To speak of 'union' or 'unity' implies a previous separation, division, and the idea that there exist entities to be united. But Buddhist practice works to uncover or awaken a healing recognition that *the nature of phenomena is from the beginning non-dual*, that causes and conditions reveal the *unconditioned*. From such a perspective, even to assert the 'oneness' of being is potentially problematic. Further, although Buddhist realization might certainly be called 'mystical', many would avoid the term since, once again, it connotes metaphysical separation and difference. So Zen paradoxically describes enlightenment as 'nothing special', and Seng Ts'an says 'not two'.

In contemporary interpretations of Buddhist teaching, there is a variety of ways of saying and experiencing this 'not two'. First, I'll refer briefly to some examples which are potentially useful for healing self/nature. They all approach the subject of healing and liberation from the assumption that 'personal' distress and global eco-social crisis are interdependent, and in each case, some form of meditation practice is assumed to be the basis for developing an experiential awareness of non-dualism and interdependence. But they also each suggest different sorts of practice which can contribute to an experienced deconstruction of dualism and awareness of *pratityasamutpada* or dependent co-arising. I will then refer to a recent book by Anne Klein which engages with traditional Buddhist teaching on this subject from an explicitly feminist standpoint. In all this, my comments are offered as signposts or references for further investigation rather than instructions for specific practice.

Intellectual analysis of 'self'

Although it sounds like a theoretical exercise, this is practised in some traditions as a tool for changing the practitioner's experience of a binary self/nature opposition. In contemporary use, it can then be directed to working with contemporary forms of suffering. For example, Sakya Trizin (Head of the Sakya lineage of Tibetan Buddhism) recently invited the audience at an international conference on Buddhism and Ecology to work through a traditional deconstruction of the concept of 'self' as a way to understanding interconnectedness.[13] In this context, the aim of the intellectual analysis is to loosen the attachment to 'I' and 'mine' of which the present global crisis is a manifestation, and motivate the practitioner to engage compassionately with the suffering of all beings.

Breathing and visualization

The Tarthang Tulku, a Tibetan lama of the Nyingma lineage, teaches the experience of non-dualism through very precise descriptions of visualization, breathing and other exercises, which are similarly designed to dissolve the attachment to belief in a world of entities, of self and other. According to this, the habitual distress of what postmodernists might recognize as Lacan's insatiable, desiring, grasping 'I' is experienced as '[a] feeling of almost continuous dissatisfaction ... a subtle form of anxiety which we can feel in the throat center as a kind of tightness, and which manifests as the "self" reaching out for experience' (Tarthang Tulku 1978: 38). In this approach, the way to transform suffering begins with releasing the 'chronic tightness' in muscles and minds.

Mindfulness of the minutiae of daily life

Another Asian exile, the Vietnamese Zen teacher and peace activist Thich Nhat Hanh, emphasizes the relationships between effective peace work in the socio-political sphere and 'being peace' in daily living. In this approach, compassionate activism is based in the realization of what Nhat Hanh calls 'interbeing', an explicitly ecological interpretation of the central concept of dependent co-arising, *pratityasamutpada*. His influential teachings focus on mindful attention in everyday activities – sitting, walking, eating a piece of fruit, using a piece of paper – as a way to discovering the emptiness/interdependence of phenomena.

Despair work

North American Buddhist Joanna Macy, who interprets dependent co-arising in terms of contemporary systems theory, explores its practical implications in the group activities she calls 'despair work'. In this context 'despair' is not nihilism, but rather, 'as it is being experienced by increasing numbers of people across a broad spectrum of society, despair is *the loss of the assumption that the species will inevitably pull through*'(Macy 1991: 17). As a facilitator of groups working to acknowledge and transform the paralysis of this despair, Macy has developed a variety of 'spiritual exercises for social activists', dealing for example with death, loving kindness, compassion, mutual power and mutual recognition. In each case the activity seeks to promote a recognition of 'the radical interdependence of all phenomena' (Macy 1991: 96) and proceeds from the assumption that if we are 'to heal our society, our psyches must heal as well' (Macy 1991: 39).[14]

Bioregionalism

Gary Snyder, a North American Buddhist and environmental activist and poet, grounds Buddhist teaching on non-dualism and *pratityasamutpada* in the programmes of bioregionalism. Critiquing the misconception that we are each a kind of 'solitary knower', Snyder interprets the Buddhist insight that 'selfhood' *is* imprisonment through an emphasis on the environments in which 'the thinking subject' is produced and sustained: 'grandparents, place, grammar, pets, friends, lovers, children, tools, the poems and songs we remember, are what we *think with....* *With no surroundings, there can be no path, and with no path one cannot become free*' (Snyder 1990: 60). In this approach, the illusion of being a clear, distinct, solitary individual mind is deconstructed through conscious, practical involvement in the life of one's local bioregion, and a committment to working for its sustainable well-being. So the field of practice is extended to learning local history, local economics, local ecology, as well as active participation in community structures.

A feminist approach

In her book *Meeting the Great Bliss Queen: Buddhists, Feminists and the Art of the Self* (Klein 1995), Anne Klein establishes a lively, scholarly 'conversation' between Buddhist teachings and feminist theories. With regard to the healing of self/nature dualisms, with which this chapter is concerned, Klein describes Buddhist practices of mindfulness and compassion, teachings on the emptiness of self and all phenomena, and the ritual of Yeshey Tsogyal (the Tibetan Great Bliss Queen) as powerful tools for contemporary women. In particular, she suggests that the theoretical debate between essentialists and postmodernists in contemporary feminism can be unstuck and transformed *in the experience* of non-dualism which Buddhist traditions make available.

The discussion of the meditative practice of mindfulness, for example, describes it as a dissolution of habitual (hierarchic) oppositions: mind and body are 'directly experienced as interactive' (Klein 1995: 72), and 'profound steadiness' is accompanied by an experience of 'unalterable flux' and particularity (Klein 1995: 66). The experience is at once a 'dismembering' and a 're-membering' of the self in that the practitioner experiences 'a visceral sense of personal continuity in the midst of clearly observed flux' (Klein 1995: 66). For feminists, this enables an experience of subjectivity that neither essentialism nor postmodernism currently offer: 'Postmodern feminist understandings emphasise particularity, but that emphasis often precludes an experience of coherence. It need not' (Klein 1995: 76).

Similarly, Klein introduces dependent arising, or the constructedness or conditioned nature of all phenomena, as a concept readily compatible with postmodernism. What is very different is the related concept of emptiness, which is both a dependent arising (participating in flux and constructedness like everything else) and unconditioned (Klein 1995: 134–5). Klein uses this perspective to suggest that 'contemporary feminist theory, like other postmodern reflection, is severely limited by its inability to take seriously the possibility of something beyond its own constructs, a silence not governed by words, a metaphysical space not conditioned by things' (Klein 1995: 143). Instead of accepting the theoretical master narratives for which women, the non-verbal and the unconditioned are non-describable, women and others can draw on Buddhist examples to 'make claims outside this "story line" by swimming past its boundaries into the deeper dimensions of subjectivity' (Klein 1995: 145).

Finally Klein proposes ritual identification with the figure of the Great Bliss Queen, who embodies the enlightened realization of various non-dualisms. As such she offers a model for integrating conditioned and unconditioned, essentialist and non-essentialist perspectives (Klein 1995: 169). Significantly, however, she is not presented as a 'goddess', 'matriarch' or 'role model' who automatically affirms or embodies the female character. Rather, 'the point of practising the Great Bliss Queen ritual is less to look at her than it is to take a fresh look at one's own potential. In this way, meeting the Great Bliss Queen is meeting one-self' (Klein 1995: 22).

Here, then, are some attempts to evoke in different areas of practice an experience which is not founded in the illusory oppositions of 'self' and 'nature': not two. Each interprets Buddhist tradition with regard to contemporary concerns, the first five emphasizing the global crisis of environment and development, while Klein addresses women (explicitly but not exclusively) and feminism in North America.

Interpreting such perspectives from my situation in the South, the diagnosis of the illness with which feminists and ecologists are concerned is fairly clear: instead of the improvements promised at the outset, the recent decades of 'development' have seriously impoverished both people and natural ecosystems. Ironically, First World models of so-called development have fuelled in many people precisely the 'self's' insatiable clinging and grasping that, for Buddhism, binds us into the suffering of dualistic existence. The whole system is clearly less healthy than before, and women inevitably experience the consequences most acutely.

So Buddhism can diagnose, but can it help us to effect a cure? Can it help us to respond compassionately to the present eco-social-spiritual crisis – as feminists (even though, in the past at least, most of the teachers have tended to be male, some even 'patriarchs'), as people in a country like South Africa (even though the intended audience is often North American or European), as health care workers? I believe it can do so, presenting as it does an alternative to essentialist goddesses and postmodern cyborgs that is both deconstructive and healing. To make this real in practice, I would hope readers might experiment with these approaches to non-dualism as inspiration for theory and practice that may be differently situated. Here are two examples of how this could work.

TWO EXAMPLES

First, in the eco-political organization I'm involved with in South Africa, the concept of 'interconnectedness', derived from Buddhist teaching on emptiness/interbeing, has become the basis of all our media: a workshop on the ecology of garbage; a factsheet about nuclear power; a book about earth, water, energy, food, ideology. All this aims to illustrate in simple terms the emptiness of 'self' as entity; that self exists only within networks of relationships with all that is not the self that 'nature' or 'the environment' can never be outside us. Throughout, we are working to develop a fairly radical perspective which sees systems, but no entities or essences; a discourse looking for a way out of the oppositions, dualisms, apartheids within which we grew up. A guiding assumption is drawn from the Buddhist view that this sort of theory can make a difference to the way people act. As Klein puts it, 'understanding [emptiness] changes the subject in desirable ways, that is, in ways that complement compassion and concentration' (Klein 1995: 137).

Second, in a different context, working with postgraduate students of literature, I have been experimenting with a similar view of interconnectedness, considering how it can inform the priorities we bring to literary/cultural criticism and theory. This has meant reconsidering the questions which inform our analysis of cultural texts, what sorts of texts we want to focus on, the way we write about such texts, and for whom. In this context, Buddhist teaching suggests a response to the master narratives of contemporary theory and a way of deconstructing theory/practice dichotomies.

In both NGO and university contexts, then, we are working to respond to the rapidly changing environment in which we are living in South Africa. Speaking of the global situation, the Dalai Lama has said that 'we are a pivotal generation'. This also seems true of the present moment in South Africa. The state-sponsored programme for healing our land is called 'Reconstruction and Development', an ambitious project which is being greeted with offers of aid and investment from the World Bank, the International Monetary Fund (IMF) and the big powers. By introducing at this time a sense of interconnectedness/emptiness into areas of the public domain, it may be possible to make a tiny intervention which situates the 'individual', 'nature', 'women' and all the others in a way that is usefully different from that which the international networks of business, money and power are interested in promoting.

WHAT IS HEALTH? A MISLEADING BUT USEFUL QUESTION

In all this I have used metaphors of healing to describe experiments in non-dualism: healing the sickness of binary epistemology, healing self/nature. But what about 'health', the concept I began with? When I began this chapter, I asked various friends working in alternative health care what the term meant for them: 'What is health?' People spoke in a sense about non-dualism, about interconnectedness and particularity: 'caring for the whole person'; 'including all of the person, "positive" and "negative" aspects, without judgement'; 'a healthy organism is connected with its environment'; or that health is 'an alignment that works for *that person*, not a perfect statue which has never lived', and so on.

Gradually I realized that the question itself is misleading, perhaps instructively so. Although it is moving in the right direction – away from an exclusive focus on disease and alienation and towards something less dualistic than mainstream medicine generally offers – it implies that 'health' is a something, an entity, a goal rather like what one tends to imagine 'enlightenment' to be. But from the perspective of *pratityasamutpada*, 'health' is (like enlightenment) as empty as everything else. At the same time, because it is also 'full' of everything else, 'health care' implies healing not only of body/mind, but also of the eco-social environment. This suggests than an approach to health care informed by Madhyamika Buddhism will see the boundaries which separate people's concern for spiritual, psychological, physical, interpersonal, social, political or environmental well-being into separate fields of 'care' as being arbitrary. And yet, of course, these arbitrary boundaries are necessary and useful. To imagine treating the whole system simultaneously is hubristic and silly. How could we negotiate this? The concept of the Truths referred to earlier is a useful beginning as it points simultaneously to the conventional truth of entities and objects and the ultimate truth of emptiness. Perhaps we can learn from this a way of grounding the work of healing and compassion in two ways of seeing, both of which are 'true': things are at once both 'empty/interconnected' (not two) and 'real' (the myriad things). And so the specialized fields of health care are also both inextricably interconnected and necessarily distinct, diverse.

And perhaps there is an analogy here, too, for a collection such as this one with our transgressions of boundaries on behalf of feminism, postmodernism or ecological politics. Our fields of specialization are certainly 'empty', interconnected, and it is useful to recognize that their boundaries are fairly arbitrary. As environmentalists know, when you take down the fences that make the fields, the animals can move freely across the land; it is better for the land and for the animals, more sustainable. And yet, if we follow this ecological metaphor, we are reminded that the environmental systems we call bioregions are also 'real', distinct and particular, and that the local inhabitants of a place, or a discipline, are generally the best informed about the ecosystems of their home. So if we wish our trans-disciplinary explorations to avoid the tyrannic delusion of another totalizing/globalizing gaze, it is useful again to remember the teaching of the Two Truths. According to this, insight into non-dualism does not conflict with recognizing difference and particularity. In the case of theory and research, this highlights the importance of local knowledge and specialization.

How do we go beyond the techno- and bioscientific constructions of nature as other? This is the question I was asked to address in this chapter. In the Buddhism I have been describing, the practice is designed to go beyond all othering; beyond fear, hatred and desire; beyond even the confident assertions of our language. Six months ago, my father died quietly among the white pillows and kind nurses of another hospital. Two years after waking from the coma, he was old and sick, wanting to go. Gone beyond, gone beyond – relinquishing at last the desire for a theory that will hold it all in place, we wake up to impermanence. No words left – and yet we speak.

NOTES

1. Now, at the end of the twentieth century, we can speak of a generalized, fairly multicultural 'Buddhism' in a way that was not possible when regional and cultural boundaries were less permeable. But when I use the term here, I am referring particularly to contemporary interpretations of Zen and Tibetan Buddhism.

2. See, for example, several of the essays in *Reweaving the World: The Emergence of Ecofeminism* (Diamond and Orenstein 1990).

3. In the case of a writer such as Vandana Shiva, Agarwal argues that a similar failure to distinguish between women of different classes, castes, races, ecological zones, and so on, leads to the equally inaccurate figure of an Essentialized Third World Woman who is seen as being 'embedded in nature' (Agarwal 1992: 125).

4. I think this is also true to some extent of Susan Griffin's justifiably influential radical/ecofeminist work, *Woman and Nature: The Roaring Inside Her* (Griffin 1978).

5. For discussion of some of the problems implicit in the image of 'Mother Earth', see the essays by Patrick Murphy (1988) and Catherine Roach (1991).

6. It is, however, possible that goddess imagery can work differently, depending on the context. In Mahayana Buddhism, for example, the wisdom which goes beyond all dualisms is paradoxically pictured as a goddess, Prajnaparamita.

7. This essay became more widely available when published in Haraway's *Simians, Cyborgs and Women*, which is the source noted in the references (Haraway 1991).

8. It is perhaps necessary to note that I don't think this is what Haraway's essay suggests the cyborg is for. My comments are offered rather as a response to the enthusiastic reception of the concept by some feminists in Europe and North America.

9. What follows is a fairly brief description. For a fuller exploration of the theory involved, see my essay 'The Snake Person Takes on the Cock-sure Boys' (Martin 1994).

10. *Majjhima-nikaya*, III, quoted in Cheng 1991, p. 84.

11. For an excellent discussion of the Twofold Truth according to the Madhyamika, as well as an introduction to Nagarjuna's approach, see Hsueh-li Cheng's *Empty Logic: Madhyamika Buddhism from Chinese Sources* (Cheng 1991). Frederic Streng (1967) also gives a clear explanation of the material, and Robert Magliola (1986) makes useful comparisons between the Madhyamika and Derridean deconstruction.

12. For an enlightening commentary on this, see the present Dalai Lama's *A Flash of Lightning in the Dark of Night: A Guide to the Bodhisattva's Way of Life*, Gyatso 1994.

13. The conference 'Ecological Responsibility: A Dialogue with Buddhism', which was held in New Delhi in October 1993, was organized by Tibet House,

the Cultural Centre of His Holiness the Dalai Lama. Sakya Trizin's paper, 'Exchanging Self for Others', is forthcoming in *The Jewelled Net: Talks and Essays on Buddhism and Ecology*, edited by myself.

14. The instructions for the exercises are too lengthy to deal with here. See 'Taking Heart: Spiritual Exercises for Social Activists', in Macy 1991, pp. 39–49.

REFERENCES

Agarwal, B. (1992) 'The Gender and Environment Debate: Lessons from India', *Feminist Studies*, vol. 18, no. 1, Spring, pp. 119–58.

Cheng, Hsueh-li (1991) *Empty Logic: Madhyamika Buddhism from Chinese Sources*, Motilal Banarsidass, Delhi.

Diamond, I. and G.F. Orenstein, eds (1990) *Reweaving the World: The Emergence of Ecofeminism*, Sierra Club, San Francisco.

Griffin, S. (1978) *Woman and Nature: The Roaring Inside Her*, The Women's Press, London.

Gyatso, T. (1994) *A Flash of Lightning in the Dark of Night: A Guide to the Bodhisattva's Way of Life*, Shambala, London.

Haraway, D. (1991) *Simians, Cyborgs and Women: The Reinvention of Nature*, Free Association Books, London.

Klein, A.C. (1995) *Meeting the Great Bliss Queen: Buddhists, Feminists and the Art of the Self*, Beacon, Boston, Mass.

Macy, J. (1991) *World as Lover, World as Self*, Parallax, Berkeley, Calif.

Magliola, R. (1986) *Derrida on the Mind*, Purdue University Press, West Lafayette (1st edn 1984).

Martin, J. (1994) 'The Snake Person Takes on the Cock-sure Boys: Buddhism/Postmodernism/South African Eco-Politics', in T. D'haen and H. Bertens, eds, *Liminal Postmodernisms: The Postmodern, the (Post-) Colonial, and the (Post-)Feminist*, Rodopi, Amsterdam and Atlanta, Ga.

Murphy, P. (1988) 'Sex-Typing the Planet: Gaia Imagery and the Problem of Subverting Patriarchy', *Environmental Ethics*, vol. 10, no. 2, pp. 155–68.

Norbu, T. (1992) *White Sail: Crossing the Waves of Ocean Mind to the Serene Continent of the Triple Gems*, Shambhala, London.

Roach, C. (1991) 'Loving Your Mother: On the Woman–Nature Relation', *Hypatia*, vol. 6, no. 1, Spring, pp. 46–59.

Salleh, A. K. (1984) 'Deeper than Deep Ecology: The Eco-Feminist Connection', *Environmental Ethics*, vol 6, Winter, pp. 339–45.

Snyder, G. (1990) *Practice of the Wild*, North Point Press, San Francisco.

Streng, F. J. (1967) *Emptiness: A Study in Religious Meaning*, Abingdon, New York.

Tarthang Tulku (1978) *Kum Nye Relaxation: Part One – Theory, Preparation, Massage*, Dharma Publishing, Berkeley, Calif.

7

DOES WOMAN SPEAK FOR NATURE?

TOWARDS A GENEALOGY OF

ECOLOGICAL FEMINISMS

Sylvia Bowerbank

> It is time to reconstitute our culture in the name of ... nature, and of
> peace and freedom, and it is women who can show the way. We have
> to be the voice of the invisible, of nature who cannot speak for herself
> in the political arenas of our society.... We are the repository of a
> sensibility which can make a future possible.
>
> Ynestra King, 'The Eco-feminist Imperative'

Important theoretical questions are now being raised among ecological
feminists in regard to the political efficacy of woman's claim to a special
link with nature. What does it mean to claim that woman speaks for
nature? Are women the 'repository' of a special ecological sensibility, as
Ynestra King puts it (Caldecott and Leland 1983: 12–13)? If so, how
might this sensibility be mobilized to save the planet? This chapter
gives these questions a historical context. The debate among women
over their appropriate relationship to 'nature' was certainly taking place
in early modern England during the rise of the scientific revolution.
Englishwomen of the early modern period, whatever their social rank
or political allegiance, recognized the symbolic power of speaking as
nature's interpreters. In this chapter, the word 'nature' is in (invisible)
quotation marks; it refers to different discourses of nature, entangled
with cultural values and interests. The use of a single term – 'nature' –
obscures the plurality and instability of its meanings (Williams 1981:
219–24). Referring to eighteenth-century aesthetics, A.O. Lovejoy long
ago pointed out that 'Nature' was (and is) the most sacred and protean

word in the English language (Lovejoy 1948: 69–70). I am writing with a sense of what Ludmilla Jordanova calls 'the historicity of nature'; that is, a sense that 'the articulation and consolidation of the idea that nature itself is inherently historical' (Jordanova 1986: 28). 'Nature' indicates historically negotiated discourses, by which a society both creates and mediates its relationship with reality. The 'nature' early modern women spoke for was often, inevitably, entangled in the contradictory cultural values and interests that gave rise to imperialism not only over nature but also over the peoples and lands of other cultures. And yet there can be found in the cultural work of early modern women anticipatory traces of a distinct ecological sensibility.

Although its articulation has been and remains a historically situated and shifting process, nevertheless the modern discourse of nature is characterized by two complementary strains of thought that have developed and changed in relationship to each other (and continue to do so). On one hand, there emerged, in the early modern period, a dominant discourse of systematic and progressive mastery over nature, whether in the psyche, in the state, or in the wild (Merchant 1980). On the other hand, an underlying sympathy for nature – at times, even an identification with nature – continued to complicate and contradict that narrative of successful mastery. From the outset, the modern discourse of nature was gendered (Keller 1985). Even as it worked to undermine modern man's connectivity with nature, it reaffirmed that of woman. It perpetuated the ancient division of intellectual labour that associated man with the higher reasoning faculties and woman with the lower feeling faculties, a division of labour that emphasized man's detachment and woman's attachment to animal and vegetative nature. The dominant 'masculine' strain is the structure of feeling associated with mastery – pride, detachment and even alienation – that fosters competitive projects of management, expansion and exploitation. The recessive 'feminine' strain is a structure of feeling associated with conservation – reverence, humility and connectivity – that tries to restrain such projects by nurturing human attachment to non-human nature. While some men – poets and prophets – might choose to dissociate themselves from the discourse of mastery, women were, in theory, restricted to an identification with and a sympathy for nature.

A number of women writers of the 1790s – some radical, some conservative – claimed to speak in the name of true nature. Yet such claims are inherently problematic. What 'nature' does woman speak for? What 'woman' is speaking for nature? The term 'woman' is itself subject to cultural determination, as is indicated by Simone de Beauvoir's quip that 'every female human being is not necessarily a woman' (De Beauvoir 1974: xvi). In practice, eighteenth-century women took diverse, even contradictory, parts in their own dialogues with and about nature. Some replicated, some rehabilitated and some repudiated the dominant discourse. They did not speak for the same 'nature'. Then, as now, 'nature' was a politicized site of struggle among women. This chapter investigates a moment in that struggle as it manifested itself in England during the 1790s. In order to show that eighteenth-century women spoke for a diversity of 'natures', this chapter will contrast the natural philosophies of Hannah More and Mary Wollstonecraft, two Englishwomen writing from opposing perspectives during the 1790s.

Roughly speaking, the debate over nature in the 1790s went on between two sets of discourses. On the one hand, a discourse of scarcity claimed that the miseries and inequities of the existing economy were inherent in nature itself. As Thomas Malthus put it in his *Essay on the Principle of Population* (1798), the suffering of the lower classes is 'an evil so deeply seated that no human ingenuity can reach it' (Malthus 1976: 43). The deserving poor could only expect to be relieved by the voluntary condescension of the fortunate and, eventually, by the just rewards of heaven. On the other hand, a discourse of progress claimed that, once the true processes of 'nature' were freed from arbitrary despotism, an equitable and free economy would inevitably evolve. This progress of man as a species, however, was to be based on the increasing mastery and exploitation of 'nature' as an abundant, indeed limitless, resource.

THE CONSTRUCTION OF
'THE TRADITIONAL WOMAN' AND 'NATURAL
HARMONY': HANNAH MORE

Englishwomen of the 1790s did not agree on what nature says: some spoke out on behalf of nature as an economy of scarcity, and others on behalf of nature as an economy of expansion. Nor did they agree on the nature of the speaking female subject. The conventional axis of conservative/radical does not suffice to explain the theoretical complexities women faced. Whatever position they took, all women had to confront the anomalous fact of their own public role; they had to articulate accounts of female subjectivity not only commensurate with competing discourses of nature but also with the new phenomenon of their own agency as female intellectuals. During the early modern period, the discourse of 'the traditional woman' faced serious challenges to its exclusive claim to naturalness and had to be reinvented for modern consumption. No doubt there would be little quarrel with the claim that 'the modern woman' – or woman defined as a self-determining subject – is a recent invention. It is harder to see that the concept of 'the traditional woman' – or woman defined as a 'naturally' determined subject – is equally a culturally situated construct with its own shifting history as a discourse of female subjectivity. To illustrate, let me cite the work of Hannah More, one of the naturalizers of the modern version of 'the traditional woman'. Fundamental to Hannah More's concept of female subjectivity is the assumption that 'the mind in each sex has some natural kind of bias' (More 1788: 8). Women who defy 'nature' will inevitably become ridiculous and miserable. Thus, in More's early pastoral, *A Search after Happiness*, Florissa, who longed to achieve fame by exercising her talent for science, is told that

> woman shines but in her proper sphere...
> So woman, born to dignify retreat,
> Unknown to flourish, and unseen be great:
> To give domestic life its sweetest charm
> With softness polish, and with virtue warm...
> (More 1773: 26–7)

Hannah More and other conservative women envisioned the universe as a hierarchy of mutual dependencies that, admittedly, subordinated woman to man. Woman was granted a special function as compassionate mediator. Compassion, however, was defined within an economy of charity as condescension. In imitation of God, superior beings condescended to care for inferiors. Thus, Hannah More felt duty-bound to intervene in public issues on behalf of the less fortunate. To give a famous example, when the poor of Bristol were suffering want and starvation in 1795 and threatening revolt, More wrote her popular poem 'The Riot; or, Half a Loaf is Better than No Bread'. In the poem, Tom seizes his pitchfork and is ready to lead a mob to pull down the mills and steal all the food, but his fellow-worker Jack convinces him to stop by blaming the hard times not on the powerful or on an unjust system, but on the weather: 'And I never yet heard, though our rulers are wise,/That they know very well how to manage the skies' (Lonsdale 1984: 809). Jack advises the poor to tighten their belts, get back to work and wait for a good potato harvest. More's poem is said to have stopped a food riot in Bristol (Todd 1985: 226).

The philosophy of natural harmony advocated by Hannah More and like-minded women is one of gendered difference and complementarity of function. Despite claims to the contrary, this philosophy of nature is not based so much on first-hand observation of true nature as it is on a shrewd appropriation of the discourse of the sublime and the beautiful, as it emerged in eighteenth-century aesthetics. Eighteenth-century commentators set out to methodize aesthetic theory. They claimed to discover certain laws of nature that established congruency between external and psychological landscapes. By 1757, Edmund Burke made explicit what was already implicit: that the qualities and effects of the sublime were essentially distinct from those of the beautiful or, as it was also called, 'the pathetick'.[1] Burke argued that the beautiful dwells in what is small, delicate and pleasing and is therefore necessarily a feminine mode. In contrast, the sublime always dwells on great and terrible objects; it is therefore necessarily a masculine mode. According to Burke, man loves what is beautiful, including woman, precisely because it is weak, arouses pathos, and submits itself to man's pleasure and use. But he does not admire what is beautiful. He only admires and submits to what is more powerful than himself – that is, the sublime (Burke 1990: 103).[2] Likewise, in an early work, *Observations on the Feeling of the Beautiful and the Sublime* (1763), Immanuel Kant found it to be a law of nature that humanity is divided into the fair and the noble sex. The fair sex is inclined to be modest, neat, charming, good-hearted and sympathetic; the noble sex is reasonable, courageous and principled (Kant 1960: 76-7). Kant claims: 'The fair sex has just as much understanding as the male, but it is a beautiful understanding, whereas … [man's] should be a deep understanding, an expression that signifies identity with the sublime.' (Kant 1960: 78). If all goes well, Kant writes, a man and a woman will form a single moral person 'governed by the understanding of the man and the taste of the wife' (Kant 1960: 95).

The ideological pattern of the sublime and the beautiful was reproduced in any number of writings by women of the late eighteenth century. This typical passage from More's *Essays on Various Subject, Principally Designed for Young Ladies* suffices to make that point:

> The female mind, in general, does not appear capable of attaining so high a degree of perfection in science as the male. … Women have generally quicker perceptions; men have juster sentiments. – Women consider how things may be prettily said; men how they may be properly said. – In women, (young ones at least) speaking accompanies, and sometimes precedes reflection; in men, reflection is the antecedent. – Women speak to shine or to please; men, to convince or confute. – Women admire what is brilliant; men what is solid. (More 1788: 4–6)

And yet, Hannah More and other traditional women of the late eighteenth century were by no means mere 'zombies of discourse', to borrow Dan Latimer's useful phrase (Latimer 1989: 280). They took strategic advantage of the compensatory powers granted them. They eagerly laid claim both to a special good nature that was capable of redeeming man's excesses and to the right to speak for that harmonic nature. According to More, the good of the whole necessitated the public expression of both sets of qualities:

> The sublime, the nervous, and the masculine, characterize their compositions; as the beautiful, the soft, and the delicate, mark those of the others. Grandeur, dignity, and force, distinguish the one species; ease, simplicity, and purity the other. Both shine from their native, distinct, unborrowed merits, not from those which are foreign, adventitious, and unnatural. (More 1788: 5–6)

If men are more dignified and judicious in their learning, argues More, women are compensated by the 'pathetick' power to move men to virtue.[3] If man may lay claim to greatness, woman may lay claim to goodness. If male intellectuals turn their attention to the scientific conquest of nature, the argument went, so female intellectuals must take on the moral role of inculcating due reverence and due restraint.

Thus, ironically, without seeming to defy traditional values, Hannah More and others made a territorial claim, in the name of nature, for certain kinds of social agency proper to women alone. In her work, More pressed remnants of the Christian system into the service of eighteenth-century theories of reality in order to naturalize what is essentially a modern justification for woman's right – or, better, woman's duty – to speak for natural beauty and harmony. Whatever the inequities of the master discourse of the sublime and the beautiful, it created asymmetrical spheres of gendered powers and therefore allowed for two distinct subject positions from which to speak for nature. It naturalized a division of labour whereby the man ventures to conquer new frontiers – the wild; the woman maintains domesticated space – the home. His sphere is intellectual; hers is moral. His landscape (the Alps) elevates the mind; her landscape (the picturesque valley) harmonizes the mind with what is. He creates the future world; she sustains the present one. His destiny is greatness; hers is goodness. Taken as a whole, the gendered discourse of the sublime and the beautiful is *par excellence* the modern discourse of nature, allowing modern humanity to claim at once dominion over and kinship with nature.

THE CONSTRUCTION OF THE 'MODERN WOMAN':
MARY WOLLSTONECRAFT

In her early books on educating girls – *Thoughts on the Education of Daughters* ([1787] 1789) and *Original Stories* ([1788] 1791) – Mary Wollstonecraft also celebrated feminine sympathy towards God's creatures: little girls should be taught gratitude for the beauty of nature as it is; they should balance the arrogant destructiveness of boys. But, by 1790, Wollstonecraft had rejected the 'nature' that constrained woman to reproduce suspect 'harmony'. Such a 'nature' was a Bastille from which the female mind must escape. She began to articulate a brilliant critique of woman's place in patriarchal holism. Ridiculing woman's claim to 'fascinating graces', she exposed the power dynamics inherent in the discourse of the sublime and the beautiful (Wollstonecraft 1988: 9). In *Vindication of the Rights of Men* (1790), she heaps scorn on Edmund Burke for his gendered theory of nature by which he reserves heroic virtues for men, while leading women to neglect their true powers in the name of 'beautiful nature':

> You may have convinced them that *littleness* and *weakness* are the very essence of beauty; and that the Supreme Being, in giving women beauty in the most supereminent degree, seemed to command them, by the powerful voice of Nature, not to cultivate the moral virtues that might chance to excite respect, and interfere with the pleasing sensations they were created to inspire. Confining thus truth, fortitude, and humanity, within the rigid pale of manly morals, they might justly argue, that to be loved, woman's high and great distinction! they should 'learn to lisp, to totter in their walk, and nick-name God's creatures'.[4] (Wollstonecraft 1790: 105–6)

Vindication of the Rights of Woman ([1792] 1988) continues Wollstonecraft's exposé of the flattering illusion that woman has natural powers that require neither thought nor self-discipline to have their beneficial effect on society. The sad lot of women is enforced not by nature, claimed Wollstonecraft, but by entrenched despotism. This critique is well known. But what positive philosophy of nature did Wollstonecraft advocate? And what subject position did Wollstonecraft advocate for woman in relationship to non-human nature?

In one way, it suffices to say that Wollstonecraft shared the philosophy of nature of the Enlightenment. What she says is often predictably along these lines. The metaphor she uses to assert the modern subject position of woman is telling: she aligns herself with the scientific construction of nature as articulated by the greatest genius of the century, the sublime Newton: 'Let there be then no coercion established in society, and the common law of gravity prevailing, the sexes will fall into their proper places' (Wollstonecraft 1988: 6). To a considerable extent, her body of work shares the same set of attitudes that reduced nature to a frontier, subject to the expansionary projects of man. In *An Historical and Moral View of the French Revolution*, she is able, for example, to take a philosophical view of the disastrous effects of the French Revolution as a necessary stage in humanity's advancement from savagery to civilization (Wollstonecraft 1795: vi). In the last words of her *An Historical and Moral View*, she writes that the horrors she witnessed are merely 'the dreadful effects' of the purging of the corrupt state, or in her words, 'the excrementitious humours exuding from the contaminated body' politic (Wollstonecraft 1795: 387).

DILEMMAS IN THE MODERN WOMAN'S APPROPRIATION OF ENLIGHTENMENT DISCOURSES ON NATURE

The inherent problems of the modern philosopher as speaking subject become manifest in Wollstonecraft's record of her 1795 journey to Scandinavia, published in the following year as *Letters Written During a Short Residence in Sweden, Norway and Denmark* ([1796] 1976). In that work, she takes on a habit of mind of empire that ranked other peoples and landscapes in accordance with the degree of their conformity to an abstract discourse of progress. According to her 'philosophic eye', the economy of free enterprise is a natural development, superior to the subsistence economy of the Swedish peasantry, which is a remnant of the golden age in a 'land of flint' (Wollstonecraft 1976: 12). Thus, she sees the peoples of Scandinavia through the lens of a temporalized chain of distinction. For example, she privileges the entrepreneurial English over the backward Swedish peasants, who

> remain so near the brute creation, as only to exert themselves to find the food necessary to sustain life, have little or no imagination to call forth the curiosity necessary to fructify the faint glimmerings of mind which entitles them to rank as lords of the creation. – Had they either, they could not contentedly remain rooted in the clods they so indolently cultivate. (Wollstonecraft 1976: 10)

In Scandinavia, Wollstonecraft's feelings of superiority to the common lot of women are unmistakable. She is the ugly tourist, an early version of the First World woman visiting her sisters in the Third World. When she is put on a desolate shore in Sweden with only her infant and

Marguerite, her French maid, as companions, she is superior to the feminine frailties of Marguerite, who fears 'robberies, murders, or the other evil, which instantly, as the sailors would have said, runs foul of a woman's imagination' (Wollstonecraft 1976: 11). Wollstonecraft demonstrates little understanding of or sympathy for the role of women in a subsistence economy. She rails against the stupidity and drudgery of the lives of Swedish women and resists any impulse to identify with their condition. The image of the peasant woman that emerges is one of an ignorant, indelicate drudge, who becomes old and fat before her time. Conditioned to confinement – shut up in overheated rooms, polluted by the continual smoking of her menfolk – she, in turn, smothers her guests with excessive hospitality as she does her babies with overswaddling. Wollstonecraft is proud to be made an exception, to be called by one host 'a woman of observation' because she asked 'men's questions' (Wollstonecraft 1976: 15).

Although Wollstonecraft announces in her 'advertisement' that what she records are her spontaneous reflections, the language she uses to describe her responses unmistakably indicates her debt, or, better, her entanglement in the discourse of the sublime and the beautiful. Even before she landed, she understood that, for refined tastes, certain emotions are appropriate to certain landscapes. The 'pathetick' mode harmonizes the soul to nature as it exists, while the sublime carries the mind beyond nature to the realm of genius and creativity. Wollstonecraft was fully aware of, and determined to take on the powers of, the masculine, sublime mode. That is why she wanted to go to Switzerland, the most sublime landscape in the world, and why she preferred the rugged landscape of Norway to the landscapes of Sweden and Denmark. Even before going, she knew the effect that such a challenging, northern landscape could have on the philosophically receptive mind. Thus on Friday, 12 June 1795, before sailing to Sweden, she wrote to Gilbert Imlay:

> the ineffable delight, the exquisite pleasure, which arises from a unison of affection and desire, when the whole soul and sense are abandoned to a lively imagination, that renders every emotion delicate and rapturous.... These emotions, more or less strong, appear to me to be the distinctive characteristic of genius, the foundation of taste, and of that exquisite relish for the beauties of nature, of which the common herd of eaters and drinkers and *child-getters*, certainly have no idea. (Wollstonecraft 1979: 291)

The position of the female subject that she assumes – in marked contrast to that which she allots to the herd of other women – is as a liberated figure in the wild landscape, transported beyond the common sentiments of womankind. She is ever escaping to be alone among the rocks – 'the sovereign of the waste', as she calls herself (Wollstonecraft 1979: 73). The landscape of the sublime – the boundless ocean, the mighty waterfall, the craggy mountain – as Kant puts it in *The Critique of Judgment* (1790), raises 'the energies of the soul above their accustomed height and discover in us a faculty of resistance ... which gives us courage to measure ourselves against the apparent almightiness of nature' (Kant 1951: 100–01). In a classic experience of the sublime, Wollstonecraft at the cataracts at Tiesdal achieves a momentary vision of the endless potential to perfect nature:

> my thoughts darted from earth to heaven, and I asked myself why I was chained to life and its misery? Still the tumultuous emotions this sublime object excited, were pleasurable; and, viewing it, my soul rose, with renewed dignity, above its cares – grasping at immortality – it seemed as impossible to stop the current of my thoughts, as of the always varying, still the same, torrent before me – I stretched out my hand to eternity, bounding over the dark speck of life to come. (Wollstonecraft 1976: 132–3)

The sublime mode challenges men – and some women, Wollstonecraft urges – to transcend the dominion of nature, as it now seems defined, and to invent new nature.

Letters Written During a Short Residence documents the remarkable process of a woman thinking her way towards a future society, while passing judgement on the existing one. What is recorded is Wollstonecraft's struggle to articulate the subject position of the modern woman in relationship to nature, or rather in relationship to the eighteenth-century discourse of the pathetic and the sublime. Clearly, she is convinced she has to make a choice *within* the dominant discourse of nature. It is a terrible choice she makes: to take up the masculine and to reject the feminine mode. The personal price of nonconformity and alienation from the present society is considerable: 'I have then considered myself as a particle broken off from the grand mass of mankind' (Wollstonecraft 1976: 17). Yet she dare not let herself be overcome by the 'imperious sympathies' which link her to the existing discourse of harmony. Particularly seductive is the experience of the feminine world. Scattered throughout the text are references to the amiable goodness of women: there is the housewife who spreads her whitest sheets for Wollstonecraft; the one who puts juniper sprigs on the bedroom floor to freshen the air; the one who rises before dawn to make Wollstonecraft coffee. There are the girls who create laughter by the age-old trick of putting a mouse in a snuff-box; there is the pregnant young woman who teaches Wollstonecraft how to row a boat; and there is Marguerite, the French servant, whose gaiety of heart Wollstonecraft finds 'worth all my philosophy' (Wollstonecraft 1976: 176). Also recorded is Wollstonecraft's overwhelming maternal attachment to baby Fanny, whom she leaves in Gothenburg while she travels. When she sees a good father playing with his child, she momentarily envies the mother making the soup (Wollstonecraft 1976: 141).

For Wollstonecraft, however, these sympathies are dangerous. They are involuntary emotions – 'the attraction of adhesion' – which threaten to make her feel at home in an unjust society. She struggles to free herself: 'I was still a part of a mighty whole, from which I could not sever myself' (Wollstonecraft 1976: 16–17). She cultivates the same wariness as she did in her reaction to the sufferings of the French during the Revolution: 'It becomes necessary to guard against the erroneous inferences of sensibility' (Wollstonecraft 1795: vi). In Scandinavia, when she considers the oppression of women – that most women live as domestic scolds married to drunken sots, or that her daughter Fanny, should she be taught to think, would be rendered 'unfit for the world she is to inhabit', Wollstonecraft rejects the pathetic mode and takes up the burden of her philosophy once more (Wollstonecraft 1976: 145, 55).

In *Letters Written During a Short Residence*, Wollstonecraft chooses the mode of progress over nature as the way to a just future. Even so, part of her is aware of the inadequacy of the choice she makes. Her ambivalence is manifested in this meditation on the wildness of the Norwegian coast at Rusoer:

> I anticipated the future improvement of the world, and observed how much man had still to do, to obtain of the earth all it could yield. I even carried my speculations so far as to advance a million or two of years to the moment when the earth would perhaps be so perfectly cultivated, and so completely peopled, as to render it necessary to inhabit every spot; yes; these bleak shores. Imagination went still farther, and pictured the state of man when the earth could no longer support him. Where was he to fly from universal famine? Do not smile: I really became distressed for these fellow-creatures, yet unborn. (Wollstonecraft 1976: 102)

What is remarkable about this passage is the way in which it hovers between the economies of progress and scarcity. Elsewhere, Wollstonecraft condemns the new tyranny of wealth in no uncertain terms. It is a species of injustice far worse than aristocracy. She ends *Letters Written*

During a Short Residence by calling herself a Cassandra who foresees that the very progressive movement with which she has aligned herself will not lead to the just society she desires.

In this chapter, I have provided a historical narrative to elucidate a striking paradox at the heart of modern culture. As Jane Jacobs notes in *The Death and Life of Great American Cities*, in its relationship with nature, Western society is the most destructive culture ever to exist and, simultaneously, the most sentimental (Jacobs 1961: 445). This paradox is deeply rooted in our social and psychological habits. The modern discourse of nature emerged in the early modern period as a gendered, two-sphered discourse, which permits the coexistence of the imperialism and sentimentalization of nature. What is needed is a fundamental revolt against the division of labour by which man conquers and woman 'loves' nature. What is needed is a new discourse of nature, a hybrid perhaps of what have been historically distinguished as the feminine and feminist modes. Or something radically new.

NOTES

1. Here I am using 'pathetick' not in the current demeaning sense, but in the positive, eighteenth-century sense of the word – although, of course, something can be learned from the degeneration of its meaning.

2. As one indication that nature is being reinvented, in the 'Cyborg Manifesto', Donna Haraway notices that the association of smallness with delicacy and submission has broken down: 'Miniaturization has turned out to be about power; small is not so much beautiful as preeminently dangerous' (Haraway 1991: 153).

3. Again, I am using 'pathetick' in the eighteenth-century sense of the word.

4. Adapted from Shakespeare's *Hamlet*, III.i.150.

REFERENCES

Burke, E. (1990) *A Philosophical Enquiry into the Origin of our Ideas of the Sublime and Beautiful*, edited by A. Phillips, Oxford University Press, Oxford.

Caldecott, L. and S. Leland, eds (1983) *Reclaim the Earth: Women Speak Out for Life on Earth*, Women's Press, London.

De Beauvoir, S. (1974) *The Second Sex*, translated by H.M. Parshley, Vintage, New York.

Haraway, D. (1991) *Simians, Cyborgs, and Women: The Reinvention of Nature*, Routledge, New York.

Jacobs, Jane (1961) *The Death and Life of Great American Cities*, Vintage, New York.

Jordanova, L.J., ed (1986) *Languages of Nature: Critical Essays on Science and Literature*, Rutgers University Press, New Brunswick, N.J.

Kant, I. (1951) *Critique of Judgment*, trans. J.H. Bernard, Haynes, New York.

———— (1960) *Observations on the Feeling of the Beautiful and Sublime*, translated by J.T. Goldthwait, University of California Press, Berkeley, Calif.

Keller, E. F. (1985) *Reflections on Gender and Science*, Yale University Press, New Haven, Conn.

King, Y. (1983) 'The Eco-feminist Imperative', in L. Caldecott and S. Leland, eds, *Reclaim the Earth: Women Speak Out for Life on Earth*, Women's Press, London, pp. 9–14.

Latimer, D., ed (1989) *Contemporary Critical Theory*, Harcourt Brace Jovanovich, San Diego, Calif.

Lonsdale, R. (1984) *The New Oxford Book of Eighteenth-Century Verse*, Oxford University Press, Oxford.

Lovejoy, A.O. (1948) '"Nature" as Aesthetic Norm', *Essays in the History of Ideas*, Johns Hopkins Press, Baltimore, Md.

Malthus, T. (1976) *An Essay on the Principle of Population*, edited by P. Appleman, Norton, New York.

Merchant, C. (1980) *The Death of Nature: Women, Ecology, and the Scientific Revolution*, Harper & Row, San Francisco, Calif.

More, H. (1788) 'Essays on Various Subject, Principally Designed for Young Ladies', *Works of Miss Hannah More in Prose and Verse*.

———— (1773) *A Search after Happiness: A Pastoral in Three Dialogues By a Young Lady*, Bristol.

Todd, J. (1985) *A Dictionary of British and American Women Writers 1660–1800*, Rowman & Littlefield, Totowa, N.J.

Williams, R. (1981) *Keywords: A Vocabulary of Culture and Society*, Fontana, London.

Wollstonecraft, M. ([1787] 1789) *Thoughts on the Education of Daughters*, J. Johnson, London.

———— (1790) *A Vindication of the Rights of Men, in a Letter to the Right Honourable Edmund Burke; occasioned by His Reflections on the Revolution in France*, J. Johnson, London.

———— ([1788] 1791) *Original Stories from Real Life with Conversations Calculated to Regulate the Affections and Form the Mind to Truth and Goodness*, J. Johnson, London.

———— (1795) *An Historical and Moral View of the Origin and Progress of the French Revolution and the Effect it has produced in Europe*.

———— ([1796] 1976) *Letters Written during a Short Residence in Sweden, Norway, and Denmark*, edited by C. Poston, University of Nebraska Press, Lincoln.

———— (1979) *Collected Letters of Mary Wollstonecraft*, edited by Ralph M. Wardle, Cornell Unversity Press, Ithaca, N.Y.

———— ([1792] 1988) *A Vindication of the Rights of Woman*, edited by C. Poston, Norton, New York.

PART TWO

MONSTERS:

BIOMEDICAL BODYGAMES

8

SIGNS OF WONDER AND TRACES OF DOUBT: ON TERATOLOGY AND EMBODIED DIFFERENCES

Rosi Braidotti

THE NON-SCIENTIFIC STATUS OF MONSTERS

Although medical accounts of monsters have been available since the eighteenth century, one can hardly speak in terms of a truly scientific discourse about them.[1] And this is precisely what makes teratology – the science of monsters – scientifically interesting. Being figures of complexity, monsters lend themselves to a layering of discourses and also to a play of the imagination which defies rationalistic reductions. Darmon puts it succinctly: 'la procréation des monstres ne se voit pas: elle s'imagine' (Darmon 1977: 8). As Canguilhem pointed out, the more fantastic or 'irrational' aspects of the discourse about monsters coexist simultaneously with the evolution of a science called 'teratology'. The simultaneity of potentially contradictory discourses about monsters is significant; it is also quite fitting because to be significant and to signify potentially contradictory meanings is precisely what the monster is supposed to do.

The Latin etymology of the term confirms it: *monster/monstrum* is primarily an object of display. This can be understood quite literally. Historically, monsters have always been exhibited in public spaces. In the Renaissance they roamed from royal courts to country fairs; in the seventeenth and eighteenth centuries they moved into pubs and coffee houses, as well as into the collection cabinets of the upper classes; in the nineteenth century, the side-shows and the circus inaugurated the commercialization of monstrous bodies, which culminated in the motion-picture industry.

In this chapter, I will analyse how teratology conveys a set of surprisingly continuous discourses which organize scientifically and socially the perception of embodied differences. We all have bodies, but not all bodies are equal: some matter more than others; some are, quite frankly, disposable. Forms of genderization and racialization of differences play an important role in this process. The monstrous body, which makes a living spectacle of itself, is eminently disposable.

The other and, in my opinion, more interesting question prompted by the etymology of the term is, however, what exactly are monsters a display of? Saint Augustine argued that *monstrum* is synonymous with *prodigum*, and thus the monster de-monstrates God's will, which may or may not be a positive thing. *Monstrum* can in fact also be associated with *moneo*, which means to warn. The warning capacity of the monster never went unnoticed in antiquity, partly because the signs of wonder usually came in clusters: a monstrous birth was accompanied by the arrival of a comet; a satanic birth, by an earthquake and so on. One could hardly ignore them. It seems to me that this astrological element is one of the keys to the longevity of the mythic quality of the monster.

It is no wonder, then, that since Babylonian times (2800 BC) monsters were used for *teratoscopy* – that is, predictions or divination based on the examination of their usually murdered bodies. Being situated as a signpost at the crossroads of the supernatural with the earthly, the monstrous body is a textual body, and this is hardly an easy task. Given that the birth of a monstrous baby was a divine warning, the best way to propitiate the gods was to offer the very same monstrous body – and often that body's mother – in sacrifice. It seems quite a paradox, though not an unfamiliar one, to be the signpost for cosmic events and to die for it.

The Greek etymology of the term again leaves us in no doubt as to what is at stake: *teras/teratos* refers both to a prodigy and to a demon. It is something which evokes both horror and fascination, aberration and adoration. It is simultaneously holy and hellish, sacred and profane. Again, the simultaneity of opposite effects is the trademark of the monstrous body. Mary Douglas and Julia Kristeva have done interesting work on this aspect of teratology.

The structural ambiguity of the monster as a figure of simultaneous and contradictory signification is not confined to antiquity. The Reformation also had a vested interest in the idea that monsters had signifying powers, which was used for anti-clerical propaganda, as proved by the famous cases of Luther's interpretation of the 'Calf-Monk' or 'Ass-

Pope'.[2] 'It is known that at the time of the religious wars, Catholics and Protestants disputed the favour of heaven by giving warrant to the authority of monsters' (Céard 1991: 183).

In 1573, Ambroise Paré, in his analysis of the 'Calf-Monk' case, no longer charged the monster with the task of denouncing the depravity of the monastic state. What emerged instead was an illustrative function of the monster as pointing out the infinite powers of the imagination. The kind of rarity represented by monsters is for Paré testimony to the ingenuity and the great variety of nature. Monsters are, therefore, not outside the natural order, but very much part of it, though they tend to represent the more fanciful and uncontrollable elements of natural life. This idea lasted well into the eighteenth century.

Because of this ambiguity, monsters in all their complexity have raised the issue as to what constitutes an object of scientific inquiry. To paraphrase Daston and Galison (1992: 82), we may not know what we mean or why we mean it when we ask questions such as 'Is objective scientific knowledge of monsters possible?' In any case, it is difficult to know what a sensible answer to this question would be.

BEYOND THE DISTINCTION BETWEEN 'HIGH' AND 'LOW' CULTURE

For one thing, scholarship about monsters blurs the distinction between 'high' or learned and 'low' or popular culture. Teratology is historically a mixed discourse; as an 'impure' non-object of scientific inquiry, the monster is not only situated in between cultures but also plays a major role in their interaction. For instance, throughout the Middle Ages and the Renaissance, broadsheets, pamphlets, songs and legends about monstrous beings flourished without regard to, and often in blatant defiance of, more 'scientific' accounts.

Park and Daston (1991) argue that, after the introduction of the printing press, teratological literature became sharply differentiated: the urban educated classes moved away from superstitious beliefs, which continued to prosper among unlettered peasants. Not only did the two categories coexist, divided along class lines, but new genres arose to cater for the restless imaginary of the sixteenth-century beau monde. It was for them that new brands of escapist literature were written: chivalric romance and fantastic travel books. Both genres are packed with monstrous beings and events.

In her analysis of popular theories of generation and how they survived the transition to the modern world-view, Blackman points to the continuity of a more or less established body of popular beliefs, 'largely oral, handed down from generation to generation, explaining natural phenomena and bodily functions and malfunctions' (Blackman 1977: 56). This popular body of established beliefs was based on the vulgarized renditions of Aristotle's biological and gynaecological ideas, which constitute the longest-standing corpus of beliefs about childbirth in European biomedical history (Trembach 1986). Although the invention of the printing press and the development of the 'scientific spirit' transformed this corpus, it never completely replaced it.

In his analysis of nineteenth-century freak-shows, Bogdan argues that they catered simultaneously for the medical doctors' curiosity over anomalous beings and the popular hunger for sensations. This represents a special form of voyeurism: 'the pornography of disability'. It is clear that freak-shows served the medical profession well, and there is also ample evidence that many medical doctors examined the exhibits and published papers about them in respectable places, such as the *American Journal of Medical Sciences*.[3]

For her part, Jordanova argues that the complicity between the vulgarity of the side-shows and the allegedly restrained medical profession became so strong that many nineteenth-century doctors made a point of publicly dissociating themselves from such practices.

A contemporary example of such mingling of 'high' and 'low' cultures is the boom of science fiction, and especially the cyberpunk phenomenon, as well as the extent to which the fictional work of someone like William Gibson – most definitely a champion of 'low or popular' culture – is a source of inspiration for scientific discourse in the biomedical sphere and in information technology. In this respect, the 'promises' of monsters, as Haraway puts it, are plentiful.

Nevertheless, complexity is not synonymous with epistemological anarchy. A working definition of the term 'monster' has been available since the late eighteenth century, when Geoffroy de Saint Hilaire organized monsters in terms of *excess*, *lack* or *displacement* of his/her organs. There can be too many parts or too few; the right ones can be in the wrong places or duplicated at random on the surface of the body. This is the definition I have adopted in my work.[4]

THE EPISTEMOPHILIC STRUCTURES OF TERATOLOGICAL DISCOURSES

Discourses about monsters are fundamentally 'epistemophilic', in that they express and explore a deep-seated curiosity about the origins of the deformed or anomalous body. Historically, the question that was asked about monsters was: 'How could such a thing happen? Who has done this?' The quest for the *origin* of monstrous bodies has motivated some of the wildest theories about them.

The epistemophilic dimension makes teratology an ideal testing ground for Freudian critiques of scientific theories in terms of dis- placed sexual curiosity. For psychoanalytic theory, the desire to know, which is the drive that sustains scientific inquiries, is marked by curiosity about one's own origins, and is consequently stamped with libidinal investments. Psychoanalysis teaches us that desire is that which remains ungraspable at the very heart of our thought, because it is that which propels our thinking in the first place. As such, it will evade us in the very act of constituting us as subjects of knowledge. This is why no science can ever be either 'pure' or 'objective' for psychoanalysis. The monstrous or hybrid body is perfect evidence of such theory. In dis- courses about monsters, the scientific and the fantasmatic dimensions intersect constantly.

There is another, more concrete side to this epistemophilic issue. Historically, monstrous bodies have served as material for experimen- tation in biomedical practices that eventually led to comparative anatomy and embryology. Disposable bodies are useful to science.

Monsters are linked to the female body in scientific discourse through the question of biological reproduction. Theories of conception of monsters are at times extreme versions of the deep-seated anxiety that surrounds the issue of women's maternal power of procreation in a patriarchal society. To say that compulsory heterosexuality is one of the issues at stake in teratology may seem far-fetched until one reads, in a famous treaty on prodigies, a scathing and rather scurrilous account of the monstrous sexual practices attributed to female hermaphrodites – living in far away places like Africa – who take advantage of their monstrosity by indulging in the filthiest of practices: same-sex sex. The year is 1573; the author is Ambroise Paré. Far-fetched?

Historical examples of the epistemophilic structure of teratology abound. Ambroise Paré concentrates his research on monsters entirely on the question of their reproduction and tells the most extraordinary fictions about their origin; however, these fictions are embedded in some of the most serious canonical texts of Western theology and biology, mostly based on Aristotle.

Paré describes the monstrous birth as a sinister sign ('mauvais augure') that expresses the guilt or sin of the parents. The most common forms of parental transgression concern the norms for acceptable sexual

*compare with womb envy?

practice, which were regulated by the Catholic Church. Thus, the practice of intercourse on a Sunday or on the eve of any major religious holiday, as well as too frequent intercourse, are quoted reasons for monstrous births.

Sexual excess, especially in the woman, is always a factor. Too much or too little semen are quoted as central causes, as is the mixing of sperm from different sources – for instance, intercourse with animals. Hereditary factors are not ruled out. Intercourse during menstruation is fatal. The influence of stars and planets also matters, as does the consumption of forbidden food, or of the right food at the wrong time. But the monster could also be conceived because of bad atmospheric conditions, or by divine or diabolic interventions.

The devil is extremely resourceful when it comes to satanic penetrations and conceptions. Saint Augustine warns us that Satan – the great simulator! – can take different forms. For instance, as succubus (the one who lies at the bottom) he can take the appearance of a beautiful woman; in this guise, he seduces a healthy young man, thus obtaining his sperm. Then he changes into an incubus (the one who lies on top) and, in this guise – as a man – and in full control of the sperm he has just extracted, he seduces and impregnates a chosen woman. Apart from showing the infinite malice of the evil genius, this would have to count as one of the earliest theories of artificial insemination.

CONTINUITIES AND SPECIFICITIES OF THEME IN TERATOLOGICAL DISCOURSES

The striking historical continuity of some themes regarding monsters is partly due to the two main features I have already pointed out: their non-objective status or 'impurity' and their epistemophilic charge. Clearly, the question 'Where do babies – however monstrous – come from?' is as transhistorical a line of inquiry as one is ever likely to get!

Park and Daston (1981) situate the continuity of teratology in a set corpus of canonical texts: first, the biological works of Aristotle and his classical followers, primarily Albertus Magnus; second, the tradition of divination canonized by Cicero in *De Divinatione*; third, the cosmographical and anthropological components. Glenister (1964) suggests instead a relative stability in the *categories* of historical analysis of monstrous births. The following seem to recur quite regularly: supernatural causes, astrological influences, seminal and menstrual factors, hybridity, mental impressions, philosophical and scientific explanations.

It seems clear that a degree of thematic consistency and order does exist. For the sake of convenience, ever since the encyclopaedic work done in the nineteenth century by Geoffrey Saint-Hilaire, the scientific history of monsters has been divided in three major periods: classical antiquity, the pre-scientific and the scientific eras. To these traditional distinctions, I would like to add a fourth one: the genetic turning point in the post-nuclear era, also known as cybernetic teratology, and the making of new monsters due to the effects of toxicity and environmental pollution.

In the rest of this chapter, I will concentrate on two themes, the continuity of which in the history of teratological discourses strikes me as particularly significant: the racialization of monstrous bodies and the question of the maternal imagination – race and gender as marks of difference. I would like to begin with an introductory remark.

As a signpost, the monster helps organize more than the interaction of heaven and earth. It also governs the production of differences here and now. The traditional – historically constant – categories of otherness are sexual difference and sexual deviation (especially homosexuality and hermaphroditism); race and ethnicity; the non-human, either on an upward trajectory (the divine, or sacred) or a downward one (the natural environment, the animal, the degenerate, the mutant). A case apart is that of the inorganic other; that is, the machine or technological body-double, the relation of which to the monstrous body is strong. Discussion of this topic would require the kind of special attention that, I regret, I cannot give here.

The peculiarity of the organic monster is that s/he is both Same and Other. The monster is neither a total stranger nor completely familiar; s/he exists in an in-between zone. I would express this as a paradox: the monstrous other is both liminal and structurally central to our perception of normal human subjectivity. The monster helps us understand the paradox of 'difference' as a ubiquitous but perennially negative preoccupation.

This mechanism of 'domestic foreignness', exemplified by the monster, finds its closest analogy in mechanisms such as sexism and racism. The woman, the Jew, the black or the homosexual are certainly 'different' from the configuration of human subjectivity based on masculinity, whiteness, heterosexuality, and Christian values which dominates our scientific thinking. Yet they are central to this thinking, linked to it by negation, and therefore structurally necessary to upholding the dominant view of subjectivity. The real enemy is within: s/he is liminal, but dwells at the heart of the matter. With this in mind, let us look at some historical cases.

THE RACIALIZATION OF 'OTHER' BODIES

One of the dominant teratological discourses in antiquity is that of the monstrous races on the edge of civilization. We find a sort of anthropological geography, the study of territories or special lands where the monstrous races live. Homer had written about cyclops and giant races, of course, but it is Herodotus that started the anthropological trend in the fifth century BC. Though he was rather reserved about neighbouring civilizations such as the Egyptian and the Persian, he went quite wild over more distant lands such as India and Ethiopia, which he thought were populated by cannibals, troglodytes and monstrously deformed people. In the fourth century BC, Ktesias described the Indian tribes of *Sciapodes*, who had one single large foot on which they could hop faster than any bipeds; descriptions of *Cynocephali* (dog-headed people) and *Blemmyae* (headless people) also abound. Through the canonization these monstrous races receive in Pliny's *Natural History*, they will become part and parcel of European medieval folklore. Medieval iconography will, of course, accentuate the monstrosity of monsters and provide moral readings of their morphological deformations.

Whence does this geographical and anthropological racist imaginary originate? Bernal (1987) suggests that the foundations for this topographic determinism of races can be found in Aristotle's *Politics*, in the following passage:

> The races that live in cold regions and those of Europe are full of courage and passion but somewhat lacking in skill and brainpower, for this reason, while remaining generally independent, they lack political cohesion and the ability to rule others. On the other hand, the Asiatic races have both brains and skill but are lacking in courage and willpower; so they have remained both enslaved and subject. The Hellenic race, occupying a mid position geographically, has a measure of both. Hence it has continued to be free, to have the best political institutions and to be capable of ruling others given a single constitution.[5]

The politics of climate and the justice of *in media res* were to have a long and rather successful history in European culture. In a set of continuous historical variations, our culture has tended to represent the furthest away as the most monstrous – that is, the least civilized, the least democratic or least law-abiding; though the actual structures of the scientific discourses conveying this idea underwent historical transformations – from the geographical discourse of the Greeks to the concern for jurisprudence in the eighteenth century, down to evolutionary anthropology in the nineteenth. The idea lived on, stubbornly and lethally.

The colonization of the North American continent, for instance, intensified the trend. Greek theories about climatic and geographical determinism of races lived on in the New World, though they underwent significant revisions. A papal bull by Paul II was needed in 1537 to affirm that Native Americans were fully human and therefore in possession of an immortal soul (de Waal Malefijt 1968), but this did not stop the European settlers from capturing them as 'specimens' and shipping them back to Europe to be placed on public display, a phenomenon which grew throughout the eighteenth century and turned into a major entertainment industry in the nineteenth.

It is worth noting the link between the exhibition of freaks and the orientalist and racist imaginary that underlies it. In the side-shows, spectators wanted to be shocked by the unsightly spectacle of primordial races, in order to be confirmed in their assumptions of racial superiority. Colonial narratives were used to aggrandize the human exhibits (Gould and Pyle 1897), using a pseudo-scientific language borrowed from that of natural-scientific imperialist explorations of unknown continents. Ethiopian, Indian, African and Asian 'monsters' came to be inscribed in these narratives of colonialist teratology.

Theories of geographical determination of monstrosity continued to be produced with stunning regularity. In the eighteenth century, the French 'philosophes', in their concern for jurisprudence, were not immune from the influence of such ideas, though on the whole they opposed slavery. Montesquieu in 1748 and Rousseau in 1764 followed the school of geographical determinism by stating that the northern regions were the ones capable of engendering true virtue and a democratic spirit (Bernal 1987).

Maupertuis (1759), on the basis of his analysis of a monstrosity called 'les nègres-blanc' (black albinos), suggests that black babies are more likely to be born to white parents than white are to blacks; it follows that white is the basic human colour, and blackness is an accidental variation which became hereditary for people living in equatorial zones.

In the nineteenth century, as suggested above, experts pointed to organic disease, intemperance and intermarriage as possible causal factors, but they never abandoned anthropological explanations and ethnographic classification systems. Through the later part of the nineteenth and the early twentieth century, the theory that certain forms of mental deficiency were a biological throwback to earlier races of humans, even to apes, was still widely believed, especially in evolutionary anthropology.

A contemporary version of the continuity of the Greek geoclimatic determination of monstrous races can be found in superstitions and legends surrounding the abominable snowman and, more significantly, in speculations about life in outer space and the colonization of other planets. Extraterrestrials, in popular science-fiction literature and films, perpetuate ancient traditions of representing far-away places as monstrously alien. They also highlight, however, the messianic or divine undertones of the monstrous other, thus reflecting the systematic dichotomy of the *teras* as both god and abjection.

That is the optimistic version of the contemporary situation. A less optimistic one was provided on the front page of the *New York Times* on 21 February 1995. In the Austrian city of Oberwart, a neo-Nazi group attacked a Gypsy settlement of 117 people and left behind a placard saying: 'Gypsies go back to India'. In an important article entitled 'Marvels of the East', Wittkower (1942) analyses the history of racialized teratology centring on India: it originates, as stated earlier, with Herodotus. However wrong the neo-Nazis may be, they are certainly accurate in their fantasmatic geography.

I do not wish to suggest that this is all there is to the racialization of monstrous bodies. Specific historical variations obviously exist – for instance, the vehemence of attacks on Jewish monstrosity throughout the sixteenth century. In his *Histoires prodigieuses et mémorables, extraites de plusieurs fameux autheurs, grecs et latins, sacrés et prophanes,* Boaistuau (1598) devotes a whole chapter to the monstrous race of the Jews. Situated between sections devoted to comets, earthquakes and organic, malformed babies, the chapter on the Jews adopts a different tone. Relying on the classical repertoire of European anti-Semitism (the killing of Christ, the poisoning of water wells, and so on), it describes in minute and rather pictorial details the capital punishment that should be inflicted to 'cette malhereuse vermine' (Book 1, ch. X: 35). No other chapter in this text displays such unabashed hatred or such dedication to violent retaliation for alleged sins of monstrosity. Clearly, the monstrousness of the European Jews is of the most negative and demonic kind, with little of the divine sense of wonder that accompanies other prodigies.

Later on, the racialization process intensified and shifted from Jews to African and Asian peoples. For instance, Linnaeus, in his classification system of all living beings, assumes a hierarchical relationship between the races, which was to become central to the European world-view. Thus, in the tenth edition of his *Systema naturae* (1759), Linnaeus postulates a race called *homo monstrosus*, which is one of the branches of *homo sapiens*, living in remote regions of the earth. Black men are classified as being at an equal distance between apes and humans (though satyrs and pygmies are closer to the former than to the latter). This will promote the idea of 'the search for a "missing link", a creature half-ape, half-man' (de Waal Malefijt 1968: 118). This creature was generally believed to roam about in Java and Africa.

The point, however, remains that, in the history of the racialization of the monstrous body, the continuity of certain themes intersects with singular and specific historical instances of teratological discourse. What is both surprising and intriguing is the recycling of the same themes and arguments through time, though they get pinned to different racial groups.

THE THEORY OF THE MATERNAL IMAGINATION

There is no doubt, however, that the 'imagination' hypothesis is the longest lasting theory of monstrous births. It attributes to the mother the capacity to undo the living capital she is carrying in her womb; the power of her imagination is such that she can actually kill or deform her creation. It must be borne in mind here that the power of the imagination has been a major issue since the seventeenth century. At that time, it had a double function: to create order through the principle of making connections or spotting resemblances, and yet also to upset that order (*Encyclopédie* 1765). This double function is to be found in Descartes' treatment of the imagination in his metaphysics. It is also fully deployed in the debates about the maternal imagination.

In his study of freak-shows, Bogdan (1988) reminds us that, as late as the nineteenth century, the explanation for the birth of the famous dwarf General Tom Thumb was the theory of maternal impression. Shortly before Tom's birth the family's puppy had drowned. The mother had been distraught and wept hysterically, causing the baby to be 'marked' and shrink.

Boucé (1985) points out that, in popular teratology, the theory of the maternal imagination continues to be used to explain sexual promiscuity. For instance, as far back as 1573 Paré recounts Hippocrates' story of a princess that was accused of adultery because she gave birth to a black baby. She was excused, however, when she pointed to a large portrait of a Moor that was hanging above the bed where she had consummated her normal, lawful and lily-white intercourse with her husband. Just looking at the picture of the black man had been enough.

In 1642 (Darmon 1977) Aldrovandi pointed out the cases of women who, during Charles V's occupation of Picardy, gave birth to dark-haired, Spanish-looking children, strikingly similar to the foreign soldiers, the sight of whom – they claimed most forcefully – had 'startled' them so. Some of these accounts are not without a sense of humour. The anti-imaginationist Blondel tells of a woman who, on 6 January, gave birth to three babies: two white and one black. Darmon quotes the case of a woman who gave birth to a boy who looked very much like the local bishop. She saved her life, however, by saying that every Sunday she had stood in that church, in pious adoration of the man, and that she 'imprinted' his features on the foetus. Swammerdam quotes the case of a pregnant woman who, startled by the sight of a black man on the street, rushed home to wash herself in warm water. Her child was consequently born white, except for the spaces between his fingers and toes. She had been unable to reach these and they had therefore turned out pitch black on her child. The most recent record I found of this sort of imbrication of teratological and racialized ac-counts of female reproductive powers dates to the period following the landing of the Allied troops in Normandy. The blonde Norman women claimed that they delivered black babies because they had been 'fright-ened' by the first black soldiers they had seen (Darmon 1977).

Crucial to this theory is the assumption that the child's entire morphological destiny is played out during conception and the period of gestation. Malebranche (1673) cites a spectacular incidence of this in his report of a pregnant woman who had watched a public hanging and gave birth to a still-born baby, strangled by the umbilical cord. It appeared, further, that even looking at a crucifix might be likely to engender a foetus with broken joints.

The case *for* the maternal imagination through the seventeenth century was upheld by Paré, Descartes and Malebranche. One implication of the importance attributed to the maternal powers of disruption is that proc-reation was not to be taken for granted but rather constituted a real 'art'. Women became especially responsible for the style and the form of their procreative powers, and many medical treatises were devoted to advising them on how to deal with their delicate situation. A great number of these medical texts concentrate on how to reproduce baby boys, and several are devoted exclusively to the reproduction of male geniuses or 'great men'.

According to common belief, pregnant women were to avoid all excitement and cultivate the serenity of their soul. A special warning was issued against reading, which was seen as the activity most likely to influence and inflame their inflammable imagination. Fraisse (1989), in her study of discourses on women during the French Revolution, focuses on the prohibition surrounding women's reading. This activity seems to be fraught with unspeakable dangers, which, in the case of pregnant women, assume catastrophic dimensions. As late as the nineteenth century, the idea that reading could inflame the female imagination and cause irreparable damage to the woman's frail nervous system remained in fashion. I cannot help being reminded of Freud's patient Dora, whose neurotic symptoms were not unrelated to her reading the 'unhealthy' texts of Mantegazza and other sexologists deemed unsuitable for such a young lady.

The key categories in the theory of the maternal imagination are female desire or wishes ('envies'), the imagination, and the optical structure of human emotions. Glenister (1964) argues that the maternal imagination or impression theory is an optical theory; it is about vision and visual powers. It contains a satanic variable in the tradition of the 'evil eye'. All it takes is for a pregnant woman to think ardently about, dream of, or quite simply long for, certain foodstuffs or for unusual or different people for these impressions to be transferred and printed upon the foetus.

In what Boucé (1985) describes as 'a pervasive epistemological haze', this concept covers phenomena as diverse as the sequels of affective traumas, strong emotions, cravings, wild fantasies and simple memories.

The case *against* the maternal imagination was upheld by Blondel, Buffon, Maupertuis and the *Encyclopédie*. The opposition attacked relentlessly the epistemological haze of the maternal theory. Blondel, of the British Royal Academy, wrote a passionate treatise refuting the theory, based on the assumption of the 'neutrality' of the foetus from the mother. He claimed that the foetus is completely isolated from all sensations or emotions experienced by the mother, thereby showing little knowledge of physiology but great rigour in his argument. Maupertuis followed a similar line.

The most systematic attack against this theory, however, comes from the *Encyclopédie*. Contrary to the view of Blondel, it is argued that the imagination is an important faculty which moves us all, especially pregnant women, quite deeply, but that there is no direct link between the movements of the imagination and physiological processes. There is a general understanding that all passions, emotions or sensations are likely to affect and enervate pregnant women. And there is no denying that these passions have bodily counterparts: the heart beating faster, the muscles contracting, and so on. What comes especially under fire is the faculty that Malebranche had called 'sympathie' (the capacity to feel with/suffer with); that is to say, the causal link between emotions and the capacity to act on other objects.

In fact, the eighteenth-century Encyclopaedists take great care to circumscribe the powers of the imagination because, being unruly, it ends up confusing our ideas and is thus an obstacle to true knowledge. In the same vein, they set out to re-educate the poor gullible women who actually believe in the power of their imaginations. They suggest the following experiment: interview pregnant women before they give birth and make a list of all their desires/'envies', and then compare these to what their newly born baby looks like in an attempt to cure them of their superstition. With customary wit, they do admit, however, that whenever they attempted this experiment, the women got very annoyed and still would not change their minds. So, could women cause monstrous births? No, says the *Encyclopédie*. Were women to have the power actually to create – or deform – life, they might use it to manufacture perfect babies for a change, instead of producing monstrous ones. Moreover, they add gingerly, if the women possessed such powers, they would probably conceive many more baby boys than girls, given that all women are at all times affected by their desire for men.

So what produces monsters? Maupertuis goes to some length in trying to provide an elaborate answer to this eternal question. He proposes a theory of magnetic correspondence between mother and foetus: their respective particles exercise a mutual fatal and foetal attraction which sets in train the process whereby babies are formed. Needless to say, whenever the particles are not strong enough, a monster will be produced by lack; in cases of overattraction of the same particles, a monster by excess is likely to be the result.

By the end of the eighteenth century, however, this question must have begun to seem quite redundant to some people, because the *Encyclopédie* responds dismissively, quoting chance or misadventure as the only possible sources of deformity. To the optical-epistemological question: 'Why do some babies look more like their mothers than their fathers?', they answer (Volume VII, entry 'foetus', p. 2): '[I]l faut bien voir que cela a lieu, sans trop nous instruire du comment ni du pourquoi.'

The theme of monstrous births began to lose scientific momentum. Within less than a century, as teratology gained scientific credibility and led to embryology, *homo monstrosus* became of little scientific relevance to embryological debates, though his place in anthropology was assured for centuries to come.

PRELIMINARY CONCLUSIONS

First, to sum up on the subject of the maternal imagination. In the eighteenth century, the pro-imagination lobby did not fail to respond to the criticism; they emphasized the powerful link between the mother and the foetus, ridiculing any suggestions of the latter's 'neutrality'. They extended this into an attack on the limitations of the rationalist approach and also adopted something of a feminist line in stating that they were taking the side of the poor women, who constantly took the blame for monstrous births. By showing that they were overwhelmed by the imagination, they could be exonerated and even helped out.

In a historical perspective, this theory was indeed a step forward for women, as it recognized their active role in the process of generation. However, scientific teratology was instrumental in creating, or strengthening, a nexus of stifling interdicts, imperatives and even, in effect, pressing advice on women. The disciplining of the maternal body that followed from all this – all 'for her own good', of course – runs parallel to the reorganization of the profession of midwifery, which has been amply documented by feminist scholarship. (Oakley 1984; Ehrenreich and English 1979).

The fundamental contradiction that lies at the heart of the quarrel about the maternal imagination concerns the understanding of the woman's body. By the end of the eighteenth century, the mother's body seems to be in a position structurally analogous to the classical monster: it is caught in a deep contradiction that splits it within itself. The female, pregnant body is posited *both* as a protective filter and as a conductor or highly sensitive conveyor of impressions, shocks and emotions. It is both a 'neutral' and a somewhat 'electrical' body. There is an insidious assimilation of the pregnant woman to an unstable, potentially sick subject, vulnerable to uncontrollable emotions. This can be linked to the eighteenth-century discourse about the pathologization of woman (Fraisse 1989).

Second, to conclude the notion of the racialization of the monstrous others. The persistence of the racial and racist overtones in teratological discourses intersects with the continuous emphasis on controlling and disciplining the woman's body. Thus, teratology shows the imbrication of genderized and racialized narratives and the role they play in constructing scientific discourses about the female body. Their interconnection is such that any analysis of female embodied experience simply needs to take into account the simultaneous – if often contradictory – effects of racialized and genderized discourses and practices.

Third, to say some final words on monsters as non-scientific objects of research. As I said at the beginning, any historical account of teratological discourses has to face up to the limitations and aporias of scientific objectivity. Monsters are not just one object of scientific inquiry. They are many objects, whose configuration, structure and content shift historically. If they can be called an object at all, they are one which is the effect of, while being also constitutive of, certain discursive practices: climatic and geographical anthropologies in antiquity; theological divination through the Renaissance; then anatomy; embryology; until we reach today's cybernetic and environmental chimio-teratology.

Clearly, the epistemophilic or imaginary charge surrounding the monster is partly responsible for this paradox of simultaneous complexity or changeability as well as continuity. The monstrous body, more than an object, is a shifter, a vehicle that constructs a web of interconnected and yet potentially contradictory discourses about his or her embodied self. Gender and race are primary operators in this process.

As a way of concluding, I would like to propose a redefinition: the monster is a process without a stable object. It makes knowledge happen by circulating, sometimes as the most irrational non-object. It is slippery enough to make the Encyclopaedists nervous; yet, in a perfectly nomadic cycle of repetitions, the monstrous other keeps emerging on the discursive scene. As such, it persists in haunting not only our imagination but also our scientific knowledge-claims. Difference will just not go away. And because this embodiment of difference moves, flows, changes; because it propels discourses without ever settling into them; because it evades us in the very process of puzzling us, it will never be known what the next monster is going to look like; nor will it be possible to guess where it will come from. And because we *cannot* know, the monster is always going to get us.

NOTES

1. An earlier version of this chapter was researched and delivered during my sabbatical leave at the School of Social Sciences, Institute for Advanced Study in Princeton, New Jersey, February 1995. I am very grateful to Joan Scott, Robert Wokkler, Peter Galison and Phillip Soergel for their comments.

2. See on this point, Soergel 1993.

3. Bogdan quotes the case of Maximo and Bartola, who were exhibited as 'The Last of the Great Aztecs'. They were examined by J. Mason Warren, MD, who published a paper about them in the *American Journal of Medical Sciences*, April 1851.

4. I have developed this idea at some length in my article: 'Mothers, Monsters and Machines' (Braidotti 1994: 75–95).

5. Aristotle, *Politics*, VII.7, quoted in Bernal 1987.

REFERENCES

Bernal, M. (1987) *Black Athena. The Afroasiatic Roots of Classical Civilization*, Vintage, London.

Blondel, J. (1727) *The Strength of the Imagination in Pregnant Women Examined*, J. Peele, London.

Blackman, J. (1977) 'Popular Theories of Generation: The Evolution of Aristotle's Works', in J. Woodward and D. Richards, eds, *Health Care and Popular Medicine in Nineteenth Century England*, Croom Helm, London, pp. 56–88.

Boaistuau, P. (1598) *Histoires prodigieuses et mémorables*, Gabriel Buon, Paris.

Bogdan, R. (1988) *Freak Show. Presenting Human Oddities for Amusement and Profit*, University of Chicago Press, Chicago.

Boucé, P.-G. (1985) 'Les jeux interdits de l'imaginaire: onanisme et culpabilisation sexuelle au XVIIIème siècle', in J. Céard, ed., *La Folie et le Corps*, Presses de l'Ecole Normale Supérieure, Paris, pp. 223–43.

Braidotti, R. (1994) *Nomadic Subjects*, Columbia University Press, New York.

Canguilhem, G. (1966) *Le Normal et le pathologique*, Presses Universitaires de France, Paris.

Céard, J. (1977) *La Nature et les Prodiges. L'insolite en France au XVIème siècle*, Librairie Droz, Genève.

———— (1991) 'The Crisis in the Science of Monsters', in P. Desan, ed., *Humanism in Crisis. The Decline of the French Renaissance*, University of Michigan Press, Ann Arbor.

Darmon, P. (1977) *Le Mythe de la Procréation à l'age baroque*, Seuil, Paris.

Daston, L. and P. Galison (1992) 'The Image of Objectivity', *Representations*, no. 40, pp. 81–128.

Encyclopédie, ou Dictionnaire Raisonné des Sciences, des Arts et des Métiers (1765) Vol. VII, Neufchatel.

Ehrenreich, B. and D. English (1979) *For Her Own Good. 150 Years of Experts' Advice to Women*, Pluto Press, London.

Fiedler, L. (1979) *Freaks: Myths and Images of the Secret Self*, Simon & Schuster, New York.

Fraisse, G. (1989) *Muse de la raison*, Alinéa, Aix-en-Provence.

Gibson, W. (1984) *Neuromancer*, Ace Books, New York.

Glenister, T.W. (1964) 'Fantasies, Facts and Foetuses: The Interplay of Fancy and Reason in Teratology', *Medical History*, vol. 8, pp. 15–30.

Gould, G. and W. Pyle (1897) *Anomalies and Curiosities of Medicine*, W.B. Saunders, Philadelphia.

Haraway, D. (1992) 'The Promises of Monsters: A Regenerative Politics for Inappropriate/d Others', in L. Grossberg, C. Nelson and A. Treichler, eds, *Cultural Studies*, Routledge, New York and London.

Linnaeus, C. ([1759] 1964) *Systema naturae*, Cramer, Weinheim.

Jordanova, L. (1985) 'Gender, Generation and Science: William Hunter's Obstetrical Atlas', in W.F. Bynum and R. Porter, eds, *William Hunter and the 18th Century Medical World*, Cambridge University Press, Cambridge, pp. 385–412.

Malebranche (1673) *De la recherche de la vérité*, reprinted, Vrin, Paris, 1946.

Maupertuis, P. L. de ([1759] 1866) *La Vénus Physique: ou Les lois de la génération*, Office de la Librairie, Paris.

Oakley, A. (1984) *The Captured Womb*, Blackwells, Oxford.

Paré, A. (1971) *Des monstres et des prodiges*, Librairie Droz, Geneva.

Park, K. and L. Daston (1981) 'Unnatural Conceptions: The Study of Monsters in 16th and 17th Century France and England', *Past and Present*, no. 92, pp. 20–54.

Saint Augustine (1972) *The City of God*, Penguin, Harmondsworth.

Saint-Hilaire, G. de (1832) *Histoire Génerale et particulière des Anomalies de l'Organization Chez l'Homme et les Animaux*, J.B. Ballière, Paris.

Soergel, P. (1993) 'The Counter-Reformation Impact on Clerical Propaganda', in P.A. Dykema and H.A. Oberman, eds, *Anticlericalism in Late Medieval and Early Modern Europe*, E.J. Brill, Leiden, pp. 639–53.

Trembach, R., ed. (1986) *Aristotle's Masterpiece*, Garland Publishing, London and New York.

de Waal Malefijt, A. (1968) 'Homo Monstrosus', *Scientific American*, vol. 219, no. 4, pp. 113–18.

Wittkower, R. (1942) 'Marvels of the East: A Study in the History of Monsters', *Journal of the Warburg and Courtauld Institutes*, London, vol. 5, pp. 159–97.

9

THE DECLINE OF THE ONE-SIZE-FITS-ALL

PARADIGM, OR, HOW REPRODUCTIVE

SCIENTISTS TRY TO COPE WITH

POSTMODERNITY

Nelly Oudshoorn

Have you ever heard of andrology? The very fact that andrology, the medical specialism concerned with the reproductive functions of men, is still a cinderella profession compared to its bigger sister, gynaecology, is one of the striking examples of the institutional and discursive processes of othering in the biomedical sciences. Feminist discourses of the last two decades have provided major challenges to these 'othering processes of scientific discourse'.[1] In this chapter I want to show how major changes in the dominant paradigm of subject–object dichotomies emerged in one specific area of the biomedical sciences: the reproductive sciences. I begin by describing how the identification of 'woman' as 'the other' eventually resulted in setting the female body apart in a separate branch of medicine. The emergence of gynaecology and sex endocrinology in the late nineteenth and early twentieth centuries established a discursive practice in which sex and repro-duction became considered as 'more fundamental to Woman's than Man's nature' (Moscucci 1990; Oudshoorn 1994b). Next, I compare the discourses on contraceptive technologies of the 1950s and 1980s. I will describe a major transformation in the reproductive paradigm, in which the emphasis on the universality of women and their bodies – the ultimate consequence of the process of othering – became re-placed by a discourse that acknowledged the diversity of human bodies. I will show how this shift meant a break in the process of othering that had dominated the reproductive sciences since the nineteenth century.[2]

THE INSTITUTIONALIZATION OF WOMAN
AS THE OTHER

The institutional process of othering in medicine has a surprisingly recent history. For our postmodern minds it is hard to imagine that, for two thousand years, male and female bodies were not conceptualized in terms of differences. Medical texts from the ancient Greeks until the late eighteenth century described male and female bodies as fundamentally similar. Women had even the same genitals as men, with one difference: 'Theirs are inside the body and not outside it.' In this approach, characterized by Thomas Laqueur as the 'one-sex model', the female body was understood as a 'male turned inside herself' – not a different sex, but a lesser version of the male body.[3]

It was only in the eighteenth century that biomedical discourse began to conceptualize the female body as the Other: a body that was to be considered as essentially different from the male body. The long established tradition that emphasized bodily similarities over differences began to be heavily criticized. In the eighteenth century, anatomists increasingly focused on bodily differences between the sexes and argued that sex was not restricted to the reproductive organs; or, as one physician put it, "[t]he essence of sex is not confined to a single organ but extends, through more or less perceptible nuances, into every part' (Schiebinger 1989: 189). The first part of the body to become sexualized was the skeleton. If sex differences could be found in 'the hardest part of the body', it would be likely that sex penetrated 'every muscle, vein, and organ attached to and molded by the skeleton' (Schiebinger 1989: 191).

In nineteenth-century cellular physiology, the medical gaze shifted from the bones to the cells (Laqueur 1990: 6, 215). By the late nineteenth century, medical scientists had extended this sexualization to every imaginable part of the body: bones, blood vessels, cells, hair and brain (Schiebinger 1989: 189). Only the eye seems to have no sex (Honegger 1991: 176). Biomedical discourse thus shows a clear shift in focus from similarities to differences. This shift seems to have been caused by epistemological and socio-political changes rather than by scientific progress. In *Making Sex*, Laqueur described this shift in the context of changes in the political climate. The French Revolution and new liberal claims in the eighteenth century led to new ideals about the social relationships between men and women in which the complementarity between the sexes was emphasized. This theory of complementarity 'taught that man and woman are not physical and moral equals but complementary opposites. Women now became viewed as fundamentally different from, and thus incomparable to, men' (Laqueur 1990: 32, 216, 217). The theory of sexual complementarity was meant to keep women out of competition with men, designing separate spheres for men and women. In this theory, which came to be known as the 'doctrine of the two spheres', the sexes were expected to complement, rather than compete with, each other.[4]

The female and the male body now became conceptualized in terms of opposite bodies with 'incommensurably different organs, functions, and feelings' (Laqueur 1990: viii). This change is visible in medical language as well. 'Organs that had shared a name, ovaries and testicles, were now linguistically distinguished. Organs that had not been distinguished by a name of their own, the vagina, for example, were given one' (Laqueur 1990: 149).

Following this shift, the female body became the medical object *par excellence* (Foucault 1981), emphasizing woman's unique sexual character. Medical scientists now started to identify the ultimate cause of woman's otherness. The medical literature of this period shows a radical naturalization of femininity in which scientists reduced woman to one specific organ. In the eighteenth and nineteenth centuries, scientists set out to localize the essence of femininity in different places in the body. Until the middle of the nineteenth century, scientists considered the uterus as the seat of femininity. This conceptualization is reflected in the statement of the German poet and naturalist Johann Wolfgang Goethe (1749–1832): 'Der Hauptpunkt der ganzen weiblichen Existenz ist die Gebaermutter' ['The uterus is the essence of the whole female existence'] (Medvei 1983: 213). In the middle of the nineteenth century, medical attention began to shift from the uterus to the ovaries, which came to be regarded as largely autonomous control centres of reproduction in the female animal, while in humans they were thought to be the essence of femininity itself (Gallagher and Laqueur 1987: 27). In 1848, Virchow (1817-1885), often portrayed as the founding father of physiology, characterized the function of the ovaries thus:

> It has been completely wrong to regard the uterus as the characteristic organ.... The womb, as part of the sexual canal, of the whole apparatus of reproduction, is merely an organ of secondary importance. Remove the ovary, and we shall have before us a masculine woman, an ugly half-form with the coarse and harsh form, the heavy bone formation, the moustache, the rough voice, the flat chest, the sour and egoistic mentality and the distorted outlook ... in short, all that we admire and respect in woman as womanly, is merely dependent on her ovaries. (Medvei 1983: 215)

In the late nineteenth century, the search for the cause of woman's otherness eventually led to setting women's bodies apart in a medical specialism: gynaecology. In her fascinating account of the rise of the 'Science of Women', Moscucci has described how 'the belief that the female body is finalised for reproduction defined the study of "natural woman" as a separate branch of medicine.' With the emergence of gynaecology, women became identified as 'a special group of patients' (Moscucci 1990: 2). The turn of the century witnessed the founding of societies, journals and hospitals specifically devoted to the diagnosis and treatment of the female body. 'Woman' thus became set apart in the discursive and institutional practices of the biomedical sciences. The growth of gynaecology was not paralleled by the establishment of a complementary 'science of masculinity'. 'As the male was the standard of the species, he could not be set apart on the basis of his sex' (Moscucci 1990: 32).[5]

This institutional process of othering was continued and reinforced by the rise of sex endocrinology, a discipline devoted to the study of sex hormones that emerged in the 1920s and 1930s. In *Beyond the Natural Body* I have described how the very existence of gynaecology facilitated a situation in which the new science of sex endocrinology focused almost exclusively on the female body. The by then established gynaecological practices had transformed the female body into an easily accessible supplier of research materials, a convenient guinea pig for tests and an organized audience for the products of sex endocrinology. Both laboratory scientists and pharmaceutical firms depended on these institutional practices to provide them with the necessary tools and materials to transform the hormonal model of the body into a new set of disease categories, diagnostic tools and drugs. Sex endocrinologists integrated the notion of the female body as a reproductive body into the hormonal model, but not without thoroughly changing it. They provided the medical profession with tools to intervene in features that had been considered inaccessible prior to the hormonal era. The introduction of diagnostic tests and drugs enabled the medical profession to intervene in the menstrual cycle and the menopause, thus bringing the 'natural' features of reproduction and ageing into the domain of medical intervention.

The introduction of the concept of sex hormones not only changed the medical treatment of the female body but also redefined the existing social configurations structuring medical practice. The field of sex endocrinology generated a set of social relationships that did not exist prior to its emergence. What changed in this episode was the question

of who was entitled to claim authoritative knowledge about the female
body. The hormonal model enabled gynaecologists to draw the female
body more and more deeply into the gynaecological clinic. Gynaecologists, however, had to share their increased medical authority with
another professional group: the laboratory scientists. With the introduction of the concept of sex hormones, scientists explicitly linked
women's diseases with laboratory practice. The study of woman as the
other thus became extended from the clinic to the laboratory and
thereby firmly rooted in the heart of the life sciences.

ONE SIZE FITS ALL

Bearing in mind this short history of the process of othering in the
biomedical sciences, it will be no surprise that the development of the
first physiological means of contraception focused exclusively on
women. The history of the contraceptive pill indicates how the process
of othering required an emphasis on similarities among women.[6]

Remarkably, this time the choice to focus on women, rather than
men, was not made by the medical profession or laboratory scientists
but by an 'outsider', Margaret Sanger, a women's rights activist and
pioneer for birth control in the United States of America. Sanger,
arrested and jailed for opening the first birth-control clinic in New
York in 1916, believed that the most important threat to women's
independence came from unwanted and unanticipated pregnancies. She
advocated birth control as a basic precondition to the liberation of
women (Christian Johnson 1977: 1). In 1951, at the age of 72, Sanger
approached Gregory Pincus, an American reproductive biologist
specializing in the study of hormones, and persuaded him to start
research on contraceptives.[7] She was very explicit about what type of
contraceptive had to be developed: it had to be a 'universal contraceptive' that could be used by all women, regardless of colour, class,
age, or educational background (Christian Johnson 1977).

These early ideas on contraception set the stage for the reproductive
paradigm of the 1960s and early 1970s. The adage 'One Size Fits All'
became the major cornerstone of R&D in contraceptives. The quest
for universal contraceptives can be considered as the ultimate consequence of the process of othering. Classifying woman as the other
directs the attention to similarities among women. Consequently, the
design of medical technology does not have to take into account the
diversity of its users. The history of the pill therefore reads as an
intriguing story of how scientists tried to construct similarities between

women. This is very obvious in the texts that Pincus and his colleagues published reporting the clinical trials of the pill. A perusal of these publications reveals a very telling picture: the women participating in the clinical trials have disappeared from the stage. They were replaced, quite simply, by the number of treated menstrual cycles. In the 1958 publication of one of the first large-scale clinical trials, Pincus concluded that 'in the 1279 cycles during which the regimen of treatment was meticulously followed, there was not a single pregnancy' (Pincus 1958: 133). In the 1959 publication in *Science*, which described all four field trials of the pill, it was reported:

> We have recently collected and analyzed the data (to November 1958) from these four projects and present here the outstanding findings derived from these data; 830 subjects took the medication for a total of 8133 menstrual cycles, or 635 woman years. (Pincus 1959: 81)

A popular writer adopted this representation strategy as well. In *The Hormone Quest*, the author concludes:

> By 1960 1600 women at the Caribbean Field Trial Centers had used Enovid as a contraceptive for from a few months to nearly four years. Their experience, as a group, with the new steroid covered nearly 40,000 menstrual cycles or – as medical staticians prefer to put it – about 3000 woman-years of exposure to the possibility of pregnancy. (Maisel 1965: 134)

This representational strategy clearly emphasizes the similarities between women. The use of such categories as 'cycle' replaces the individual subject by the group, suggesting a continuity that did not exist in the trials. That suggestion simultaneously affirms continuity while obscuring discontinuity by framing new scientific categories for data measurement. A representation in terms of cycles implies an abstraction from the bodies of individual women to the universal category of a physical process. Here we see how scientific texts are not simply a reflection of the proceedings of research. Texts are a far stronger tool than that: they are a representation which creates a new reality. The discourse of pill researchers constructed women's bodies as universal with respect to their reproductive functions.

The construction of similarities between women is not just a matter of discourse. During the testing of the pill, similarities were literally created by the introduction of a specific regimen of medication. In one of the first clinical trials, women were quite distressed when they noticed that their menstruations ceased during the treatment with oral progestins (Maisel 1965: 119). If these women were distressed, Pincus reflected, it would be very likely that women taking progestins for contraceptive purposes would experience similar reactions to cessation. A contraceptive that suppresses menstruation did not meet the requirements of a 'universal' contraceptive. Pincus therefore changed the medication. The pills should be taken for twenty days, starting on the fifth day after menstruation, as was the practice in the hormonal treatment of menstrual irregularities in the 1940s (McLaughlin 1982: 110). This suggestion set the standard for the administration of progestins in all later trials and eventually for the use of the contraceptive pill in the 1960s.

The choice of this regimen of medication was shaped by moral objections to any drugs that would interfere with menstruation. Pincus was directly confronted with this norm by Searle, the pharmaceutical firm which put the pill on the market. Searle's director of biological research let Pincus know that he did not want to take part in the development of any compound that might interfere with the menstrual cycle (McLauglin 1982: 111). In later publications, Pincus presented the effect of progestin on menstruation as a way of mimicking nature: women would still have their menstrual periods. In 1958, Pincus legitimated the regimen of medication as follows:

> Actually, in view of the ability of this compound to prevent menstrual bleeding as long as it is taken, a cycle of any desired length could presumably be produced. We had chosen our standard day 5 through day 24 regime in the expectation that 'normal' cycle length would occur. (Pincus 1958: 1338)

This quotation illustrates that concepts such as 'normality' and 'similarity' are medical constructs, rather than rooted in nature. Pincus could have made a menstrual cycle of any desired length. He chose to make a 'normal' menstrual cycle that subsequently became materialized in the pill. This diminished the variety in menstrual patterns among women: all pill-users have a regular cycle of four weeks. The pill thus literally created similarities in women's reproductive functions.

The next step toward creating similarities in women's reproductive functions was to adjust women to the demands of the new technology. Women had to learn to follow the relatively complicated instructions of 'one tablet a day, beginning on day 5 of the menstrual cycle until one vial of 20 tablets was consumed, i.e. through day 24 of the cycle' (Pincus 1958: 1335). During the trials in Puerto Rico, the control to ensure a strict adherence to this regimen of medication was assigned to a team of trained social workers. In one of the reports of this trial, published in the *American Journal of Obstetrics and Gynaecology* in 1958, Pincus described this regimen as follows:

A schedule of visits by a trained social worker was arranged so that in every medication cycle each subject was seen shortly after she should have taken the last tablet. Initially only one vial was distributed to each woman. This was replaced on the social worker's visit. Since, in a number of instances, the housewives were not at home when she called, it was decided, after a few months, to leave two vials with each subject so that the continuity of the regime of medication (day 5 through day 24) might not be broken. (Pincus 1958: 1335)

During the visits of the social worker, the women were asked to cooperate in interviews as well.

At each consultation, information was elicited concerning the length of the menstrual cycle, the occurrence of side effects, the frequency of coitus, and the number of missed tablets. A rough check, in some instances, on the number of tablets omitted was made by counting those remaining in the vial. (Pincus 1958: 1335)

This strategy to ensure that women would adhere to the required test protocols did not work in all cases. In the publications of this trial, Pincus reported 17 pregnancies due to what he described as 'patient failure': these women had missed some days of tablet-taking (Pincus 1958: 1335; Pincus 1959: 81). Obviously only women can fail, not the technology.[8]

The most obvious illustration of scientists' emphasis on similarities, however, is their choice of test subjects. The quotations cited earlier show that the testing of hormones as contraceptives did not take place in the continental USA (where the laboratory research took place) but in the Caribbean Islands. In the late 1950s and early 1960s, four large-scale field trials were organized (three in Puerto Rico and one in Haiti) in which more than 1,600 women participated. So it was women of colour, especially in former colonial settings, who entered this history as the guinea pigs of one of the most revolutionary drugs in the history of medicine. Most importantly, the choice to test hormones on women of colour could only be made because scientists did not recognize any fundamental differences between women.

The emphasis on similarities in the development of medical technologies such as the pill is not unproblematic. The concept of similarity functions as the cornerstone for the development of universal technologies, technologies that can be used by women all over the world. The theoretical assumption underlying the idea of universal technologies is that technologies can be made to work everywhere because scientific knowledge is universal by nature. The case-study of the pill exemplifies the failure of this claim. Despite all the emphasis on similarities, the pill has not developed into a universal technology. The dream of making the ideal contraceptive for any woman, regardless of her specific background, was not fulfilled. The main acceptance of the pill had been among middle- and upper-class women in the Western, industrialized world, with one exception: China. Most women in countries of the South had adopted sterilization and intra-uterine devices as means of contraception (Seaman and Seaman 1978: 76). Scientists may explain this failure by saying that women are to blame. My argument is that, if anything is to blame, it is the technology. I suggest that we may be able to understand the failures of science and technology by adopting a social constructivist approach that emphasizes the contextual nature of science and technology. In this perspective, every technology contains a configured user.[9] Consequently, technologies cannot simply be transported elsewhere.

The case of the contraceptive pill illustrates the complications that emerge when Western technologies are introduced into developing countries. Although the pill was developed as a universal, context-independent contraceptive, it nevertheless contained a specific user: a woman, medicalized enough to take medication regularly, who is accustomed to gynaecological examinations and regular visits to the physician, and who does not have to hide contraception from her partner. It goes without saying that this portrait of the ideal pill user is highly culturally specific (with varieties even within one culture). This user is more likely to be found in Western, industrialized countries with well-developed health-care systems. From this perspective it can be understood that the pill has not found a universal acceptance. Actually, the user-specificity of the envisioned universal contraceptive pill was already manifest during the clinical testing in the Caribbean Islands. The early trials witnessed a high percentage of drop-outs. Disciplining women to the conditions of the tests was not always successful. Many women did not participate in the gynaecological examinations, 'forgot' to take the pills, or simply quit the programme because they preferred other contraceptive methods, particularly sterilization. The Caribbean trials provided the pill researchers with information indicating that the pill did not meet with universal acceptance. These test conditions were, of course, a much heavier burden than the conditions of using the pill after it had been approved by the Food and Drug Administration. Two conditions remained the same, however: frequent visits to a physician (the pill was only available by prescription) and regular gynaecological examinations (women using the pill had to have regular gynaecological examinations, including blood-pressure tests and vaginal smears to check for adverse health effects).[10]

The making of the pill into a successful contraceptive technology thus required a specific context, in which:

- there exists an easily accessible, well-developed health-care infrastructure;

- people are accustomed to taking prescription drugs (many countries in the Two-Third's World mainly use 'over the counter' drugs, which people can buy in shops);

- women are accustomed to regular medical controls; and

- women and men are free to negotiate the use of contraceptives.

The pill could only be made into a universal contraceptive if its producers put great effort into mobilizing and disciplining people and institutions to meet the specific requirements of the new technology. Needless to say, many of the required transformations were beyond the power of the inventors of the pill.

THE CAFETERIA DISCOURSE

In the 1970s, scientists concluded that the development of 'a magic bullet' – that is, a perfect contraceptive for everyone – had failed (Harper 1983: 212). The previous twenty years of experience with the pill had made it clear that this method had significant limitations, not only with respect to acceptability but also to safety and continuity of use (Greep 1976: 3). In the 1970s, the safety issue became of central concern because feminist health advocates and physicians reported serious side-effects of both oral contraception and intra-uterine devices (Seaman and Seaman 1978; Boston Health Collective 1971). In this period we see the emergence of a totally different type of contraceptive discourse. In *Reproduction and Human Welfare* (1976), the first extensive review of the reproductive sciences and contraceptive development initiated and funded by the Ford Foundation in the United States of America, the authors evaluated the experiences with birth control methods as follows:

> Thus, current technology cannot be regarded as adequate to meet individual or societal needs in either industrial or developing nations.... The heterogeneity of personal, cultural, religious, and economic circumstances of human life, as well as the varying needs of individuals at different stages in the life

cycle, impose diverse demands upon the technology. It is thus likely that there will never be an 'ideal' contraceptive for all circumstances. (Greep et al. 1976: 4)

The bulky report on the state of the art of contraceptive technology concluded with a list of recommendations addressed to 'biomedical scientists and those who act for the general public on Capitol Hill and in the White House' (Greep 1976: xvii) which opened with the following statement:

> A variety of safe and effective methods of fertility regulation beyond those now available is urgently needed by the world's diverse population living under different conditions and circumstances. This requires increased efforts ranging from fundamental research on reproductive processes to targeted activities in contraceptive development. (Greep et al. 1976: 25)

This drastic shift in the reproductive paradigm coincided with broader cultural changes in the late 1970s: the collapse of the dreams of modernity. The declining belief in grand theories and ideologies to understand and control the world led to a situation in which locality and individuality became of central concern in Western culture. The notion of differences became an important theme. Feminists, among others, acknowledged the importance of the vast differences among women's experiences and characteristics in different cultural settings (hooks 1982). The crisis in modernity eroded the belief in one technological fix to improve the human condition (Smart 1992). Reproductive scientists readily adopted the postmodern acknowledgement of differences, not least because it enabled them to expand their research programme. They used the voiced need for a wider variety of contraceptive methods to negotiate an increase in financial support for fundamental research in the reproductive sciences. To industry, the recognition of diversity among users indicated a variety of new markets.[11] To quote Adele Clarke's felicitous phrase, 'In postmodernity, capital has fallen in love with difference' (Clarke 1995: 10).

In the 1980s, contraceptive R&D resulted in the introduction of a wider variety of contraceptive methods. On the one hand, scientists put great effort into differentiating the existing methods. The pill was now produced in many different types consisting of varying sorts and doses of hormones, tailored to the various physiological and psychological reactions of the user. Similarly, industry started marketing new types of intra-uterine device (IUD). One of these new IUDs nicely exemplifies industry's adjustment to the changing paradigm: Organon advertised an IUD which is able to adjust to differences in size of the uterus as 'the flexible alternative'.[12] Besides this differentiation of existing methods, scientists developed new contraceptive methods such as long-acting injectable contraceptives, subdermal implants (devices which have to be inserted under the skin) and vaginal rings. The most recent innovations include the possibility of developing vaccines against pregnancy and nonsurgical methods of sterilization. In *Birth Control Technologies: Prospects by the Year 2000*, the author aptly describes the new reproductive paradigm for the last decades of the twentieth century:

> Family planning programs need to have available for consumers a variety of safe and effective methods, so that in a 'cafeteria' style, self-selection by consumers will lead to greater individual motivation to use any particular method and ensure continued widespread use of birth control methods. (Harper 1983: 9)[13]

Most remarkably, the acknowledgement of the need 'to modify technology to fit people, rather than modifying people to fit technology' (Marshall 1977: 65) broadened contraceptive R&D to include a new group: men. Since the introduction of the condom and sterilization, both methods that date from the nineteenth century, no new means of contraception for men had been developed. A review of the state of the art of contraceptive development in 1977 concluded that,

> although there were as many as 14 methods available for limitation of fertility, only 3 of these were ones that could be used by men: coitus interruptus, condoms and vasectomy. (Schearer 1977: 178)

At present, it is estimated that worldwide only 21 per cent of contraceptive-using couples rely on male methods – that is, condoms and vasectomies (Hatcher 1990). Reproductive scientists suggest that research on reproductive functions of the male has lagged at least fifteen years behind that on the female (Greep et al. 1976: 15), one of the most striking consequences of the process of othering in the reproductive sciences.[14] Until the late 1970s, scientists and culture at large – including feminists! – considered the female as the sex responsible for contraception. Rather ironically, reproductive biologists have argued that, in terms of population control, it would have been more efficient to choose men as the major target for controlling fertility because men have a much longer fertile life than women (Spilman et al. 1975: 2, 3).

History repeats itself. As in the case of the pill for women, the request for developing new male contraceptives came from outside the scientific community. In this case, social pressures came from two different sides: feminists in the Western, industrialized world; and governments of the

Southern world, most notably China and India. Feminists demanded that men share the responsibilities and health hazards of contraception, whereas governmental agencies urged the inclusion of 'the forgotten 50% of family planning' as a target for contraceptive development (Handelsman 1991: 230; Wu 1988: 443). In the 1970s and 1980s, the question 'What about a male pill?' appeared at regular intervals in newspaper headlines, particularly in periods during which the serious health risks of the female pill were reported (*The Lancet* 1984: 1108). Although research in male reproduction has increased due to these pressures, the pill's 'male twin' has not yet appeared on the market. Reproductive scientists estimate that it is very unlikely that new male contraceptives will be available before well into the twenty-first century (Mastroianni et al. 1990: 483). Nevertheless, the male has definitely been put on the scientific and political agenda.[15] The United Nations' International Conference on Population and Development, held recently in Cairo, addressed male responsibilities in family planning as one of its goals.[16]

The shift in the reproductive paradigm toward acknowledging differences among users thus coincided with an erosion of the gendered subject–object relations in scientific discources in which men traditionally possessed the subject position and women were the target. For the first time in the history of the reproductive sciences, male scientists are testing contraceptive compounds on their own sex.[17] The reverse also happened: women have increasingly adopted the subject position. Since the 1980s, women are represented in substantial numbers in decision-making bodies dealing with contraception, and the number of women scientists has increased as well (Djerassi 1989: 358).

CONTROL OR CHOICE?

After this short retrospective view of the history of contraceptives, it is time to reflect on the meaning of the shift in the reproductive paradigm. Is the cafeteria discourse really so different from the one-size-fits-all discourse? I have argued that there is an important difference: the cafeteria discourse acknowledges the diversity of users, whereas the one-size-fits-all discourse emphasizes the universality of women and their bodies, a discourse which largely erased diversities. We may therefore conclude that the shift in discourses does matter a lot. It meant a break in the process of othering that had dominated the reproductive sciences since the nineteenth century. The universal category of 'woman' became replaced by human bodies in all their diversities.

Nevertheless, if you make such neat distinctions, continuities will inevitably be discovered between these discourses as well. Adele Clarke recently described another distinctive feature of modern approaches to human reproduction: their quest to achieve control over reproductive processes (Clarke 1988, 1995). If we compare the cafeteria discourse with the one-size-fits-all discourse from the perspective of control, the two discourses seem to conflate. In the discourse on the pill, control was of central concern. In his own account of what made him decide to begin contraceptive research, Pincus cited 'two overtly ascertainable factors: a visit from Mrs. Margaret Sanger in 1951, and the emergence of the appreciation of the importance of the population explosion' (Pincus 1965: 5). The pill was thus called into existence as a technological fix to solve what was perceived as 'the population problem'. From the viewpoint of control, the cafeteria discourse is more ambiguous. Here reproductive scientists frequently adopt double talk: their reports are couched in terms of individual choice while they simultaneously emphasize the need to control population growth. In this type of discourse, individual control is on uneasy terms with population control by the state. The aim to lower birth rates has to be attuned to the individual's reproductive health needs. The volume mentioned earlier, *Reproduction and Human Welfare,* exemplifies my point. Discussing the problem of the 'current unprecedented rate of world population growth', the authors concluded:

> Reproductive research aimed at improved methods of fertility regulation thus links the search for solutions of the personal problems of individuals and the social problems of societies with some of the most critical overarching problems facing the world as a whole. (Greep et al. 1976: 2)

This ambiguity of the cafeteria discourse is clearly visible in one of the recently developed contraceptive methods, contraceptive implants. Contraceptive implants (like Norplant) are long-acting methods (five years) which are inserted under the skin of a woman's upper arm. Although this contraceptive method is presented as a technology to increase the freedom of women to choose the contraceptive they prefer, it facilitates a situation in which the individual's control over her fertility is replaced with control by family-planning organizations or the state. Similarly, as in the case of the pill, contraceptive implants are not a 'neutral' device; they contain a specific type of user – a woman who is considered likely to forget to take her contraceptives. By introducing long-acting implants, the continuity of use is guaranteed because it is embedded in the technology itself. The contraceptive is now delivered in a form that ensures that women will continue contraception over a specific period. This type of contraceptive is a nice example of 'technical delegates': artefacts that are designed to compensate for the perceived deficiences of their users.[18] Feminist health activists have noted the danger of abuse of this type of contraceptive because the user depends on the assistance of health workers to remove the device if she wants to get pregnant (Mintzes 1992; Mintzes et al. 1993).[19] The new generation of provider-dependent long-acting contraceptives aims at 'minimizing user failure', but simultaneously 'minimizes women's control' (Hartmann 1992: 6; Hardon 1992).

The cafeteria discourse can thus be portrayed as simultaneously modern and postmodern. This is in line with Clarke's argument which questions the robustness of the boundary between modern and postmodern approaches and points to 'the simultaneity in time and space of modern and postmodern approaches' (Clarke 1995: 3). However, in reproductive discourses the modern and postmodern conflate only in time, not in space. If we look more closely at the cafeteria discourse, we can see an important differentiation between that part of the population deemed worthy of a greater individual choice, and that part in need of a stricter fertility control. The rhetoric of individual choice seems to be addressed to users all over the world, whereas the rhetoric of population control is more exclusively centred on the countries of the South.[20] To quote Hartmann:

> We in the industrialized countries have the right to voluntary choice as to whether and when to bear children, but their rights are subordinate to the overriding imperative of population control. (Hartmann 1987: 14)

Modernistic tendencies are thus still very much alive in reproductive discourses concerned with countries of the Two-Third's World. Although the cafeteria discourse has disrupted the former scientific representations of the gendered subject–object relations, it has reinforced the othering of people of colour. The focus on 'woman' as the responsible sex has been replaced with a focus on a specific category of women and men who are considered more responsible than others. In the present political climate, in which population control in countries of the South is deemed a precondition for the solution of environmental problems, this politics of othering will remain a crucial issue in the biomedical sciences.[21]

NOTES

1. See the Introduction to this volume.
2. I wish especially to thank Adele Clarke and the women present at the

conference 'Between Mother Goddesses, Monsters, and Cyborgs. Feminist Perspectives on Science, Technology and Health Care', held at Odense University, Denmark, 2–5 November 1994, for their useful comments on an earlier version of this chapter.

3. For thousands of years the 'one-sex model' dominated biomedical discourse, even to such an extent that medical texts lacked a specific anatomical nomenclature for female reproductive organs. The ovary, for instance, did not have a name of its own, but was described as a female testicle, thus referring to the male organ. The words we are now familiar with, such as vagina and clitoris, simply did not exist (Laqueur 1990: 5, 96). According to Laqueur, this stress on similarities, representing the female body as just a variation on one basic male type, was inextricably intertwined with patriarchal thinking, reflecting the values of an overwhelmingly male public world in which 'man is the measure of all things, and woman does not exist as an ontologically distinct category' (Laqueur 1990: 62).

4. The shift from studying similarities to differences was not caused by new scientific findings; to the contrary, Laqueur described how scientific literature provided many new discoveries which could have strengthened the one-sex model. The new field of embryology, for instance, claimed that reproductive organs 'begin from one and the same embryonic structure', offering support to the earlier belief in the similarity between male and female reproductive systems (Laqueur 1990: 169). However, Laqueur does not present a simple causal model for scientific and political changes: 'These social and political changes are not, in themselves, explanations for the reinterpretation of bodies … none of these things caused the making of a new sex body. Instead, the remaking of the body is itself intrinsic to each of these developments' (Laqueur 1990: 11).

5. Although there were two previous attempts to establish a medical specialism devoted to the study of the male reproductive functions, it was not until the late 1970s that andrology became a definite branch of medical science (Niemi 1987; Moscucci 1990: 32, 33).

6. See Oudshoorn 1994b for a more extended analysis of the development of the pill in the 1950s and the 1960s.

7. Pincus was easily convinced by Sanger to use his knowledge of hormones for the development of a contraceptive method, not least because she provided him with the required funds. Sanger raised $150,000 mainly from her friend Katherine Dexter McCormick (Seaman and Seaman 1978: 63). In the 1920s and 1930s Sanger had promoted the diaphragm with spermicide as a universal means to enhance women's power over their reproduction. In the 1950s, Sanger switched to promote hormonal contraceptives, but she did not give up her advocacy of the diaphragm. For a much more extended analysis of Sanger's ideas on contraceptives, see Chesler 1992; McCann 1994; and Reed 1984.

8. In more recent discourses on contraceptive technologies, the term 'patient failure' has been replaced by the terms 'user compliance' and 'noncompliance', which nevertheless have a similar connotation: it is the user that is problematic, not the technology. I thank Adele Clarke for this observation.

9. The concept of the configured user has been introduced by Steve Woolgar. See Woolgar 1991.

10. Such regular medical examinations of pill users were normal medical practice in all countries in which the pill was introduced until the mid-1980s.

11. The role of industry in the development of new contraceptives remained, however, very restricted due to a number of constraints that I have described elsewhere (Oudshoorn 1994a).

12. Advertisement for Multiload Cu 250, released by Organon (Australia). I want to thank Adele Clarke for sending me this advertisement.

13. The implicit assumption in the cafeteria discourse is 'that more technologies automatically equal more choices'. Feminist health advocates have argued that contraceptive choice is not such a simple matter. Individual choices are defined and constrained by power relations in sexual relationships, dependencies between users and providers, and the availability of methods (Hartmann 1992: 3, 4).

14. This applies not only to contraceptive research but also to research on the causes of infertility. In *The Stork and the Syringe*, Naomi Pfeffer concludes that 'although doctors acknowledged that it takes both a woman and a man to make a baby, medical theory and practice focused almost exclusively on the female body' (Pfeffer 1993: 30).

15. However, there still exists a disproportionate expenditure on contraceptive R&D for women. In 1986 only 8 per cent of the funding for contraceptive research was earmarked for male methods (Atkinson and Atkinson 1986). In an overview of 1983 it was concluded that only 8 of the 31 contraceptive methods being developed were male methods (Harper 1983: 5). For an analysis of the constraints on the development of male contraceptives, see Oudshoorn 1994a.

16. Women's Environment and Development Organization 1994.

17. With one exception: one of the first clinical trials that Pincus performed to investigate the contraceptive activity of hormones included eight men, all patients from a mental institution. Despite the fact that the hormone preparations had a definite contraceptive effect in these male patients, men were not included in later trials due to the occurrence of side-effects (Oudshoorn 1994b).

18. Madeleine Akrich, 'Comment decrire les objets techniques', *Technique et Culture*, vol. 5, 1987, pp. 49–63; Bruno Latour, 'Mixing Humans and Non-humans Together: The Sociology of a Door-Closer', *Social Problems*, vol. 35, 1988, pp. 298–310.

19. A study of the Population Council (1990) which evaluated the use of Norplant in Indonesia actually revealed cases of coercive use; women were refused removal of the implant, and there were not enough practitioners with the required skill to remove the implants (Hartmann 1992: 6). Coercive use is not restricted to developing countries. In the USA one legislator in the state of Kansas has tried to introduce a bill 'to pay $500 to any mother on welfare who uses Norplant. Under the bill, believed to be the first of its kind considered by a state, Kansas would also pay for implanting the device and for annual check ups' (Hardon 1992: 26; Lewin 1991). In California, a judge ordered that Norplant be implanted in the case of a woman who had pleaded guilty to child abuse in exchange for a shorter jail sentence (Cantwell 1991).

20. See, amongst others, Greep et al. 1976: xviii, 1, 4.

21. This is not to say that the promotion of population control for women of colour is restricted to Southern countries. In the USA, women of colour (and poor women) have been a major target in family-planning programmes since the 1930s.

REFERENCES

Atkinson, L. and F. Atkinson (1986) 'The Next Contraceptive Revolution', *Family Planning Perspectives*, vol. 18, pp. 19-26.

Boston Health Collective (1971) *Our Bodies, Ourselves*, Simon & Schuster, New York.

Cantwell, M. (1991) 'Coercion and Contraception', *New York Times*, 27 January.

Chesler, E. (1992) *Women of Valor: Margaret Sanger and the Birth Control Movement in America*, Simon & Schuster, New York.

Christian Johnson, R. (1977) 'Feminism, Philanthropy and Science in the Development of the Oral Contraceptive Pill', *Pharmacy in History*, vol. 19, no. 2, pp. 63–79.

Clarke, A. (1988) 'The Industrialization of Human Reproduction, 1889–1989', Keynote Address, Conference on Athena Meets Prometheus: Gender and Technoscience, University of California – Davis.

——— (1995) 'Modernity, Postmodernity and Reproductive Processes, 1890–1990 or, "Mommy, Where Do Cyborgs Come from Anyway?"', forthcoming in C.H. Gray, J. Figueroa-Sarriera and S. Mentor, *The Cyborg Handbook*, Routledge, New York.

Djerassi, C. (1989) 'The Bitter Pill', *Science*, vol. 245, pp. 356–61.

Foucault, M. (1981) *The History of Sexuality Volume 1: An Introduction*, trans. Robert Hurley, Penguin Books, Harmondsworth.

Gallagher, C. and T. Laqueur, eds (1987) *The Making of the Modern Body: Sexuality and Society in the Nineteenth Century*, University of Chicago Press, London, Berkeley and Los Angeles.

Greep, R.O., M. Koblisky and F. Jaffe (1976) *Reproduction and Human Welfare: A Challenge to Research. A Review of the Reproductive Sciences and Contraceptive Development*, MIT Press, Cambridge, Mass. and London.

Handelsman, D.J. (1991) 'Bridging the Gender Gap in Contraception; Another Hurdle Cleared,' *The Medical Journal of Australia*, vol. 154, no. 4, pp. 230–33.

Hardon, A. (1992) 'Norplant: Conflicting Views on its Safety and Acceptability', in H.B. Holmes, ed., *Issues in Reproductive Technology: An Anthology*, Garland Publishing Inc., New York and London, pp. 11–31.

Harper, M.J.K. (1983) *Birth Control Technologies: Prospects by the Year 2000*, University of Texas Press, Austin.

Hartmann, B. (1987) *Reproductive Rights and Wrongs: The Global Politics of Population Control and Contraceptive Choice*, Harper & Row, New York.

——— (1992) 'Contraceptive Choice: A Multitude of Meanings', in H.B. Holmes, ed., *Issues in Reproductive Technology: An Anthology*, Garland Publishing Inc., New York and London, pp. 3–9.

Hatcher, R. (1990) *Contraceptive Technology: 1990–1992*, Irvington, N.Y.

Honegger, C. (1991) *Die Ordnung der Geschlechter: Die Wissenschaften vom Menschen und das Weib,* Campus Verlag, Frankfurt and New York.

hooks, b. (1982) *Ain't I a Woman: Black Women and Feminism,* Pluto Press, London.

The Lancet (1984) 'Gossypol Prospects', vol. 8386, pp. 1108–9.

Laqueur, T. (1990) *Making Sex: Body and Gender from the Greeks to Freud,* Harvard University Press, Cambridge, Mass. and London.

Lewin, T. (1991) 'A Plan to Pay Welfare Mothers for Birth Control', *New York Times,* 9 February 1991, pp. 8, 9.

Maisel, A.Q. (1965) *The Hormone Quest,* Random House, New York.

Marshall, J.F. (1977) 'Acceptability of Fertility Regulating Methods: Designing Technology to Fit People', *Preventive Medicine,* vol. 6, pp. 65–73.

Mastroianni, L., P.F. Donaldson and T.T. Kane (1990) Development of Contraceptives – Obstacles and Opportunities', *The New England Journal of Medicine,* vol. 322, 15 February, pp. 482–5.

McCann, P. (1994) *Birth Control Politics 1925–1945,* Cornell University Press, Ithaca, N.Y.

McLaughlin, L. (1982) *The Pill, John Rock and the Church: The Biography of a Revolution,* Little Brown, Boston, Mass. and Toronto.

Medvei, V.C. (1983) *A History of Endocrinology,* MTP Press, The Hague.

Mintzes, B., ed. (1992) *A Question of Control. Women's Perspectives on the Development and Use of Contraceptive Technologies,* Report of an International Conference held in Woudschoten, The Netherlands, April 1991, WEMOS Women and Pharmaceuticals Project and Health Action International, Amsterdam.

Mintzes, B., A. Hardon and J. Hanhart (1993) *Norplant: Under Her Skin,* Eburon, Delft.

Moscucci, O. (1990) *The Science of Woman. Gynaecology and Gender in England, 1800–1929,* Cambridge University Press, Cambridge.

Niemi, S. (1987) 'Andrology as a Specialty: Its Origin', *Journal of Andrology,* vol. 8, pp. 210–13.

Oudshoorn, N. (1994a) 'The Role of New Organizations in Contraceptive R&D, or How to Organize a World-Wide Laboratory', paper presented at the INSERM/CNRS workshop 'The Invisible Industrialist, or Manufactures and the Construction of Scientific Knowledge', Paris, May 19–21.

—— (1994b) *Beyond the Natural Body. An Archeology of Sex Hormones,* Routledge, London and New York.

Pfeffer, N. (1993) *The Stork and the Syringe: A Political History of Reproductive Medicine,* Polity Press, Cambridge.

Pincus, G. (1958) 'Fertility Control with Oral Medication', *American Journal of Obstetrics and Gynaecology,* vol. 75, pp. 1333–47.

—— (1959) 'Progestational Agents and the Control of Fertility', *Vitamins and Hormones,* vol. 169, pp. 307–25.

—— (1965) *The Control of Fertility,* Academic Press, New York and London.

Reed, J. (1984) *The Birth Control Movement and American Society: From Private Vice to Public Virtue,* Princeton University Press, Princeton, N.J.

Schearer, S.B (1977) 'Pharmacological Approach to Contraception in Men', *Drug Therapy,* vol. 5, no. 2, pp. 72–7.

Schiebinger, L. (1989) *The Mind Has No Sex? Women in the Origins of Modern Science*, Harvard University Press, Cambridge, Mass. and London.

Seaman B. (1969) *The Doctor's Case against the Pill*, Peter H. Wyden, New York.

Seaman, B. and G. Seaman (1978) *Women and the Crisis in Sex Hormones. An Investigation of the Dangerous Uses of Hormones: From Birth Control to Menopause and the Safe Alternatives*, Harvester, Brighton, Sussex.

Smart, B. (1992) *Modern Conditions, Postmodern Controversies*, Routledge, London and New York.

Spilman, C.H., T.J. Lobl and K.T. Kirton (1976) *Regulatory Mechanisms of Male Reproductive Physiology*, Sixth Brook Lodge Workshop on Problems of Reproductive Biology (Amsterdam), Excerpta Medica, Oxford.

Women's Environment and Development Organization (1994) 'Women at Center of UN Population', *News and Views*, vol. 6, no. 1, p. 3.

Woolgar, S. (1991) 'Configuring the User: The Case of Usability Trials', in J. Law, ed., *A Sociology of Monsters: Essays on Power, Technology and Domination*, Routledge, London.

Wu, F.C.W. (1988) 'Male Contraception: Current Status and Future Prospects', *Clinical Endocrinology*, vol. 29, pp. 443–65.

✒ 10 ✒

MEDICALIZATION OF MENOPAUSE:

FROM 'FEMININE FOREVER'

TO 'HEALTHY FOREVER'

Bettina Leysen

Is menopause a natural phenomenon in the life of a woman, just like menarche, pregnancy, giving birth and death? Social scientists, some feminists, and part of the medical profession consider menopause a normal developmental stage. Or is menopause a deficiency disease, an endocrinopathy (disease of a hormone-producing organ), for which hormones have to be administered, just as insulin is given to diabetics? An increasing number of gynaecologists and some feminists hold the latter view. In the first case, there is a spectrum of possible attitudes, covering passive suffering as well as acceptance and integration of the risks life inevitably entails. In the second case, menopause becomes a medical affair. Medicalization is a sign of the times; sickness, ageing, death and pain are almost no longer regarded as natural facts of life in our Western culture, and every effort is taken to banish thoughts of these phenomena from our daily lives. The message of popular culture is to be fit, healthy and active at whatever age or stage in life.

Against this background, it is no surprise that menopause has become the target of public and medical interest. Biomedical knowledge and practice are a product of a social and cultural milieu, the values and beliefs of which are, in turn, reinforced. For the woman, hormonal replacement therapy seems to help her live up to the demands of our society: to stay young, feminine and healthy. Hormonal replacement therapy is not limited to relief of symptoms caused by the deprivation of oestrogens due to menopause. It is now promoted on a large scale for preventing osteoporosis and cardiovascular diseases. If a consensus is reached in biomedical science that menopause is a deficiency disease, this will have important implications for physicians and women alike. If the physician wants to act according to good medical practice, the prescription of hormonal replacement therapy is not only legitimated, but will be imperative. On the other hand, it is conceivable that the woman suffering from one of the aforementioned diseases, and who declines to take hormonal replacement therapy, will be held responsible for her condition.

The present chapter examines critically the concept of menopause, the related symptoms and, in particular, the scientific evidence supporting prophylactic treatment, in the light of the importance and scale of the issue and the implications involved for women in the future.

DEFINITION

Strictly speaking, menopause refers to the last menstrual period, although by convention it is defined in retrospect: one year after the last menstrual period. However, the word 'menopause' is often used to denote the time from before menopause, when cycle irregularities are common, until several years after menopause when oestrogen-deprivation symptoms have ceased (oestrogen is the female sex hormone produced in the ovaries during the menstrual cycle and pregnancy). For this entire period, the word 'climacteric' is also used. Menopause is caused by the cessation of the ovarian production of oestrogens and progesterone (progesterone is the female sex hormone produced in the ovaries during the second half of the menstrual cycle and during pregnancy). The age at which menopause occurs varies between 42 years (Yucatan Mayan) and 51.4 years (the Netherlands) according to culture. It is unknown whether this variability is due to genetic or environmental factors, or whether it is the result of methodological problems in the assessment of age (Flint 1994:17). Globally, there are today an estimated 470 million women aged 50 and older (Barrett-Connor 1993).

What symptoms are characteristic of menopause? The only symptom experienced by all women is cessation of menstruation. Over four hundred effects of oestrogens are known, but there is no consensus in medicine about the menopausal syndrome. According to minimalists, only menstrual irregularities, hot flushes and genito-urinary atrophy (that is, atrophy of genitals and/or the urinary system) are true signs of menopause (van Hall 1993). Maximalists, on the other hand, include a whole range of somatic changes and psychic complaints, occurring from before menopause to decades later. In total, about forty different symptoms have been named.

As medical textbooks on menopause usually dwell on psychological difficulties, it is worthwhile taking a closer look at them. A German manual from 1987 (Kuhl and Taubert 1987) lists depressive symptomatology, sleeplessness, reduced energy level, irritability, headaches, decreased libido, feelings of loneliness and poor memory; an English manual adds loss of self-esteem (Whitehead and Godfree 1992).

AETIOLOGY

Depending on the author, this symptomatology is attributed more or less to hormone deprivation or to role changes during this stage of life. It is evident that culture influences cognition of the meaning of menopause. In cultures where the status and the self-esteem of women increases after menopause, women will welcome its advent. In most Western societies, menopause is feared and regarded as punishment.

Wilbush formulates the interesting hypothesis that,

> The expression of climacteric stress, like any other communication, needs a 'code' to transmit its message. The West has evolved a code which equates social injustice with physical injury. (Wilbush 1982: 20)

In other words, social injustice becomes medicalized. Having a good social network and some income of their own was found to protect women against certain climacteric complaints. The impact of menopause is related to the social position of women in our society, women in lower socio-economic categories being particularly vulnerable (Severne 1977).

Medicalization, by which a normal physiological process becomes a medical affair, can be distinguished on three levels, according to Conrad and Schneider: the conceptual, the institutional and the interactional. On the conceptual level, medicalization occurs when a problem is defined in medical terminology. On the institutional level, medicalization occurs when the medical profession legally controls the problem. On the interactional level, medicalization occurs when the problem of the patient is diagnosed and/or treated as a medical problem (Bell 1990).

HISTORY

Womens' experiences of menopause, as expressed in letters and diaries, have yet to be explored, according to Susan Bell (Bell 1990). Wilbush

(1979) states that the menopausal syndrome was apparently created around 1800 in the writings of the medical men in France. Gardanne proposed the name 'ménespausie', which he later changed to 'ménopause', for the cessation of menses. Furthermore, Wilbush argues that menopause as a disease began with upper-class women who lost their status and privileges after the French Revolution. This loss made them all the more dependent on their physical attractiveness. Menopause for them was equal to neglect and social death. More than today, medical literature was aware of the social factors in disease. Ruth Formanek (1990) argues that the medical view of menopause has historical antecedents in the humoral theory of ancient Greece. Retained blood was thought to rise to the brain and cause mental illness and other diseases. By the end of the nineteenth century, most male physicians believed that mental symptoms, hot flushes and perspiration were due to the undischarged blood entering the brain.

MEDICALIZATION

Susan Bell (1987) argues that medicalization of menopause on the conceptual level took place in the 1930s and 1940s in the USA. Several factors were involved in this development: biomedical researchers' construction of a theoretical framework and a scientific methodology for understanding the role of oestrogens in menopause; the availability of the cheap synthetic hormone diethylstilbestrol; and the belief of some doctors that gynaecology would become more scientific and, therefore, safer by adopting theories and tools of the sex endocrinologists. According to the paradigm of sex endocrinology, form, function and behaviour of the sexes was attributable to biological processes, thereby releasing women from responsibility for their behaviour.

The loss of ovarian function at the time of menopause, accompanied by oestrogen-deprivation symptoms, was regarded as a biological deficiency which had to be corrected artificially by supplementing the lacking oestrogens. A professor of gynaecology, R.T. Frank, stated that 'estrogenic relief of the menopause' was 'a major triumph, second only to the treatment of hypothyroidism [insufficient production of the thyroid hormone] by thyroid [the gland responsible for metabolism] medication, and of diabetes by insulin'(Frank 1941). In this view, a woman's experience during menopause was reduced to an individual somatic deficiency, demonstrating once again the inferiority of the female body. In 1943, James Goodall was able to extract conjugated oestrogens from the urine of pregnant mares (McCrea 1983). Since then these have become the leading oestrogen supplement in the USA, peaking in 1976, when 26.7 million prescriptions were issued.

The medicalization of menopause on all three levels – conceptual, institutional and interactional – came about in the 1960s in the USA. The promotor of menopause as a deficiency disease, which could be cured by oestrogen-replacement therapy, was gynaecologist Robert Wilson. He succeeded in convincing the medical community, as well as women in mid-life, of the many advantages of such therapy in preventing the symptoms of menopause and ageing. In his popular book *Feminine Forever* (1966), Wilson shows himself to be concerned not only about womens' loss of good health through menopause, but also about the effect of oestrogen deprivation on their temperament (see McCrea 1983). Oestrogens are even promoted as an efficient remedy for restoring peace in the family, by stabilizing the mood of the wife. Moreover, Wilson was not the only one to concentrate on the loss of femininity during menopause. An even more denigrating and, at the same time, moralizing attitude is expressed in another bestseller of the 1960s, *Everything You Wanted To Know About Sex* (Reuben 1969):

> As estrogen is shut off, a woman comes as close as she can to being a man. Increased facial hair, deepened voice, obesity, and decline of breasts and female genitalia all contribute to a masculine appearance. Not really a man, but no longer a functional woman, these individuals live in a world of intersex. Having outlived their ovaries, they have outlived their usefulness as human beings. (Reuben 1969)

Decades earlier, Helene Deutsch, a female psychoanalyst, had described the postmenopausal woman as the 'third sex' (Oldenhave 1991: 116).

According to Nelly Oudshoorn (Oudshoorn 1991; and Chapter 9 in this volume), the fact that the female, and not the male, body became the central focus of the hormone industry is due to the existence of the medical specialism of gynaecology, dealing with the female reproductive organs. That gynaecology has been and still is the specialism which most strongly propagates the use of female hormones is beyond question. The advent of andrology has not been followed by a comparable interest in hormone therapy for males. Biological differences between the sexes must be taken into account to explain this different evolution (no abrupt decline of testosterone production in males and a greater anxiety on the part of urologists about causing side-effects in men by the administration of the hormone).

As regards the sexist and misogynistic arguments cited earlier, they are advanced less often in present-day medical and psychoanalytic literature. Nowadays the eternal conservation of health has become the goal. The watchword '*feminine forever* through oestrogens' has been replaced by '*healthy forever* through hormonal replacement therapy'.

FEMINIST CRITIQUE ON THE CONCEPTUAL LEVEL

Feminist critique of the medical model of menopause has been directed against the concept of the deficiency model in contrast to the concept of menopause as a normal life transition or ageing process. The medical model stresses the dependence of women on hormones for their physical and mental equilibrium and emphasizes a deficiency in biological make-up. Instead of regarding the end of ovarian production of female hormones and ova as a protection on the part of nature against the physical demands of pregnancy, for which the ageing body is less well suited, a different conclusion is drawn: woman was not meant to outlive her ovaries. Once the reproductive task is fulfilled, she becomes useless. This reductionist view of women is still common in gynaecology. The uterus and ovaries are frequently regarded as useless organs after menopause and can therefore be disposed of surgically, in order to prevent cancer, for instance. When, during a conference on menopause in 1981 in Ostende, Belgium, some critical women in the audience ironically proposed the same line of reasoning for bilateral mastectomy (surgical removal of the breast) in order to prevent the much more frequent breast cancer, cries of derision from the established medical profession could be heard.

FEMINIST CRITIQUE OF SAFETY AND EFFICACY

After the debacle of the increased incidence of endometrial cancer (cancer of the lining of the uterus), which was epidemiologically linked to a prolonged intake of oestrogens only, oestrogen therapy was replaced by combined oestrogen and progestin replacement, thereby imitating the normal menstrual cycle. This therapy, however, brings about the shedding of the endometrium (lining of the uterus). In other words, the woman is faced with ongoing blood loss at regular intervals (every month or every three months). To the regret of the pharmaceutical industry, compliance with this mode of replacement is low, because many women do not want to menstruate for the rest of their lives.

In the USA, hysterectomy (surgical removal of the uterus) has become the most common operation among women. By the age of

60, one out of three women will have had a hysterectomy. In six European countries, the number of hysterectomies per 100,000 female inhabitants lies between 126 in Sweden and 371 in the Netherlands. Corresponding figures from the USA and Canada are 549 and 619 (Wijma and Boeke 1985: 148). Although there are differences in the incidence of pathology, which justify some variation in hysterectomy rates (blacks are more likely to develop fibroids – benign tumours of the uterus), these are insufficient to explain the magnitude of the difference between the two continents. One is tempted to ask whether hysterectomies have not become a convenience operation in North America, allowing hormone replacement without the inconvenient bleedings. For one of the decisive factors regarding compliance with hormonal replacement therapy is the fact that the woman has had a hysterectomy (Cauley et al. 1990).

Feminists are also critical about the safety of current hormonal replacement therapy. While there is no longer doubt about the safety of combined oestrogen–progestin replacement therapy with regard to endometrium cancer, the question is far from settled as far as breast-cancer risk is concerned. Nevertheless, lifelong hormonal replacement therapy is advocated by some experts on menopause. Increased breast-cancer rates are even acknowledged in publications on risk/benefit considerations of long-term hormonal replacement therapy in healthy postmenopausal women (Gorsky et al. 1994; Miller 1991). Even the quality of a year spent with breast cancer seems to be numerically quantifiable. To the affected women, the following equation to be found in Gorsky's text must sound cynical:

> To adjust for the quality of life after a coronary heart disease or breast cancer event, we assumed that each woman experiencing these events would live her remaining years at a relative value or 0,8 rather than 1; that is a quality adjusted life year after such a nonfatal event was assumed to be worth 80% of a healthy year life. (Gorsky 1994)

HEALTH FOREVER ON MEDICAL PRESCRIPTION, OR, THE CONSTRUCTION OF A NEW INDICATION FOR HORMONAL REPLACEMENT THERAPY

In critically examining the indication and efficacy of hormonal replacement therapy, we must distinguish between symptomatic treatment and prophylactic treatment (treatment of symptoms as opposed to preventive treatment before symptoms develop). Notwithstanding the important implications for women, prophylactic hormonal replacement therapy has not yet been critically analysed by feminists.

Oestrogens, with or without the addition of progestins, are efficient in treating true oestrogen-deprivation symptoms like hot flushes and symptoms of urogenital atrophy like vaginal dryness and burning. Treatment duration depends on the duration of the symptoms. Whereas between 50 and 80 per cent of all menopausal women experience these symptoms, only some 10 to 25 per cent suffer enough from them to warrant treatment.

In the last decade, the medical indication of hormonal replacement therapy was widened from cure to prevention. This was the logical result of adding arterial and skeletal diseases to the list of symptoms associated with oestrogen deficiency (Whitehead and Godfree 1992: 14). Initially, hormonal replacement therapy was advocated for the prevention of osteoporosis (bone disease resulting in frail bones with increased risk of fracture); it was subsequently extended to treatment of coronary heart disease (disease of the blood vessels of the heart), thereby increasing the potential customer group enormously. Close examination of medical literature on these topics makes it clear that promises stand in for proofs, and that many questions remain unsolved.

OSTEOPOROSIS

Osteoporosis is a chronic condition characterized by a reduced amount of bone, which leads to diminished physical strength of the skeleton and increased susceptibility to fractures (Christiansen 1993). Bone is not a dead substance, but the site of considerable metabolic exchange, with bone resorption and formation continuing throughout life. As Ineke van Wingerden (see Chapter 11 of this volume) points out, osteoporosis has become known as a female condition. One of the reasons women are more prone to osteoporosis is because they experience the withdrawal of female hormones around mid-life. In men the decline of male hormones is more gradual over decades. Ineke van Wingerden describes two competing theories regarding the development of osteoporosis. From these she constructs two different female bodies: the hormonal body and the mineral body. In fact, there are two different types of osteoporosis, each with a different locus in the body, a different age group and a different sex ratio.

Post-menopausal osteoporosis affects women mainly between the ages of 50 and 70. Fracture sites include the spine and the forearm. The sex ratio is one man to six women. This type of bone loss is related to post-menopausal oestrogen deprivation, with an average incidence of 2 per cent bone loss over the first five to ten post-menopausal years. This fact, together with the relatively lower bone mass in women, explains why osteoporosis affects more women than men. Vertebral osteoporosis causes shortening and stooping: the well-known dowager's hump. Many women suffer numerous asymptomatic fractures before the diagnosis is established.

The second type is senile osteoporosis, which affects people over the age of 70. The sex ratio here is one man to two women. The typical fracture site is the hip. Factors related to the ageing process play an important role. Structural bone strength, which is related to exercise, and body-fat padding are modifying protective factors.

Osteoporosis in itself is asymptomatic; it causes no pain. Osteoporosis is not equal to fracture, just as hypertension is not equal to a stroke or myocardial infarct. Blacks have denser bones and lower fracture rates than whites or Asian women. Recently, the lifetime incidence of fractures of the wrist, vertebra or hip in women has been found to be one in three in the USA (Melton et al. 1992). In other words, the majority of women will not suffer a fracture. It is important to point this out, because many healthy menopausal women think that unless they undergo hormonal replacement therapy they will break bones later on.

In order to decide who is likely to develop osteoporosis, measurement of bone density and the rate of metabolic turnover of the bone can help in identifying those women with a low bone mass and an increased risk of osteoporosis. Ineke van Wingerden shows us the profound impact of new technology – *in casu* bone densitometry – on womens' lives on the conceptual, individual and socio-economic levels. To cite Sandra Coney: 'Before 1960 osteoporosis was a problem of bones, now it is a problem of women' (Coney 1994). In fact, the term 'osteoporosis' has become almost as well known as hypercholesterolemia (increased level of cholesterol in the blood) and hypertension. Indeed, there are parallels with these other two conditions: namely, the impact of lifestyle on their development; the lack of symptoms of these technically discovered abnormalities; and the existence of therapeutic strategies.

Two of Coney's statements can, however, be questioned: the tendency to consider the issue of prevention as a consequence of the densitometric conceptualization of the female body; and the so-called seduction coming from the statistical risk shown by the densitometric measurement. For this is turning things the other way around. If one is not interested in carrying out appropriate measures to decrease the risk of the fractures, one simply should not do a bone densitometry. What is the use of measuring cholesterol in the blood, if you are not inclined to change your dietary habits? Furthermore, bone densitometry has become such a widely used (and abused) technique because prevention is possible. But what is the use of a test, when you cannot change the future course of a disease? It will only result in anxiety.

Contrary to the multitude of publications on the protective effect of oestrogen or combined replacement therapy on bone density, there is a dearth of publications on the actual prevention of fractures. This is understandable because of the large number of women who have to be followed for 25 years before definite statements on reduction of fracture rate by hormonal replacement therapy can be made. A recent publication in the *New England Journal of Medicine* (Felson et al. 1993) shows that a period of at least seven years of hormonal replacement therapy is necessary to conserve bone density in old age. Even this duration has little residual effect on women aged 75 or older, known to be at greatest risk of fractures. In other words, the protective effect is lost gradually after stopping treatment, an argument favouring long-term, even lifelong, treatment.

In the debate about osteoporosis it should not be forgotten that women have to ensure an adequate calcium intake. The need for calcium increases with age from 500 mg during adult years to 1,500 mg in old age. Some of the controversy accompanying findings on the protective effect of calcium on bones can be explained by the fact that calcium intake must occur before bedtime (Blumsohn et al. 1994). It is during night that calcium is stolen from the bones (see van Wingerden, Chapter 11 of this volume, where the calcium theory is compared to the hormone theory). Both calcium and hormones are necessary for bone remodelling, however; the calcium is lost from the bones when the calcium concentration in the blood is not high enough. Furthermore, bone density is built up during childhood and adolescence; thus primary prevention should be aimed at young girls, motivating them to exercise and to ensure adequate intake of dairy products.

CARDIOVASCULAR DISEASES

Recently, hormonal replacement therapy has been promoted for the prevention of cardiovascular diseases, the chief cause of death among women in all industrialized countries. A critical analysis of the evidence of the protective effect is unconvincing. Nevertheless, at least in Belgium, organizations have been founded with the goal of informing the general public about the many advantages of hormonal replacement therapy. Needless to say, they are financed by the pharmaceutical industry. For the following remarks, I am indebted to the articles on oestrogens and coronary heart disease by Elisabeth Barrett-Connor. A review of the studies of oestrogen use in women and relation to cardio-vascular disease informs us that eleven out of the twenty-four published reports show statistically significant reductions, amounting on average to 50 per cent (Barrett-Connor 1991a).

There are, however, several limitations to these studies. First, practically all the studies are observational. This means that we have no information about why these women were prescribed oestrogens, or about how they differ from women who refused or stopped oestrogen-replacement therapy. In general, women taking oestrogen-replacement therapy are more likely to be educated, upper middle class and slim. In other words, there is already a lower risk of these women contracting coronary heart disease without taking hormones.

Furthermore, women who continue with hormonal replacement therapy are, by definition, compliant women. Compliance is used in medical literature to denote the willingness of the patient to stick to his/her therapy. Research has shown that compliant subjects have a significantly lower risk of heart disease when taking a placebo (a dummy pill) than subjects not compliant with their placebo. The reason is probably that the former subjects are more health conscious and have a lifestyle which includes a healthy diet and physical activity. This was even true in a socio-economically homogeneous group with ready access to medical care (Barrett-Connor 1991b).

Further flaws in the argument include the link between cholesterol and risk of coronary heart disease (Barrett-Connor 1992). Hyper-cholesterolemia produces early death from coronary heart disease in elderly men but not in women. All too often, women are not investigated as a separate category, and results applying to men are incorrectly transferred to women. The same goes for age. Even in medicine the statement of Evelyn Sullerot holds true: 'On ne compte, ce qui compte' (Only that is counted which is worthwhile counting).

In conclusion, let me emphasize that even if some evidence suggests that unopposed oestrogen replacement reduces the risk of coronary heart disease, we need valid trials (randomized, placebo-controlled trials, in which known and unknown biases are randomly distributed). *For the moment, there is no reason to advise all women to go on hormonal replacement therapy for prophylactic reasons.* Instead of labelling all women as potential patients in need of hormonal replacement therapy, public health efforts should be directed elsewhere – for example, towards the prevention of smoking among women.

CRITICAL VOICES IN MEDICAL LITERATURE

Voices critical of hormonal replacement therapy and the claim that it prevents disease can even be found in medical literature, if one searches hard enough. The problem is that general practitioners derive a substantial part of their information from the pharmaceutical industry. Critical comments are difficult to find in the journals aimed at gynaecologists.

An eye-opening article on the prolongation of life by hormonal replacement therapy, published in a journal for specialists in internal medicine, was brought to my attention by a professor of bone disease, who urged gynaecologists to inform their women patients about it. The authors of this critical review (Grady 1992) examined 265 English-language articles published since 1970. The risks and benefits of long-term hormonal replacement treatment for an asymptomatic post-menopausal woman (that is, a woman not suffering from hot flushes and genito-urinary atrophy) was assessed. The net gain in life expectancy was *one* year; the lifetime probability of developing cardiovascular disease was decreased by 12.1 per cent, and of hip fracture by only 2.5 per cent. The authors conclude:

> A woman must be fully informed of the risks and benefits of hormone therapy and play an important role in deciding whether to take hormones and which regimen to use. A woman's risk factors for coronary heart disease, hip fracture, and breast cancer and whether she has had a hysterectomy may affect the decision. For many women, however, the value placed on prevention of coronary heart disease compared with the desire to avoid cancer will probably determine whether she takes hormones as preventive therapy. (Grady 1992)

A comment from a 'master of menopause' who runs a Climacteric Clinic in Florida is worth quoting, since it is a viewpoint one has difficulty in finding in the abundant medical literature on the topic. That it is an unusual standpoint is prefigured in the title: 'Estrogen in Postmenopausal Women: An Opposing View'.

> Both conditions [osteoporosis and arterial disease] are modulated by the presence or absence of estrogen, but both are also heavily influenced by the individual's genetic make-up, lifestyle, social habits, and physical activity. Women who enter their menopause with adequate bone mass do not develop osteoporosis. Women who are normotensive, have appropriate lipid and

lipoprotein profiles, are physically active, and do not smoke are unlikely to experience significant atherogenic disease. Why then should one treat all post-menopausal women with estrogen therapy? (Notelovitz 1989)

While it was not so difficult for feminists to be critical of the role-conforming and sexist ('feminine forever') objectives of oestrogen replacement as promoted by Wilson in the 1960s, ideological criticism alone is no longer sufficient. When future health is at stake, the validity of scientific investigation has to be questioned. Without a background in biomedical sciences, this is difficult. As Jane Lewis argues (1993), it is difficult for women to weigh the pros and cons of high-tech medicine, to decide whether to accept or reject it, and, in the former case, how to exercise some degree of control over it. Furthermore, if feedback to the medical world is the objective, the debate has to be held on women's terms.

THE GOLD-EFFECT

As far as prevention of cardiovascular diseases by hormonal replacement therapy is concerned, we are confronted with an example of the 'Gold-effect', as described by Peter Skrabanek and James McCormick in their book *Follies and Fallacies in Medicine* (1989: 59). 'The Gold-effect' describes how an opinion, held by some experts, is able to become an established concept in medicine. It all starts when some experts, so convinced about an idea that their conviction might be termed 'faith', organize a conference on the subject. Having attracted more people who are favourable to the new concept than those who are not inter-ested in it, the conference agrees that a committee should be formed to promote the new concept. The articles from this conference will show a considerable degree of consensus. Soon, a new medical journal specializing in the subject will be founded. (Examples are *Maturitas* in 1978 and *European Menopause Journal* in 1994.) Naturally articles in line with the ideological line of the journal are more likely to be published. Once the new concept is transmitted by the established journals, it becomes increasingly difficult to eradicate it because most readers like to give credit to what is published by 'authorities'. The phrase 'there is more and more evidence that' is soon replaced by 'it is generally accepted' or 'it is a well-known fact that'.

The fact that there is increasing evidence of the protective effect of oestrogen-replacement therapy on cardiovascular diseases is, for example, about to become generally accepted. This has far-reaching consequences.

At the Figo Congress in Singapore in 1991 (International Federation of Gynaecology and Obstetrics), the motion was issued that hormonal replacement therapy should be made available to all women when they reach their menopause. If consensus is reached that menopause is a deficiency disease resulting in cardiovascular diseases and osteoporosis, hormonal replacement therapy will not only be legitimated, but will be considered imperative if the physician wants to act according to good clinical practice.

MEDICALIZATION: A DOUBLE-EDGED SWORD

Paraphrasing Michel Foucault, we might ask whether it will be drugs that discipline us to health in old age or diet, exercise and lifestyle? Everywhere in Europe, cost–benefit calculations of hormonal replacement therapy are being made. They stress the fact that the cost of treating women with fractures exceeds the cost of hormonal replacement therapy with the concomittant medical check-ups (usually pointing out that the net gain will be much greater if the cost for the treatment of cardiovascular diseases is included in the calculation). Presenting hormonal replacement therapy in economic terms is likely to turn it into a political issue. In the worst of all scenarios, one can imagine that social security will penalize women for diseases or invalidity allegedly due to hormone deprivation.

In the meantime, women in Europe do not seem as keen on hormonal replacement therapy as in the USA, where up to 42 per cent of menopausal women are reported to take it. This is an important factor for drug companies which have invested heavily in the marketing of new hormone preparations for menopausal women. Whereas there was only one combined oestrogen–progestin preparation available in Belgium ten years ago, physicians in the country can now choose between eight different ones. Not surprisingly, one of the topics of the last International Congress on Menopause in Stockholm in 1993 was compliance or willingness of women to take the prescribed medication correctly.

A phenomenon which is increasingly used at international conferences is the organization of symposia featuring international authorities sponsored by the pharmaceutical industry. 'Why do women prefer to gather information from the writings of the Madames of Menopause, instead of following the advice of the Masters of Menopause?', exclaimed one 'master' disdainfully as a response to the discussion of women's (lack of) compliance. Although it will never be openly admitted, it is questionable how far these speakers are totally free in the choice and content of their lectures.

The medicalization of menopause can be viewed from different angles. It has caused a renewed interest in the biology and psychology of mid-life women, who, together with the elderly, are the part of our society with least status. It is characteristic of our society that one of the primary reasons for this new wave of medicalization is the fact that mid-life women have been discovered as an enormous market for the pharmaceutical industry. By becoming an interesting economic target, and not only for drug companies, mid-life women as a group gain in importance. In 1994, the leading Flemish news magazine (*Weekend Knack* 1994) organized a poll about menopause among its readers, female and male, together with five articles on the topic.

The problem with media coverage is, however, that the information obtained is heavily dependent on the opinion of the interviewed expert. In several countries the popular media are the main source of information (Mansfield and Boyer 1990). The repercussions from this kind of information-gathering might be quite substantial. The same holds true for feminist analysis of menopause, but here the content of the information can be evaluated in the light of the explicit ideological background. Medical journalism, on the other hand, should deal in objective information. Furthermore, we should be aware of the fact that sponsors can also influence the choice or content of the articles. By inviting journalists to conferences on menopause where a new drug is introduced, drug companies ensure advertisement in the report on the conference. Lately, the cosmetics industry is likewise invading journalism and the gynaecological world.

Sandra Coney describes in her book *The Menopause Industry* (1994) 'the intertwining between pharmaceutical industry and "authorities" on menopause and the media'. Another source of concern in the medicalization of menopause is distortion of the image of the menopausal woman. If we believe textbooks and authorities on menopause, it is a period characterized by depression and psychological symptoms. The latter include deficient activity, decreased drive, irritability, anxiety attacks, feelings of loneliness, headache, sleeplessness, decreased libido and forgetfulness (Kuhl and Tauber 1987: 15). A Dutch gynaecologist pointed out jokingly that most of these symptoms could also be found in middle-aged men who indulge too heavily in alcohol. Comparing symptoms in men and women of different age groups within the general population, he was subsequently able to show that women between 45 and 54 differ from the other categories with respect to only one symptom: transpiration (van Hall et al. 1993).

How is it then that the 'Masters of Menopause' time and again depict psychological complaints as typical for menopause. These 'Masters', who forget that they are confronted with a highly selected group of self-referred women, generalize their findings from a menopause clinic to the general population. Anderson (1987) was able to show that more than 60 per cent of women in a menopause clinic were depressed. It is obvious that the overrepresentation of self-selected women with more severe complaints does not tell us anything about the true incidence of psychological complaints during menopause.

To shed some light on the relationship between mood disorders and menopause, we need to look at prospective longitudinal cohort studies, where women are investigated from before menopause until they have entered menopause. Those studies do not find an increased incidence of mood disorders or depression, but rather lack of enjoyment in things and a reduction in the sense of happiness, life satisfaction and the feeling that life is meaningful, worthwhile and rewarding (McKinlay et al. 1992; Matthews et al. 1990; Hunter 1992; Holte 1994: 169).

Instead of labelling these latter feelings mood disorder, we can better regard them as aspects of a developmental crisis, accompanying the transition from one stage of life to another. Feminists have pointed out the resemblance with another life-transition, puberty, which is accepted as such and not medicalized. Cross-cultural research reveals the absence of symptoms of depression in traditional societies, where menopause raises the status of women. In these societies, menopause is welcomed as a time to reward a woman's achievements and publicly acknowledge her new, socially valued role (Kaiser 1990). This finding once again points to the conclusion that a woman's experience of menopause is heavily dependent on the socio-cultural environment. In this light, we can understand that 50 per cent of Norwegian women find their life less rewarding on becoming menopausal (Holte 1994: 169).

In contrast to the dreadful image of menopausal women propagated by Western medical experts on menopause, the advertisements of companies producing hormones feature active, dynamic middle-class women in mid-life. The underlying message is, of course, that their state is due to the benefit of hormonal replacement therapy. Physicians are indoctrinated to accept that their younger patients on the contraceptive pill will, in the end, become menopausal. 'In 30 years she will be 50' and 'Estrogens and progestins are now already the commonest thing in the world, this will later also be the case with X and Y for their climacteric', are the actual slogans in two commercial advertisements targeted at physicians (for the contraceptive pill Cilest, manufactured by Cilag; and for Zumenon and Duphaston, manufactured by Duphar).

'Feminine forever' has ceased to be a slogan for the medicalization of menopause. 'Healthy forever' has just begun to be promoted. Let us hope that the latter promise will not once again be followed by a debacle like that of an increased incidence of cancer of the female genital organs.

REFERENCES

Anderson (1987) 'Characteristics of Menopausal Women Seeking Assistance', *American Journal of Obstetrics and Gynecology*, vol. 156, no. 2, p. 428.

Barrett-Connor, E. (1991a) 'Estrogen and Coronary Heart Disease in Women', *Journal of the American Medical Association*, vol. 265, no. 14, pp. 1861–7.

———— (1991b) 'Postmenopausal Estrogen and Prevention Bias', *Annals of Internal Medicine* 115, pp. 455–6.

———— (1992) 'Hypercholesterolemia Predicts Early Death from Coronary Heart Disease in Elderly Men but Not Women', The Rancho Bernardo Study, *Annals in Epidemiology* 2, pp. 77–83.

———— (1993) 'Epidemiology and the Menopause: A Global Overview', *International Journal of Fertility* 38, Supplement 1, pp. 6–14.

Bell, S.E. (1987) 'Changing Ideas: The Medicalization of Menopause', *Social Sciences in Medicine* 24, pp. 535–42.

———— (1990) 'Sociological Perspectives on the Medicalization of Menopause', *Annals of the New York Academy of Sciences* 592, pp. 173–8.

Blumsohn et al. (1994) *Journal of Endocrinology and Metabolism*, vol. 79, pp. 730–35.

Cauley, J.A., S.R. Cummings, D.M. Black et al. (1990) 'Prevalence and Determinants of Estrogen Replacement Therapy in Elderly Women', *Annals of the Journal of Obstetrics and Gynecology* 163, pp. 1438–44.

Christiansen, C. (1993) 'Prevention and Treatment of Osteoporosis with Hormone Replacement Therapy', *International Journal of Fertility* 38, Supplement 1, pp. 45–54.

Coney, S. (1994) *The Menopause Industry: How the Medical Establishment Exploits Women*, Hunter House, Alameda, Calif.

Felson, D.T. et al. (1993) 'The Effect of Postmenopausal Estrogen Therapy on Bone Density in Elderly Women', *New England Journal of Medicine* 329, pp. 1141–6.

Flint, M. (1994) 'Menopause – The Global Aspect', in G. Berg and M. Hammar, eds, *The Modern Management of Menopause*, Parthenon Publishing Group, Casterton Hall.

Formanek, R. (1990) 'Menopause: Two Views', *Annals of the New York Academy of Sciences*, vol. 592, no. 9, p. 173.

Frank, R.T. (1941) 'Treatment of Disorders of the Menopause', *Bulletin of the*

New York Academy of Medicine 17, p. 856.

Gorsky et al. (1994) 'Relative Risks and Benefits of Long-Term Estrogen Replacement Therapy: A Decision Analysis', *Obstetrics and Gynaecology* 83, pp. 161–6.

Grady, D. (1992) 'Hormone Therapy to Prevent Disease and Prolong Life in Postmenopausal Women', *Annals of Internal Medicine* 117, pp. 1016–37.

Holte, A. (1994) 'Psychosocial Factors and the Menopause: Results from the Norwegian Menopause Project', in G. Berg and M. Hammar, eds, *The Modern Management of Menopause*, Parthenon Publishing Group, Casterton Hall.

Hunter, M. (1992) 'The South-East England Longitudinal Study of the Climacteric and Postmenopause', *Maturitas* 14, pp. 117–26.

Kaiser, K. (1990) Cross-Cultural Perspectives on Menopause, *Annals of the New York Academy of Sciences*, pp. 430–32.

Kuhl, H. and A. Taubert (1987) *Das Klimakterium*, Georg Thieme Verlag, Stuttgart.

Lewis, J. (1993) 'Feminism, the Menopause and Hormone Replacement Therapy', *Feminist Review* 43, pp. 38–55.

Leysen, B. et al. (1992) 'Image of the Climacteric Woman: A Comparison of Women Attending a University Menopause Clinic and Women Participating in a Self-Help Group', *Journal of Psychosomatic Obstetrics and Gynaecology* 13, pp. 299–309.

Mansfield, P. and B. Boyer (1990) 'The Experiences, Concerns and Health Care Needs of Women in the Menopausal Transition', *Annals of the New York Academy of Sciences*, pp. 448–9.

Matthews, K. et al. (1990) 'Influences of Natural Menopause on Psychological Characteristics and Symptoms of Middle-Aged Healthy Women', *Journal of Consultative Clinical Psychiatry*, vol. 58, no. 3, pp. 345–51.

McCrea, F. (1983) 'The Politics of Menopause: The "Discovery" of a Deficiency Disease', *Social Problems* 13, pp. 111–23.

McKinlay, S. et al. (1992) 'The Normal Menopause Transition', *Maturitas* 14, pp. 103–15.

Melton, L.J. et al. (1992) 'How Many Women Have Osteoporosis?', *Journal of Bone and Mineral Research* 9, pp. 1005–10.

Miller, A.B. (1991) 'Risk/Benefit Considerations of Antioestrogen/Estrogen Therapy in Healthy Postmenopausal Women', *Preventive Medicine* 20, pp. 79–85.

Notelovitz, M. (1989) 'Estrogen in Postmenopausal Women: An Opposing View', *Journal of Family Practice*, vol. 29, no. 4, pp. 410–15.

Oldenhave, A. (1991) 'Well-Being and Sexuality in the Climacteric', Ph.D. thesis, Rijksuniversiteit, Utrecht.

Oudshoorn, N. (1991) 'The Making of the Hormonal Body: A Contextual History of the Study of Sex Hormones 1923–1940', *Tijdschrift voor Vrouwenstudies* 47, pp. 418–21.

Reuben, D. (1969) *Everything You Wanted to Know about Sex*, David McKay, New York.

Severne, L. (1977) 'De overgangsjaren: een onderzoek in België bij 922 vrouwen tussen 45 en 55 jaar', International Health Foundation, Brussels.

Skrabanek, P. and J. McCormick (1989) *Follies and Fallacies in Medicine,* Tarragon Press, Ravenstone Withorn.

Udris, I. (1987) 'V.I.M. Vrouwen in de middenleeftijd: Focus op specifiek vrouwenvormingswerk', Hoger instituut voor Readaptatiewetenschappen, Catholic University of Louvain.

van Hall, E.V. (1993) 'Hormonale mythologie rond de overgang', lecture: 'De Balie', Amsterdam, 18 November.

van Hall, E.V. et al. (1993) 'Medicalisering van de overgang', *Medisch Contact* 48, pp. 179–81.

van Wingerden, I. (1993) 'Hormonaal of mineraal? Osteoporose en het vrouwenlichaam, *Tijdschrift voor Vrouwenstudies*, vol. 14, no. 2, pp. 149–71.

Weekend Knack (1994) 4 artikels over de menopause en menopause enquete: de resultaten.

Whitehead, M. and V. Godfree (1992) *Hormone Replacement Therapy*, Edinburgh Churchill Livingstone, Edinburgh.

Wijma, K. and P.E. Boeke (1985) *Psychologische aspekten van obstetrische en gynaecologische (ziekte-)beelden*, Van Loghum Slaterus, Deventer.

Wilbush, J. (1979) 'La Ménespausie – the Birth of a Syndrome', *Maturitas* 1, pp. 145–51.

—— (1982) 'Sociological Aspects of Midlife', in P. Van Keep et al., eds, *The Controversial Climacteric*, MTP Press, Lancaster, pp. 20–21.

Wilson, R. (1966) *Forever Feminine*, M. Evans.

POSTMODERN VISIONS OF THE MENOPAUSAL BODY: THE APPARATUS OF BODILY PRODUCTION AND THE CASE OF BRITTLE BONES

Ineke van Wingerden

For women in our society ageing has become an issue that deserves serious attention. Menopause and brittle bones are looming on the horizon. The Change or ageing no longer ushers in a relatively relaxed and simple phase in life without periods or pregnancies. On the contrary: suddenly, women have become 'perimenopausal' and are confronted with a body that requires their undivided attention. Women are being urged to anticipate the 'postmenopause' and associated phenomena. Osteoporosis or brittle bones has become a major issue for ageing women and they are encouraged to look after their bones. Women are required to reconsider their relationship to their body.

THE MENOPAUSAL BODY

Within the life sciences, the body can be 'discovered' by biomedical research. Biomedicine has defined the menopausal body in hormonal terms and has split it into a premenopausal, a perimenopausal and a postmenopausal body. Social studies of science and technology, however, have criticized this notion of 'discovering' the body (and nature) (Latour 1987).[1] Starting from these criticisms, Donna Haraway elaborates on a metaphor of production. Instead of being discovered, bodies are being *produced*. She has illustrated her point in 'Situated Knowledges' and in 'The Biopolitics of Postmodern Bodies' (Haraway 1988, 1989). In the latter she describes how 'immunological bodies' are the result of what she has called the *apparatus of bodily production* in which immunological discourse, technology, matter and language are knotted together. The body that is produced is never ahistorical, but bears the marks of time and the place of its production.[2] Many authors have given examples of the way in which bodies are produced by biomedical discourse and have focused on a variety of the (f)actors involved.[3] Haraway in particular has stressed the power of these productions; they determine how medicine and we ourselves deal with our body.

Drawing on my research on the osteoporosis debate and inspired by Haraway's apparatus of bodily production, I will make a detailed analysis of the way in which bodies are produced in this specific area of biomedical research and medical practice.[4] I have gathered my data by doing ethnographic fieldwork in an outpatient clinic for bone metabolism. In that clinic I observed doctor–patient consultations and interviewed the medical staff. In addition, I analysed consensus-development texts, clinic protocols and information material. In order to analyse women's reactions to biomedical discourse concerning the menopause and osteoporosis, I followed a year of women's e-mail communication on the Internet (Menopause Discussion List).

I intend to show that the bodies produced are not innocent productions. A certain conceptualization of the body becomes connected with ways of intervening in the bodily matter (Foucault 1979; Bordo 1989). To quote the latter: '[T]he scientific representations form a set of practical rules and regulations through which the body is trained, shaped, obeys and responds.' Women who talk to their doctor about brittle bones are given advice about nutrition and lifestyle and may be prescribed drugs (usually hormones). In addition, I will discuss the concept of apparatus of bodily production in relation to the constructivism versus objectivity dilemma. My special concern will be the articulation of matter and materiality. Finally, I will assess the implications of divergent fragments of knowledge and outline the issues relating to postmodern ways of coping with the menopausal body.

THE DEBATE ON OSTEOPOROSIS

Osteoporosis is the loss of bone mass or the phenomenon of bones becoming brittle. It is a much debated and controversial issue in biomedical literature and in medical and other practices. Osteoporosis has become known mainly as a female condition, affecting women more frequently and more severely than men. However, the way of representing the severity of the problem of osteoporosis depends on historical, material-technical conditions.

In my research project I am focusing on various practices concerning osteoporosis. I first made an analysis of research practices by studying biomedical texts and concentrating on how the condition of osteoporosis is defined, and on the material conditions involved in the definitions. The second part of my research is concerned with intervention practices and will be central to this chapter. By intervention I mean strategies of prevention and the variety of therapeutic regimes that are recommended to women in the course of counselling. The main issue here is how knowledge about osteoporosis and the female body is transformed into therapeutic solutions. The third practice under study concerns information and communication. What knowledge about osteoporosis is communicated to women, and how is this done? There is an enormous amount of information on osteoporosis, both in writing and on videotape. In the Netherlands, where I am doing my research, this material has been distributed by all kinds of channels. The brochures and fact-sheets can be found in waiting rooms of general practitioners and in pharmacies; leaflets and brochures are spread by women's health centres and health food stores. The result of this widespread distribution is that the issue of osteoporosis has become a pervasive one, forcing women to relate to it. It seems impossible to escape the issue of brittle bones.

THE BONE MASS BODY

Central to this section is the apparatus of bodily production in clinical settings. Before analysing the production of the female body in the clinic, I will briefly summarize the production of the female body in research practices. The biomedical literature on osteoporosis in women can be said to be dominated by two competing theories on the primary event in the process of osteoporosis, each theory invoking one specific event as the primary cause of osteoporosis. According to one theory, lack of oestrogen is responsible for the decrease in bone mass; according to the other, it is a lack of calcium which triggers the pathophysiological process. I have described how the availability of certain experimental compounds (like synthetic oestrogens), the use of particular measurements (of height or calcium balance) and the set-up of experiments have produced a so-called 'hormonal osteoporosis' and a 'mineral osteoporosis' (van Wingerden 1993). Two conceptualizations of the female body emerge simultaneously. The female body is conceptualized as a 'hormonal body', and the process of osteoporosis becomes strongly tied to the event of the menopause; or, in research focusing on the

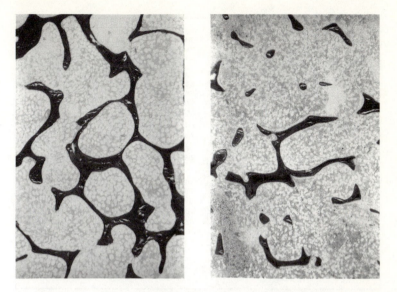

PLATE 11.1 (a and b) Representation of osteoporosis: microscopic preparation of a biopsy from the hip (iliac crest) bone. It visualizes the thinning and loss of internal tissue structure.

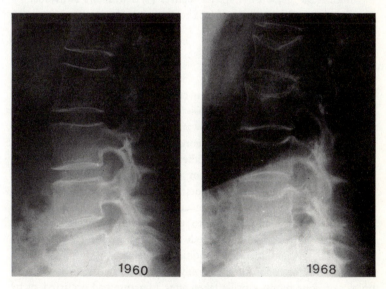

PLATE 11.2 (a and b) Representation of osteoporosis: X-ray photographs of a spine. The 1968 photograph makes a fracture visible.

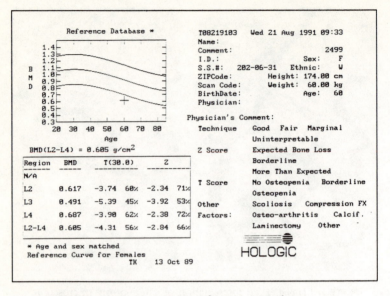

PLATE 11.3 Representation of osteoporosis: bone mass (BMD: 0.605 g/cm²) measured by densitometry of the spine (lumbar vertebrae L2–L4). It visualizes (+) a woman's individual risk compared to a reference database.

role of calcium, the female body is conceptualized as a 'mineral body' in which the process of osteoporosis is part of an ageing process, with perhaps some special features for women. Research practice on osteoporosis thus produces a pluriform conceptualization of the female body: not one body, but two different bodies are produced. As a consequence, different solutions to the problem of osteoporosis are suggested: a hormonal solution consisting of oestrogen supplement and a mineral solution consisting of calcium supplement.[5]

We now turn our attention to the clinic in order to study the conceptualization of the female body there. Again my focus will be on the technology and material conditions involved in this production. Until recently, osteoporosis could only be assessed by the invasive technology of bone biopsy, usually taken after a fracture had occurred, or by the non-invasive, but rather insensitive, X-ray technology. Recently, a new technology (densitometry or absorptiometry) has been developed which is based on the absorption of energy by particular bones of the body, usually the wrist, spinal vertebrae or hip (these are the places where most fractures occur). The absorbed energy is a measure of the amount of bone mass present. It should be stressed that the three technologies mentioned represent osteoporosis in very different ways. Bone biopsies visualize cells and the intercellular matrix. X-rays visualize bones as thicker or thinner shadows, and this technology can make a fracture visible. Densitometry visualizes the bone mass (and not the fractures) and expresses it in bone mineral density per square centimetre.

Today the special outpatient clinics for bone metabolism are all equipped with this densitometry technology. When a woman attends a clinic, a diagnosis has to be made. Is she osteoporotic? This question is answered by measuring her bone mass by densitometry. The diagnostic procedure of measuring bone mass produces a new conceptualization of the body. It visualizes a process of bones becoming brittle, a process which a woman may not be aware of. I have called the body produced by densitometry the 'bone mass body'. In the following section, I will assess the implications of the 'bone mass body' at the level of individual interventions (prevention and monitoring of therapies) and at a political level.

PREVENTION

Densitometry is propagated as a more sensitive method than X-ray photography. Densitometry means that smaller changes in the amount of bone mass are detectable. This has brought women into a new relationship with the condition of osteoporosis. With X-ray technology, osteoporosis enters a woman's life after a fracture. Now a woman no longer has to wait for a fracture to discover that she is osteoporotic: she can learn from her bone-mass measurement that she is *at risk* of osteoporosis. In the Netherlands, a debate has started on the subject of whether a bone-mass measurement should be offered to all perimenopausal women.[6] Being at risk, however, does not necessarily mean that you will develop the condition. The confrontation with a measurement (obtained on request or by participating in a screening programme) means that you will have to make a decision about osteoporosis. The first consequence of the densitometric conceptualization of the female body is, therefore, *the urge to consider the issue of prevention*.

On the basis of the measurement of bone mass, a decision has to be made about whether further action should be undertaken. Should a woman consider preventive strategies? To answer this question, one needs to have a point of reference. It is necessary to have a cut-off point for normal and abnormal bone mass. This point is constructed by pooling bone-mass values obtained by measurements in healthy women. An individual measurement will be compared either to measurements of peak bone mass (the bone mass reached around the age of 35) or to bone-mass measurements in the woman's own age group. 'Your' risk is based on these normal bone-mass measurements and could lead your physician to start counselling you on the prevention of osteoporosis. The statistical procedures of creating normal values produce concepts like 'danger area' and 'fracture threshold', constructions which are negotiated among medical specialists. In the clinic, however, the statistical risk produced by the densitometric measurement *may tempt you to intervene* in your risk story. By executing preventive strategies you may attain risk reduction. Consequently, the story of osteoporotic fractures has changed into a risk story of possible future fractures. A woman's body is now conceived of as a 'body at risk'. Talking about risks has already pervaded conversation among women. Analysis of the e-mail discussion illustrates that thinking in terms of risks and risk factors has become an ordinary topic.

> I think it makes sense to be on HRT [hormonal replacement therapy – IvW] if one has risk factors for osteoporosis.... Even though I do weightbearing exercises, don't smoke, eat a pretty ideal diet and ensure an adequate calcium intake with supplements, the thought of ending up in pain, shaped like a comma, breaking bones every year is enough for me to want the extra protection HRT affords.

> After reading all this stuff about mood swings, weight gain, headaches and assorted oddities, I decided I'd much rather take my risks on osteoporosis and heart disease, than risk messing up my very happy body and mind by taking HRT.

MONITORING

Another group of women attending the clinic are already receiving therapy for osteoporosis. I will not go into the details of the various therapies that are available, but will focus on the issue of how the 'bone-mass body' – the body produced by densitometry – is involved in the monitoring of therapies.[7] The conceptualization of the female body as a 'bone-mass body' leads to an intervention in a woman's bodily materiality. These interventions are meant to increase her bone mass; she is intervening in her risk story. But the therapies cannot guarantee her a fracture-free life. Will she comply with the therapies offered to her? The densitometric measurement is used in a variety of ways; I will consider three aspects:

1. It can be used to *motivate* a woman to continue her therapy. Some therapeutic regimes are hard to practise in daily life, and some drugs have severe side-effects. The doctor, therefore, often asks a woman to have confidence in the technology, expressing his own belief in the bone-mass measurement and telling her that the next measurement should make progress visible: 'we cannot make your back the same length as before, but we can prevent further crushed vertebrae; I can hardly believe that the next measurement will not show some progress.'

2. Densitometric technology asks a woman to *focus on her osseous system* and to make other organs or other conditions subordinate to the condition of her bones. When asked by their doctor to make a decision on the therapeutic possibilities, women often reply: 'What is best for my bones?' Other parts of the body, like the uterus and the breasts, and the cancer risks associated with certain types of treatment, seem to have become only marginal topics.

3. And finally the 'bone-mass' body has the potential to *signal the end* of a therapy if a measurement is above the fracture threshold: 'the results of your bone mass are beautiful, very steady ... you are above the risk limit. We will now stop the therapy, congratulations, no more pills; you will not have any more crushed vertebrae'.

The above examples illustrate the power effects of the 'bone-mass body'. This body is not an innocent production. Women are asked to go along with therapeutic regimes aimed at increasing their bone mass. Regimes may consist of a number of different drugs (up to five different ones) and are to be accompanied by physical exercise. The 'bone-mass body' thus entails a disciplining of the body, and sometimes lifelong management. Body management comes in many different forms: hormonal therapies stress 'femininity' and simultaneously offer a solution to the possible loss of sexual attractiveness, while other therapies focus on nutrition and conscientious physical exercise.[8]

A constructivist approach to biomedical knowledge and the availability of analytical tools like the apparatus of bodily production allow for a reconstruction of the way in which various bodies are produced. The apparatus of bodily production provides insight into the intertwined knot of discourse, technology, language and matter. In clinical settings, however, the bodies produced – for example, the 'bone-mass body' – seem to contradict the woman's experience of matter resulting in pain. This becomes paramount in the execution of body management, no matter in what form. In many conversations between doctors and women, the tension between the conceptualization of matter as 'bone mass' and the experience of matter in terms of pain has come to the fore. The two rarely correspond. For instance, there can be an important improvement in bone mass, but the pain does not go away. Or a woman who takes the prescribed drugs and manages her pain through compulsory exercise does not see her endeavors reflected in an increased bone mass.[9] The articulation of this tension between the densitometric 'bone-mass body' and the experience of pain brings us to the more theoretical question of what constitutes an adequate approach to the body, especially in medicine. How can we address the question of 'matter' and materiality of the body? The issue has been of concern to many theoreticians of the body. Turner proposes that one can approach the body in three ways: as a symbolic representation, as an organic basis and as lived experience. According to him, these approaches are not mutually exclusive but complementary, depending on the question under study (Turner 1992). The philosopher and feminist theoretician Braidotti acknowledges the materiality of the body in her notion of embodiment, but she does not go into questions of changing or painful matter (Braidotti 1994). An objection often made against poststructuralist analyses of the body is that the matter/flesh is denied. Butler (1993), however, argues that insight into the construction of bodily materiality does not imply a denial of this materiality.[10] My study of biomedical practice and especially of the practice of intervention has revealed tension between the representation of matter and the experience of pain. I would very much like to develop an approach to the body which incorporates its socially constructed character but, at the same time, develops the notion of materiality beyond the mere acknowledgement that it matters.[11]

LIFELONG BODY MANAGEMENT

In the earlier part of this chapter I identified some of the disciplining effects of the densitometric body for the individual woman in a therapeutic setting. I would now like to turn to the political implications of the 'bone-mass body'. The medical interview has been described by medical sociologist Armstrong as the place where doctor and patient are constituted (Armstrong 1982). Advocating various preventive and therapeutic measures can be regarded as offering a woman a variety of subject positions in which, I expect, conceptualizations of her changing body matter are involved. Subsequently a woman will have to relate to these subject positions which are descriptions/prescriptions of the 'woman-as'. For instance, the woman is defined as firm, active in pain management, well organized, calculating pros and cons, but, most importantly, as *responsible for* making choices concerning prevention and therapy and as *willing to engage in* lifelong body management.

The theme of responsibility is closely tied to present-day health-care policies. These policies have become strongly influenced by economic motives. I would argue that, in the case of osteoporosis, the prevention paradigm strongly exploits the fear of future fractures.[12] Another trend that I noticed was the readiness to take over and use themes and concerns of the women's health movement ('it's a woman's decision'). In much of the information material, the issue of guilt comes to the fore. We now know about brittle bones, and we do not have to undergo passively a 'brittle' future. The underlying theme of striving for savings in health care is incorporated in a story about the quality of life. A normative quality is striking in advertisements for hormonal therapies. These adverts address today's baby-boom generation in the following way: 'The creative hotshots of the sixties do not want to slow down. They do not want to become that irritated, depressive, and a-sexual woman plagued by hot flushes and brittle bones due to her hormone deficiency.' They promote their hormonal products with a picture of the Mona Lisa 'captured by the spell of life', or with a picture of 'the woman who never ages'. They are also preparing the next generation for hormone use in an advertisement featuring young women under 30. The advertisement reads: 'Already used to taking hormones, they will continue to do so after the menopause.'

BONES AND WOMEN

We now need to address the question of how women relate to the subject positions offered to them. How do they relate to the themes of a brittle future and of responsibility and guilt? Do they go along with the 'brittle body', and will they behave as 'responsible women'? Analysis of the Internet e-mail discussion on the menopause and osteoporosis revealed many different attitudes and reactions. Some of the participants displayed feminist assertiveness. Some claimed that extensive medical interference with the third phase of life is justified:

> Now that women are living longer and assuming their rightful place in public life, most of us do not want to be laid low by menopausal symptoms if this can be avoided.

> It is hard for me to see how this [being on hormonal replacement treatment – IvW] is a feminist issue even though I have read most of the literature. It's a health issue.

On the other hand, some participants strongly resisted or rejected biomedical conceptualizations of the female body and the focus on bones. I also noted a substantial resistance to the terminology used. The women who joined in the discussion coined creative new expressions; for instance, they disliked the term 'symptoms' and suggested instead 'signs', 'markers' or 'growing pains'. They also felt free to accept medical advice or to modify it and attune it to their personal priorities. Women seem to make their own evaluation of risks. They resist the biomedical construction of risk and replace it with an individual construction of risk.

> Maybe I'll regret it some day when my bones shatter as I fall onto the concrete with a heart attack, but I decided...

From this material, I conclude that the simple notion of disciplining by biomedical discourse does not apply here. The cited quotations demonstrate that there is no passive production of docile bodies or subjects in clinical practice. On the contrary, women actively negotiate the subject positions offered to them, draw up their own risk assessment, and coin other expressions for the postmenopausal phenomena. According to Sawicki (1991), it is in the negotiation about the offered subject positions that resistance and agency become visible. The e-mail discussion also included numerous references to poetry and fiction by elderly crones and stories about strong mothers and grandmothers.

THE APPARATUS OF BODILY PRODUCTION

In this chapter I have tried to highlight the epistemological, individual and political implications of the apparatus of bodily production. Haraway is convincing when she argues that there is no unmediated knowledge of the body. Bodies are not objects in nature that can be discovered. On the contrary, bodies are produced. Her concept forces us to focus attention on the production conditions for bodies in different settings, on the role of technology, and on the consequences of the bodies produced. The 'apparatus of bodily production' produces bodies that are multiple and local but never innocent. It has been useful for me to analyse the production of various bodies in biomedical discourse on osteoporosis. Different practices produce different bodies. The 'hormonal body' and 'mineral body' produced in research practices bear the marks of this practice concerned with causal relationships. The 'bone-mass body', on the other hand, bears the marks of a practice concerned with finding a solution to osteoporosis and a therapeutic regimen that 'works'. The focus on technology has stressed the power effects of these bodies. Densitometry has made the internal structure of bones visible and accessible to intervention and has led to extensive body management.

One could argue that my analysis describing the existence of pluriform knowledge practices and multiple bodies implies a relativistic point of view. How will women ever be able to deal with this pluriformity of bodies? I do agree that it requires a certain skill to make one's own assessment on these conditions. On the other hand, I think it is misleading to expect everything from 'better' studies or 'better' information and communication. A recent report by the Office of Technology Assessment of the American Congress (US Congress 1994) states that it is a good thing to expose and express the biomedical uncertainties in information materials because 'most simple messages about the prevention and treatment of osteoporosis are likely to be incorrect and conversely, the correct message is likely to be complex.'

Finally, Haraway has drawn our attention to another aspect of 'the apparatus of bodily production'. Once we have analysed the networks of power operating in the construction of bodies, it becomes possible to intervene in the process. She stresses the need for women to enter the field of knowledge production and is optimistic about the possibility of creating new coalitions and about the production of other knowledges.[13] I would very much welcome this kind of intervention in the biopolitics of the postmenopausal body, in the production of knowledge, representation and practices of the body.

NOTES

1. For a critique on the various 'menopausal bodies', see P. Kaufert, 'Menopause as Process or Event: The Creation of Definitions in Biomedicine', in M. Lock and D. Gordon, eds, *Biomedicine Examined*, Kluwer Academic Publishers, Dordrecht, 1988, pp. 331–49.

2. Immunological discourse has frequently drawn on war metaphors in explanations of immunological processes. See also E. Martin, 'Histories of Immune Systems', *Culture, Medicine and Psychiatry* 17, 1993, pp. 67–76. She states that characteristics of our society pervade immunological theories. In our present-day information society where things become obsolete and are replaced at high speed, immunological theory reflects these characteristics and describes the immunological response in terms of agility and flexibility.

3. See T. Laqueur, *Making Sex: Body and Gender from the Greeks to Freud*, Harvard University Press, Cambridge, Mass. and London, 1990; A. Mol, '"Sekse" en "Wetenschap": een vergelijking met twee onbekenden', in L. Boon and E. de Vries, eds, *Wetenschapstheorie, de empirische wending,* Wolters Noordhof, Groningen, 1989, pp. 97–107; N. Oudshoorn, *Beyond the Natural Body: An Archeology of Sex Hormones,* Routledge, London, 1994; M. van den Wijngaard, *Reinventing the Sexes: Feminism and the Biomedical Construction of Femininity and Masculinity, 1959–1985,* Amsterdam, 1991.

4. In medicine, a process of consensus development usually starts when there is a need. This need becomes articulated in times of controversy. Controversial issues in biomedical practice are characterized by the existence of a debate on the scientific value of research data or when actual practices do not correspond to a scientific standard and large differences between local practices emerge. The collective process of consensus development is aimed at the drawing up of guidelines for medical practice.

5. In Chapter 10 of this volume, Bettina Leysen also refers to calcium and hormones as compounds, which are *both* necessary for bone remodelling. My constructivist approach, however, is above all aimed at analysing the production conditions and effects of different conceptualizations of osteoporosis and the body. In intervention practices the pivotal question is 'What can we do about osteoporosis?' As a result, pacifications between different conceptualizations emerge. See I. van Wingerden, 'Female Bodies and Brittle Bones: An Analysis of the Intervention Practice for Osteoporosis', in T. Eberhart and C. Wächter, eds, *Feminist Perspectives on Technology, Work and Ecology. 2nd European Feminist Research Conference,* IFZ, Graz, 1994, pp. 68–74, for an analysis of the relationship between different conceptualizations, especially in processes of consensus development.

6. This is one of the recommendations put forward in the report *Preventie van osteoporose* (Prevention of Osteoporosis) of the Gezondheidsraad (Dutch Health Council, an advisory body of the government), which appeared in 1991. However, the state secretary of the Ministry of Welfare, Health and Cultural Affairs disregarded this advice.

7. In the clinic we encounter a hormonal and a mineral solution to the problem of osteoporosis, in which we can see a continuity with the conceptualizations of the female body in research practices. But other treatment modalities, not connected to a specific pathophysiological factor, have become important in the treatment of osteoporosis; for example, sodium fluoride, bisphosphonates and calcitonin.

8. Of late the emphasis in hormone therapies on femininity, as in 'Feminine Forever', seems to have shifted towards the emphasis on 'healthy forever' (see Chapter 10 of this volume). I think the issue of femininity has never disappeared because in advertisements the 'healthy woman' is also portrayed as a very attractive woman. Furthermore, in addition to 'health' the theme of 'emancipation' is used extensively in co-optation strategies of pharmaceutical entrepreneurs which are targeted at the baby-boom generation.

9. One could argue that the scientific representation of the body in terms of bone mass and experience of (skeletal) pain are completely different things, and

hence the tension between the two is not unexpected. I am aware that the 'bone mass body' does not coincide with the entity 'osteoporosis'. However, it is the pivotal aspect in clinical settings. For the patients, the experience of pain in this changing body mass also belongs to the entity 'osteoporosis'.

10. The body historian Barbara Duden has attacked the dismissal of the senses, especially touch, in poststructuralist analyses of the body. See B. Duden, 'Die Frau ohne Unterleib: Zu Judith Butlers Entkörperung. Ein Zeitdokument', *Feministische Studien*, vol. 11, no. 2, 1993, pp. 24–34; for a reply, see J. Butler 1993.

11. See also N.J. Fox, *Postmodernism, Sociology and Health*, Open University Press, Milton Keynes and Philadelphia, 1993, for what I think is an unsatisfactory articulation of materiality. Fox states that in his book he focuses not on the medical, anatomical body, but on the body as a non-organic, political surface. Yet he stresses that the inscription of this surface (with power) is 'material' because the inscription can be 'read'. However, it is not the 'materiality' of the body that is addressed in this activity. What I would like to see concerns the notion of embodiment. According to Braidotti, embodiment – for example, having a female body – is crucial to a feminist redefinition of subjectivity. I would like to explore how in my case study, a changing materiality can be incorporated in the construction of subjectivity.

12. See also N. Worcester and M.H. Whatley, 'The Selling of HRT: Playing on the Fear Factor', *Feminist Review* 41, 1992, pp. 1–26.

13. To quote Susan Leigh Star ('Power, Technology and the Phenomenology of Conventions: On Being Allergic to Onions', in J. Law, ed., *A Sociology of Monsters: Essays on Power, Technology and Domination*, Routledge, London and New York, 1991, pp. 26–56): 'the power of feminist analysis is to move from the experience of being a non-user, an outcast or a castaway, to the analysis of ... many ... technologies and implicitly to the fact that "it might have been otherwise"'.

REFERENCES

Armstrong, D. (1982) 'The Doctor–Patient Relationship 1930–1980', in P. Wright and A. Treacher, eds, *The Problem of Medical Knowledge*, Edinburgh University Press, Edinburgh, pp. 109–22.

Bordo, S.R. (1989) 'The Body and the Reproduction of Femininity: A Feminist Appropriation of Foucault', in A.M. Jagger and S.R. Bordo, eds, *Gender/Body/Knowledge: Feminist Reconstructions of Being and Knowing*, Rutgers University Press, London and New Brunswick, N.J., pp. 13–33.

Braidotti, R. (1994) *Nomadic Subjects: Embodiment and Sexual Difference in Contemporary Feminist Theory*, Columbia University Press, New York.

Butler, J. (1993) *Bodies that Matter: On the Discursive Limits of 'Sex'*, Routledge, New York and London.

Foucault, M. (1979) *Discipline and Punish: Birth of the Prison*, trans. A. Sheridan, Vintage/Random House, New York.

Haraway, D. (1988) 'Situated Knowledges: The Science Question in Feminism and the Privilege of Partial Perspective', *Feminist Studies*, vol. 14, no. 3, pp. 575–99.

————— (1989) 'The Biopolitics of Postmodern Bodies: Determinations of Self in Immune System Discourse', *Differences*, vol. 1, no. 1, pp. 3–43.

Latour, B. (1987) *Science in Action: How to Follow Scientists and Engineers through Society*, Harvard University Press, Cambridge, Mass.

Sawicki, J. (1991) 'Disciplining Mothers', in J. Sawicki, ed., *Disciplining Foucault: Feminism, Power and the Body*, Routledge, New York, pp. 67–94.

Turner, B.S. (1992) *Regulating Bodies: Essays in Medical Sociology*, Routledge, London and New York.

US Congress, Office of Technology Assessment (1994) *Public Information about Osteoporosis: What's Available, What's Needed?* Background paper, OTA-BP-H-131, Government Printing Office, Washington DC, July.

van Wingerden, I. (1993) 'Hormonaal of mineraal? Osteoporose en het vrouwen-lichaam', *Tijdschrift voor Vrouwenstudies*, vol. 14, no. 2, pp. 149–71.

THE SALUTARY TALE OF

THE PRE-EMBRYO

Pat Spallone

A new word appeared in Britain in 1985 to describe the human embryo from the point of fertilization to fourteen days after. The word was 'pre-embryo', and it was coined at the height of public unease over test-tube babies and human embryo research. The new word and its scientific rationale were promoted vigorously, first by scientists and later by others campaigning for the cause of human embryo research against the claims of politicians who wished to ban the research altogether. It was taken up in other countries, too, including Australia, Denmark and the USA.

The term 'pre-embryo' was used by an important subset of speakers and writers in Britain when the threat of legal sanctions against human embryo research was greatest. It was used strategically between 1985 and 1990, until the enactment of legislation which allowed regulated human embryo research, thus bringing the threat of an absolute ban to an end.

How and why the 'pre-embryo' arose is a complicated matter. This chapter is a sociological historical analysis of the radical redefinition of the embryo in Britain. It describes and documents the evolution of the term and analyses its promotion and its power.

As the term 'pre-embryo' was coined in the context of moral debates on human embryo research, let me explain briefly that human embryo research is experimentation on, or research utilizing, human embryos created by *in vitro* fertilization (the test-tube baby technique), the joining of egg and sperm outside a woman's body and in a laboratory dish. *In vitro* fertilization defined the newness of new reproductive technologies, a phrase which includes a range of techniques of fertility and infertility control, as well as those used in biological and medical research into mammalian development.

My two main theoretical bearings are as follows. First, the evolution of the term 'pre-embryo' expresses the socio-technical or heterogeneous nature of scientific knowledge. Bijker and Law (1992), among others, argue that technology is never purely technological, it is also social; while the social is never purely social, it is also technological. A major theme of this chapter is that the pre-embryo is a case of a socio-technical process in that it is the outcome of interactions in a network of actors involved with human embryo research in particular and reproductive technologies generally.

My second theoretical bearing comes from Donna Haraway's work in *Primate Visions*, in which she encapsulates,

> Biology as a way of knowing the world is kin to Romantic literature, with its discourse about organic form and function. Biology is the fiction appropriate to objects called organisms; biology fashions the facts 'discovered' from organic beings. Organisms perform for the biologist, who transforms that performance into a truth attested by disciplined experience; i.e., into a fact, the jointly accomplished deed or feat of the scientist and the organism. Romanticism passes into realism, and realism into naturalism, genius into progress, insight into fact. *Both* the scientist and the organism are actors in a story-telling practice. (Haraway 1989: 4–5)

The pre-embryo is an origins story, the origin of the embryo, in the discipline of embryology: a discipline which, as primatology, is structured as one of the great Western myths of paternity, sex and the origins of man. The dichotomized organism embryo/pre-embryo may be seen as an actor in a story-telling practice, although its role here is not the same as that of the human actors in the social network described. This consideration opened my mind to the possibility of seeing the power of the pre-embryo as an idea, but I am mindful of a complicating factor. The pre-embryo has a material reality and material conditions of living. As an organism-construct, it may be a work of fiction, but as a material reality with material conditions of living (however socially and environmentally shaped they may be), it is also a work of science.

The two theoretical bearings inform one another. Both reflect in their different ways an interest in relationships among technological innovations, people and nature (however defined). Together they helped inform a central consideration of this chapter: namely, the processes by

which embryos are objectified and subjectified as well as the implications for knowledge, human identities and relationships. I began this
project particularly interested in how the dichotomy embryo/pre-
embryo sustains an ancient dichotomy embryo/woman. The latter is
perhaps most familiar from anti-abortion rhetorics, but also apparent in
biomedical discourse. Historian Barbara Duden (1993), for instance,
argues that the foetus has become an emblem, an image of life itself
and the true person, thus leaving out the life, body, and person of the
pregnant woman.

'BACKGROUND' TO THE PRE-EMBRYO

The Public Debate: Embryos and Progress

With the birth of the first test-tube baby in Britain in 1978, there was
a heightened public unease over the work of *in vitro* fertilization and
human embryo research. The ensuing public debate became highly
polarized between two central terms. Ethical attention focused on the
embryo, the recognized subject of embryo research. The counterpoise
to the embryo was the need for scientific progress (Spallone 1989, 1994).

The debate followed an age-old concern in Western thought with
the question, 'When does life begin?' Focusing as it did on the human
subjectivity of human embryos, the rhetoric largely fell into line with
abortion debate rhetorics, but also diverged from it. The questions of
import concerned the status of the human embryo, and how far society
should allow scientists to go in using human embryos for research.
Coincidentally, other questions remained marginal, such as the matter
of infertility services as a whole (Pfeffer and Quick 1988).

In the course of the debate, a practical problem facing authorities
was whether to place a time limit on human embryo research, and
how to set such a limit. There was an often-made argument that current
scientific understanding of life makes the question 'When does life
begin?' an irrelevance. There is no moment when life begins; rather,
life is a continuum and a process. Sperm and egg are alive, and the life
of the embryo is continuous from them. The message was that the
original question 'When does life begin?' is based on a faulty understanding of embryology.

The Royal College of Obstetricians and Gynaecologists, the major
organization representing these specialists, offered a related but somewhat contradictory argument. They stated that 'When does life begin?'
is a physical question, not a moral one. The proper moral question is,

'At what point in the development of the embryo do we attribute it the protection due to a human being?' Science can inform the physical question 'When does human life begin?' by identifying demarcation lines in the process of embryo development (Royal College of Obstetricians and Gynaecologists 1983: 13).

A similar approach was taken by the government's Committee of Inquiry into Human Fertilization and Embryology, appointed in 1982 to investigate these matters and make recommendations to the Department of Health and Social Security. Composed of fifteen members from various professions, the committee published a report, famously known as the Warnock Report after the chairperson, philosopher Mary Warnock. It recommended legislation to regulate assisted reproduction practices of *in vitro* fertilization, donor insemination, surrogacy and human embryo research. As the first national report of its kind, it became influential worldwide.

Thus, despite attempts by many spokespersons to undermine the question 'When does life begin?' with the scientific understanding that life is a continuum, the old question remained in a new guise: When do embryos begin?

A Fourteen-Day Limit Is Set

A fourteen-day time limit on human embryo research was eventually recommended, not by the medical scientific establishment, but by the Warnock Report, published in July 1984. Why fourteen days? Mary Warnock explained in an interview,

> I persuaded my colleagues not to use the criterion of the fetus feeling pain used by the British Medical Association because I was afraid some smart surgeon would come along and say, 'My embryo doesn't feel pain because I've anaesthetised it'. The genetic composition of the resulting child isn't determined for 14 days. Therefore you might say that continuity with your past begins at 14 days. This seems to me to be the important point, rather than when the embryo is alive. (Dunn 1985)

Thus the setting of a fourteen-day limit was in line with technical facts about embryos, but also indicates how knowledge is mediated by social and cultural ideas such as 'continuity with your past'. The Warnock Report itself explained that the time limit was based on the knowledge that at around the fifteenth day after fertilization, an entity called the primitive streak, the emergent spinal column, forms; this event signals the change in identity to which Warnock referred in the interview.

Mary Warnock was following a line of reasoning being pursued elsewhere and by others. It was argued that developmental individuality is not established at fertilization because at these early stages an embryo can split into twins, or two or more *in vitro* embryos can be fused together to form a single embryo. Thus unique individuality is said to be established when the embryo can no longer become more or less than one, at around two weeks. A second argument stressed another way of looking at the same thing. At about two weeks, differentiation begins; differentiation refers to the changes in cells directed by the genes, which specialize cells into specific kinds of tissue and organs. These explanations allowed a distinction to be made between fertilization and individual embryonic formation.

However, the chosen fourteen-day limit was not the only scientifically sound option. Indeed it was only one of several options being offered. The Council for Science and Society (1984) recommended a six-week limit, arguing that it is slightly before the stage at which the embryo reacts to stimuli and therefore feels pain. The Royal Society (1983), comparable to the national academies of science in other countries, argued for an open-ended time limit, maintaining that the setting of a definite end-point is unduly restrictive. The Royal College of Obstetricians and Gynaecologists, which maintained a powerful voice in the debate, stated that *in vitro* human embryos 'should not be allowed to develop beyond the stage of early neural development (Day 17 after conception: Carnegie Stage 8)' (Royal College of Obstetricians and Gynaecologists 1983: 17). After the fourteen-day limit was set, some embryologists emphasized that they did not want it to be an immovable obstacle 'for research on older embryos' (Connor 1985: 21).

There is another interesting tension in the setting of a fourteen-day limit. Many commentators pointed out that the primitive streak might or might not form at exactly the fifteenth day, after all. The Medical Research Council, the major public funding body for biological research, voiced support for the setting of a developmental stage limit on embryo research, but they argued that it should be worded differently than as a number of days because of variations in the rate of development of individual embryos (Medical Research Council 1985: 5). Nevertheless, the fourteen-day limit, which reflected a clear and definite boundary which could be enforced in law, remained.

In summary, scientific knowledge about embryos informed the ethics debate on embryo research from the beginning; but that knowledge was, as ever, plastic and adapted to circumstances, and imbued with legal, social and cultural values. While the setting of a fourteen-day limit was not arbitrary, neither was it inevitable.

At this point, there was no indication that the scientific establishment wished to redefine the embryo. On the contrary, the scientific body which was eventually to initiate a redefinition, the Medical Research Council, seemed content with an 'old-fashioned' definition. In their official response to the Warnock Report, they simply asked that the 'old' definition be confirmed: '"Embryo" is not defined in the [Warnock] Report; the Council would welcome confirmation of their understanding that this refers to a viable conceptus developed from a fertilised egg...' (Medical Research Council 1985: 5).

Thus, although the Medical Research Council was conscious of the need to define precisely the embryo of embryo research, it did not suggest that a redefinition of it was necessary. Nor did any other scientific spokesperson. This was soon to change.

The Unborn Children (Protection) Bill Wins a Majority

At the first available opportunity, in November 1984, arch-conservative Member of Parliament Enoch Powell, avowedly anti-abortion and anti-divorce, announced his intention to introduce a Private Member's Bill banning all human embryo research on the grounds that the embryo is a fully fledged human being. Powell's Unborn Children (Protection) Bill won a large majority after its second reading in February 1985. It was supported by the same strange mixture of political alliances that occurs during proceedings on abortion laws. The possibility that it could actually win in a final vote was real.

The explicit threat that the Powell bill posed to scientific research, and the implicit threat it posed to women's abortion rights, prompted the organization of a vigorous pro-embryo-research lobby which endorsed the recommendations of the Warnock Report. Whether or not scientific sensibilities found some of the Warnock recommendations problematic, and whether or not women's health and reproductive rights groups perceived a tension with the traditionally paternalistic medical establishment, political lines were clearly drawn. The fight was to be between a pro-research lobby with its generally pro-science sentiment, and an anti-research lobby, with its generally anti-abortionist sentiment. Each side could argue that its case was supported by embryological facts of life. The anti-research lobby argued that the genetic identity of an embryo was present at fertilization; the pro-research lobby would soon be arguing, as Mary Warnock had, that individual identity was not set until fourteen days after fertilization. At this juncture, the redefinition of the embryo appears.

THE EMBRYO REDEFINED

Enter the Definitive Embryo

A radical redefinition of the embryo first appeared in the popular weekly *New Scientist*, in April 1985, in a short article by the then president of the Royal Society, Nobel Prize winning physiologist Sir Andrew Huxley. Sir Andrew began by warning that Enoch Powell's Bill, if passed, was 'likely to prevent any research being undertaken on human embryos' (Huxley 1985: 2). He proceeded to list medical benefits which have arisen from research and then redefined the embryo. He did not speak of pre-embryos (the word had not yet been coined), but of 'definitive embryos' and an 'embryo proper':

> Unfortunately, the public debate ... is taking place against a background of widespread ignorance about the earliest stages of development of the fertilised egg.... This ignorance causes much confusion, which is made worse by an unfortunate ambiguity in the word 'embryo'.... The ambiguity arises because the word 'embryo' is also used to denote the whole of the collection of cells formed by repeated division of the fertilised egg during the first weeks or so, although only a few per cent of these cells are destined to become the embryo proper; by far the greater number of them will turn into extra-embryonic tissue and ultimately into the structures that are discarded as the afterbirth.... The embryo proper is first recognisable at about the 15th day after fertilisation, when a specialised region of cells called the 'primitive streak' first appears. Before that stage, it cannot be said that a definitive embryo exists. (Huxley 1985: 2)

The distinctions 'embryo' (with inverted commas), embryo proper and definitive embryo had not been made before in such discussions. Huxley redefined the embryo by singling out an event (the formation of the primitive streak) and by relying on percentages (the destiny of the majority of cells defined the organism).

Huxley, as others (*Nature* 1982; Ironside 1985), noted that people were confused or ignorant about the scientific facts of embryology; there was a deficit of knowledge among the uninitiated. One assumption was that some people still thought of the embryo as a homunculus, a tiny fully formed human being, and that this was why these people found embryo research repugnant. Hence people needed technical information on which to base their moral judgements.

The message was that scientific facts help dispel cultural myths. But this position hardly does justice to another fact: that the new definition of the embryo coincided exactly and conveniently with the fourteen-day time limit placed on human embryo research. If the Warnock

Committee had decided on a different time limit – say, six weeks – then it is likely that the redefinition of the embryo either would not have occurred, or it would have looked very different.

I am not arguing that a redefinition of the embryo was wholly manufactured or a cynical response of the scientific establishment. The redefinition was perfectly in line with scientific knowledge, and moreover it could be argued that there were already existing ideas in science about embryonic structures which precede true embryos. Furthermore, if people misunderstand facts, information was in order. However, my point is that the idea of a 'definitive embryo' at the fifteenth day after fertilization acquired force, not on the basis of the natural facts, but because it was empowered (finally) by the Warnock Committee. The idea of a definitive embryo at the fifteenth day would have had little or no force if a different time limit had been set. The new origins story of the embryo accommodated an entwinement of developments which, had they been different, so too would the definition of the embryo. The public debate on embryo research, the recommendations of the Warnock Report, the threat of the Powell Bill, and the need to enrol support to the cause of research were all factors in the evolution of a redefined embryo. Huxley's radical redefinition of the embryo appeared shortly after the Medical Research Council announced the intention to redefine the embryo. Two months later, the word 'pre-embryo' made its debut.

The Pre-Embryo Appears

The word 'pre-embryo' was presented to the general public in the first week of June 1985, in 'Guidelines for Both Clinical and Research Application of Human In Vitro Fertilisation', from a newly formed body called The Voluntary Licensing Authority for Human In Vitro Fertilisation and Embryology. The Voluntary Licensing Authority was set up by the Medical Research Council and the Royal College of Obstetricians and Gynaecologists, who jointly appointed its members; these included medical doctors, research scientists and lay (non-medical, non-science) members. Its aim was to oversee *in vitro* fertilization and human embryo research until the government acted to create a statutory authority.

When the formation of the Voluntary Licensing Authority was announced at the end of March 1985, the Medical Research Council articulated its wish to redefine the embryo (Clarke 1985: 397). More than at any other time, a deficit of knowledge among 'the uninitiated' was perceived to be causing much misunderstanding about embryo research. The Powell Bill had won a majority of supporters in parliament the month before; and although the Bill would eventually fail (on June 7, when it was 'talked out' in a procedural manoeuvre backed by the Conservative government), other anti-research parliamentarians were waiting in the wings to act similarly. In any event, the government would at some stage introduce its own legislation on new reproductive technologies. It was imperative to attract greater support for embryo research.

The Medical Research Council immediately handed over the task of redefining the embryo to the Voluntary Licensing Authority. The term 'pre-embryo' was coined at one of its early meetings by one of the lay members. A majority of the Voluntary Licensing Authority favoured it over other possibilities.[1]

Enter the Pre-Embryo

The paragraph in which the term 'pre-embryo' was first defined reads:

> During their discussion the Voluntary Licensing Authority considered it was important to define the term 'pre-embryo' used in these Guidelines. The term 'embryo' has traditionally been used to describe the stage reached in development where organogenesis has started, as shown by the appearance of the primitive streak and the certainty that thereafter a single individual is developing rather than twins or a hydatidiform mole [an abnormal growth which ends the embryo as such], for example. To the collection of dividing cells up to the determination of the primitive streak we propose to give the name 'pre-embryo'. (Voluntary Licensing Authority 1985, unpaged)

Note how a traditional meaning of the embryo was posited (which was to be repeated in later promotions of the pre-embryo). It is particularly interesting because the opposite might reasonably have been stated. The professional usages of the terms 'embryo' and 'foetus' have never been fixed, not in dictionaries and not even among contemporary embryologists. Authors are usually careful to define their usage clearly from the outset. There has never been any one traditional definition of embryo.

The identification of a scientific tradition regarding the embryo is not emphatically wrong. Embryology may well suggest both a general term 'embryo', from the time of fertilization onward, and an embryo proper which appears a bit later. But why posit or construct a tradition at this moment in history? What is clear is that the positing of a tradition supports the (new) origins story of the embryo. I am interested here in a double process of unconscious and conscious shaping of language, meaning and natural reality, which is illustrated in the following example of the promotion of the pre-embryo.

THE PROMOTION OF THE PRE-EMBRYO

Aiming to Clarify

The most vigorous, influential, and adept promoter of the term 'pre-embryo' was Anne McLaren, an embryologist renowned for her pioneering work in mammalian embryo development; a fellow of the Royal Society; a director of the Medical Research Council Mammalian Development Unit; a member of the Warnock Committee; and a member of the Voluntary Licensing Authority. In an article in *New Scientist* in 1986, Anne McLaren explained the fourteen-day limit on human embryo research in similar terms as Sir Andrew Huxley's article the year before. This time, the term 'pre-embryo' appears:

> If this entity forming around the primitive streak is the embryo (as is generally agreed), what are we to call the entire collection of cells derived from the fertilised egg, of which the embryo is a tiny subset? In recent years, we researchers have developed the bad habit of calling the whole set of cells, at each prior stage, the embryo as well. To the non-specialist this is confusing.... Other words for the totality of cells derived from the fertilised egg, prior to the appearance of the embryo, are conceptus, zygote, pre-embryo, and pro-embryo (see *Henderson's Dictionary of Biological Terms*, 9th edition, 1985). I shall use the term pre-embryo to refer to the first three major stages of development. (McLaren 1986a: 49)

The term 'pre-embryo' was new at this point in time, although this is not very clear from the passage. Notice how the word is integrated with the other terms, as if all are equivalent, and as if pre-embryo might well appear in *Henderson's Dictionary* along with pro-embryo. But the term 'pre-embryo' did not appear in any dictionaries of biology and technical terms at that time, nor in dictionaries of English.[2] By contrast, the other words mentioned in the passage – 'conceptus', 'zygote' and 'pro-embryo' – are established terms which could be found in various dictionaries of science or the English language, but none means precisely the fertilized egg up to fourteen days. 'Pro-embryo' is indeed found in *Henderson's Dictionary*, but refers to plant life, not mammals. 'Zygote' refers to a fertilized female gamete in plants or animals. The word 'conceptus' is not a technical term of the same order as 'zygote' or 'pro-embryo'; it means the early embryo but does not refer to a specific stage in its development. To the non-specialist, the new explanation might well be as confusing as the old.

I am not suggesting that promoters of the pre-embryo cynically attempted to mystify the truth. However, 'pre-embryo' is not an innocent word either. The coining of the term 'pre-embryo' was both an astute (conscious) political move and a reflection of the more subtle (unconscious?) processes of naturalization; that is, a reflection of how scientific knowledge becomes natural fact. Rather than clarifying matters, the term 'pre-embryo' obscured them. It obscured the history of the decision about the fourteen-day limit. It made it appear to those unfamiliar with the history or the science that the decision was inevitable, as if embryos have never really existed until fourteen days after fertilization. Part of the process of mystification rests in the belief that scientific facts help dispel cultural myths about embryos. But the pre-embryo is itself a myth, not because it is a lie or false, but because it is devoid of its history. The pre-embryo takes on mythic proportions and becomes a natural fact. Obscured are the processes by which natural knowledge is mediated by culture, politics and psychological predispositions.

McLaren, as others, stressed that the motive behind the term 'pre-embryo' was to end the ambiguity which accompanied the word 'embryo'. In response to a colleague who dissented over the use of 'pre-embryo' as the 'introduction of cosmetic words' into the public debate (Davies 1986), McLaren raised an example of ambiguity in a scientific paper on marsupial embryology. The researcher referred to stages of the early embryo as '2-cell embryos' and so on, but then called these 'The cells that will later give rise to the embryo...' (McLaren 1986b).

One can see the confusion in the implication that embryos give rise to embryos. However, the word 'pre-embryo' does not end an existing ambiguity, but reproduces it. I shall offer my own example from a *Nature* news item reporting on 'a test to identify accurately healthy pre-embryos. The identification of gross embryo abnormalities in the laboratory will lead to a better chance of live births from replaced embryos...' (Clarke 1986: 349). Are they embryos or pre-embryos? Or are they both at the same time, perhaps? Such linguistic ambiguity and confusion in the discourse on new reproductive technologies is not the provenance of embryos alone. Consider the following definition of 'couple' in a report from the American Fertility Society (USA). The report adopted the term 'preembryo' (*sic*) in order to avoid confusion, as the authors emphasized. Then they proceeded to define 'couple': 'The Committee uses the word couple to mean a heterosexual couple living together in a stable relationship. In some instances in this report, the context of a recommendation will make clear that the word couple also refers to single persons' (American Fertility Society 1986: vii).

No words in the debate – not 'embryos', 'pre-embryos', 'couples', nor even 'mother' (who is the mother – the woman from whom the egg came, or the woman who gives birth?) – are clear of ambiguity. The confusion is not the result of a deficit of scientific knowledge about embryo development, but of far more complicated matters.

To promoters of pre-embryo, my analysis may sound absurd because the pre-embryo has a material reality. It is true that the embryo was redefined on the basis of data about its material conditions of living. And we do need ways to talk about these things. In addition, one might reasonably argue that the act of naming was egalitarian; it was a non-scientist who coined the term, which is arguably more accessible and user-friendly than, say, 'zygote'. But the rub here is not that my critical arguments do not refer to the pre-embryo's material conditions of living at all, but that they do not constantly revolve around them as *the* central reference point.

I am interested in how both understandings of the pre-embryo, as a work of fiction (an organism-construct) and as a work of science (an organism with material conditions of living), work together. The crux of my argument is this. The coining of the term 'pre-embryo' allowed the ideology of the embryo to stay the same; the embryo remained *the* central human subject of human procreation, an image to which woman's ethical being and human subjectivity is implicitly deferred. Society could have its 'embryo', an unchanging ideological apparition, while science could experiment on embryos (pre-embryos) by shifting the origin point of the embryo to a later date. This is the new origins story. The embryo has a double identity here. The embryo created in a laboratory dish by scientists is the reification of the embryo: the making real of an ideological apparition. Yet it is also an organism with material conditions of living. The new origins story embodies both these identities. The embryo remains an unchanging ideological apparition in the face of human embryo research by shifting the origin point to a later stage.

Redefining Pregnancy, Redefining Kinship?

Let me explain what I mean by the ideology of the embryo which was allowed to stay the same; I will then reflect on some of the implications of the double identity of the embryo in relation to maternity and kinship.

The preoccupation with the status of the embryo in the debate on human embryo research harks back to the Ancient Greek concern with the value of embryonic life expressed in theories of generation, specifi-

cally Aristotelian ideas. In these theories, which focused so conspicuously on an isolated embryo, the female as progenitor contributes matter
and is the passive principle, while the male possesses intellect and is the
active principle of generation.

Aristotle's embryology is rejected today, but the principle motion of
its account of life has not disappeared. It remains part of the narrative
of embryology. You can see evidence of it in many places. For example,
in her study of the British parliamentary debates on embryo research,
Sarah Franklin found that statements which placed the embryo in a
social context or in relation to the mother were exceptional; the mother
was 'more commonly referred to as the embryo's "source of nutrition"
or its "environment"' (Franklin 1993: 108). Furthermore, when women's
experiences and needs were admitted to the discussion, they were
selectively represented. Some women's experiences of fertility, infertility
or motherhood were recognized, but not others.

Fall-out from Aristotelian accounts of life can be seen in the promotion of the pre-embryo itself, as in an appendix in the First Report
of the Voluntary Licensing Authority, entitled 'Human In Vitro Fertilisation', described as 'an explanatory note prepared by Dr Penelope
Leach', a member of the Authority and a well-known research psy-
chologist and author. She described in some detail the principles behind the fourteen-day limit and the term 'pre-embryo' in similar terms
to the others we have seen, but her explanation becomes particularly
interesting because it is spun out to take in babies and pregnancies in
more explicit ways. The explanation not only redefined the beginning
of the embryo, but the beginnings of babies:

> The belief in instant individuality and the consequent anxiety about the study
> of fertilised eggs is understandable because common parlance terms the moment
> of fertilisation 'conception', calls a woman who has conceived 'pregnant' and
> defines pregnancy as 'carrying a baby'. This is a vitally important over-
> simplification. An individual baby cannot begin *without* fertilisation but fer-
> tilisation does not start an individual baby but merely sets in motion a train
> of events which can lead to such a beginning. (Voluntary Licensing Authority
> 1986: 39)

This is an example of how the pre-embryo sustains the principle motion
of Aristotelian accounts of life. A woman who is pregnant is not even
pregnant anymore, because the pre-embryo is not the beginning of a
baby.

The passage reaches back to the 'life is a continuum' argument,
which appeared so often in the early 1980s, in emphasizing that there

is no point of instant individuality. Yet, the passage remains devoted to pinpointing a true beginning. Thus it raises the inherent contradiction of positing a certain boundary between pre-embryo and embryo as the beginning of a baby. It also begins to suggest that, far from being ethically neutral, the pre-embryo (its conceptual framework, that is) is making demands on human relationships to procreation, such as what counts as pregnancy, but not only such relationships of female fertility and motherhood. Far more. There are processes of othering implicit in the conception of the pre-embryo. That is, there is much the pre-embryo narrative does not explicitly show. I shall concentrate on one example.

I mentioned earlier that there was a perception among advocates of embryo research that many people were ignorant of the facts about embryos. There was no recognition that there might be other sorts of facts which bear on the debate, and affect people's attitudes toward the technology. A study by social anthropologist Jeanette Edwards, which was part of a group project of new reproductive technology in the context of kinship (Edwards et al. 1993), shows otherwise and informs my understanding of how ideas such as pre-embryo make demands on human relationships.

Jeanette Edwards talked to people in a town in the north-west of England, which she calls Alltown, about their views and concerns. Family relationships and relatedness were found to be important; this came through in how people discussed the problems, benefits or implications of methods such as egg and sperm donation or freezing embryos. People were concerned with who would be responsible to resulting children and the kinship ties between gamete donors and resulting child. The study showed that, far from being ignorant, people were well-aware of changes in human relationships which were implicated, although no one opinion or perspective was expressed. Edwards concluded that the people whom she interviewed had a 'relational view of human existence' (Edwards 1993: 11).

When this relational view of human existence is compared to the promotion of the pre-embryo, a contradiction is outstanding. The pre-embryo of the embryology narrative is related to no one. The promotion of the pre-embryo may be seen as a process of objectifying, while the considerations of the Alltown people may be seen as processes of subjectifying. The particularistic concerns about relationships and relatedness are of a different order than the concern in the professional debate with a universal embryo/pre-embryo related to nobody. Jeanette Edwards concluded her study thus:

> People interpret what they see as the implications of NRT [new reproductive technologies] not through what they know of the techniques and philosophies of reproductive medicine, but through what they know about the practice and predictabilities of kinship. They do not, in other words, have to be technologically literate in the methods of NRT in order to think about the implications of certain reproductive possibilities for the social relationships they create and/or influence. The Alltown people whose views are presented here ground their ideas about NRT in what they already know and, indeed, in what they are expert at. (Edwards 1993: 63)

My purpose in making the comparison with Edwards's study is to fill out the story of the pre-embryo. First, it helps show what the construction of the concept pre-embryo in itself cannot show. The embryo remains unchanged and things seem to stay the same in the face of unprecedented changes in human identities and relationships.[3]

Second, the scientific, philosophical and legal discourses on reproductive technologies shared a way of thinking, scientism, which privileges objects and events (here, embryos and the formation of the primitive streak) above relationships and processes. The universalistic discourse of science is hard pressed to recognize the particularistic discourse of the Alltown people, except to identify it as opinions rather than knowledge.[4] This, too, is a process of othering.

Complicating my analysis is the matter of contradictory processes of objectifying and subjectifying of embryos. We have pre-embryos related to nobody in embryology, but also pre-embryos related to somebody as far as the people of Alltown are concerned. Yet, at the same time, the principle notion of Aristotelian accounts of life, as well as other powerful ideas and relationships, must influence both. How do the many ideas and processes – the othering of women, the othering of a relational pre-embryo, the objectifying of pre-embryos, the subjectifying of embryos – relate to or influence each other? The people of Alltown are part of the same society and culture as are the members of the Warnock Committee and Medical Research Council. Clearly there is a lot going on which complicates a neat and tidy reading of the pre-embryo as a duality that is both related to nobody and somebody somewhere.

There is a tension here, and an exercise of power; some ideas acquire power, while others do not. How can we understand these in ways which take account of their complexity? I am particularly interested in how a consideration of that which changes, that which stays the same, the processes which allow it to happen, and the demands which these make on medical practice and other practices, may help us build theoretical and analytical bridges.

ASSESSING THE SUCCESS OF THE PRE-EMBRYO

The term 'pre-embryo' was used by the Voluntary Licensing Authority in all of its reports and texts for the whole of its existence. The term arose in other places too, but not consistently. Mary Warnock never used the term to my knowledge; nor did the *British Medical Journal* in their editorial promotion of embryo research. The journal *Nature* used it briefly but then refused it in an editorial in 1987, commenting, 'This usage [pre-embryo] is a cop-out.... The fact is that a fertilised human egg is as much deserving of being called an embryo as is a fertilised frog's egg' (*Nature* 1987: 87).

The term 'pre-embryo' was most often used in the promotion of human embryo research, as by the lobby group 'Progress, campaign for research into reproduction', formed in 1985 in response to the anti-research Powell bill. An information leaflet began, 'WHAT IS AN EMBRYO? What has popularly been called "embryo" research is not really that at all. It is research using "pre-embryos" (conceptuses)...' (Progress, undated).

Similarly, journalist Virginia Ironside wrote in a newspaper article on the 'Progress' campaign, 'Research is not actually done on embryos. It's done on pre-embryos. Between around day fourteen of a woman's cycle and the date she misses her first period is the life of the pre-embryo – before it fully implants in the womb and probably becomes an embryo' (Ironside 1985).

The most impressive evidence of the success of the pre-embryo is that it changed the hearts and minds of many of the British parliamentarians who had initially objected to human embryo research. Evidence of this is given by professor of sociology Michael Mulkay, who analysed the parliamentary debates on embryo research. The most typical view of parliamentarians opposed to embryo research was that the embryo has the spiritual status of a full human being. Lady Saltoun was one such member, but she eventually changed her views after visiting research facilities and talking to researchers. She wholeheartedly embraced the pre-embryo, giving testimony, 'I have taken steps to inform myself on the exact nature of the so-called embryo research which is being done.... Even if I were persuaded that pre-embryo research is wrong...'. The acceptance of the new definition of the embryo made it possible for those who had been opposed to the research to reconsider its medical benefits (Mulkay 1994: 199–200).

In the end, a majority of parliamentarians voted in favour of embryo research in conjunction with the government's Human Fertilization and

Embryology Bill 1989; it was a far cry from that first vote back in February 1985 in which the majority had dissented. Hence, although the term 'pre-embryo' never became universally used, it performed convincingly for the very group in British society who counted most, the parliamentarians who would vote for or against human embryo research. Thus the redefinition of the embryo is an exemplary case of how technologies come to be accepted. The pre-embryo was meant to enrol support for a contested innovation, human embryo research, and it did. Once it did, the use of the term diminished, although one may still find it used occasionally.

Finally, the current edition of *Henderson's Dictionary of Biological Terms* includes the entry 'pre-embryo n. in mammals name sometimes given to the fertilised ovum and its cleavage stages up to blastocyst formation and the specification of the cells of the inner cell mass that will develop into the embryo proper.' The Tenth Edition of *Henderson's* – first published in 1989, the first edition in which 'pre-embryo' appears – applies a term coined for human embryos to the whole of the mammalian community. Since 1989, the word 'pre-embryo' has been included in new editions of a few English language dictionaries. The pre-embryo has truly become a naturalized fact.

It has been interesting for me to see where the promotion of the pre-embryo was linked explicitly to the body of a woman or to maternity, which did occur at times. As quoted above, Penelope Leach did so, and so did Virginia Ironside, who specializes in women's issues. Anne McLaren also referred to the maternity of real women at times, although not in the texts cited in this chapter. All of these speakers are women, but it remains, according to my reading, that woman's body largely remained outside representations of the pre-embryo, only to be relocated when the story is spun out.

CONCLUDING REMARKS

The redefinition of the embryo and the neologism 'pre-embryo' are not straightforward reflections of what happens in nature, but reflect a complicated social and political network within which the scientific establishment and others were operating. The redefinition of the embryo is a case of a process whereby 'outsiders' who were sceptical of an innovation were enrolled to become 'insiders' who accept it. These points support a heterogeneous understanding of the relationship between the technical and the social, whereas the scientific promotion of the pre-embryo reflected a model which bifurcates the technical and the social, knowledge and ethics. Both models help explain how the fictions of embryology narratives are sustained. The latter sustains the belief in natural facts. The former illuminates the process by which facts are naturalized and beings are objectified.

The radical redefinition of the embryo created a dichotomy embryo/pre-embryo. I do not see this as evidence of a paradigm shift in biomedical science. Rather, I see it as illustrating how science makes use of what is handed down, the lesson of evolution. There is an adaptive continuity here.

One result is the tension between the ideology of the embryo (as both symbolic and real self) and the reification of the *in vitro* embryo in a laboratory dish. The pre-embryo allows both the 'old' embryo and 'new' embryo to exist together, a double identity. As a pre-embryo, related to nobody, and as an embryo, related to somebody by genetics and by wider considerations of culture, the embryo has a double identity. As a pre-self and a self, the embryo has a double identity. As 'other' and as 'self', the embryo has a double identity. The organism with material conditions of living is the ideological apparition of history. The two are one, and the one is both. The new origins story embodies both these identities. The embryo remains an unchanging ideological apparition in the face of human embryo research simply by shifting the origin point to a later stage.

A final reflection is in order. When I returned to the subject of the pre-embryo recently after being away from it for a few years, upon rereading the scientific promotion of the term, I was persuaded by Anne McLaren's arguments. They were convincing; the term 'embryo' was terribly ambiguous, and a new term was needed. I had to rethink my position. And so I returned to my bulging files from the 1980s, and newly acquired notes and references. Shortly thereafter, reviewing the entirety of the terrain, I reclaimed a critical reading.

The episode remains for me a lesson in the power of scientism: I, as others, may readily privilege knowledge of objects and events over wider considerations of human relationships and processes. I could so easily lose my sense of the wonderfully messy, the human, the political and the social to the issue of a technical ambiguity which, after all, is real enough too.

NOTES

1. This information comes from a private conversation with Anne McLaren, 15 February 1987, at a women's health meeting in Oxford.

2. The entry 'pre-embryo' could be found in one dictionary, it must be said. It appears as an obscure entry in the first edition of the encyclopaedic *Oxford English Dictionary*, published in 1933 (a second edition did not appear until 1992). The entry does not offer a definition; it simply gives two archaic quotations from 1894 and 1904. The word 'pre-embryo' existed, but it was neither used nor generally known in the second half of the twentieth century. It was presumed to be a new coinage in 1985.

3. Thanks to Professor Marilyn Strathern for the insight that while things appear to stay the same, great changes in human relationships are occurring.

4. My use of the idea of a universalistic versus particularistic discourse is informed by Emily Martin's *The Women in the Body* (Open University Press, Milton Keynes, 1989), in which she compares and contrasts scientific discourse on events of female fertility such as menstruation, which universalizes them, and women's different experiences which are particular and diverse.

REFERENCES

Reports

Committee of Inquiry into Human Fertilisation and Embryology Report (1984) HMSO, London [The Warnock Report].
American Fertility Society Ethics Committee (1986) 'Ethical Considerations of the New Reproductive Technologies', *Fertility and Sterility*, Supplement 1, vol. 46, no. 3.
Council for Science and Society (1984) *Human Procreation*, London.
Medical Research Council (1985) *Report of Inquiry into Human Fertilisation and Embryology, Medical Research Council Response*, London.
Voluntary Licensing Authority for Human In Vitro Fertilisation and Embryology (1985) *Guidelines for Both Clinical and Research Applications of Human In Vitro Fertilisation*, London.
—— (1986) *The First Report of the Voluntary Licensing Authority for Human In Vitro Fertilisation and Embryology*, London.
Royal College of Obstetricians and Gynaecologists (1983) *Report of the RCOG Ethics Committee on In Vitro Fertilisation and Embryo Replacement or Transfer*, Chamelion Press, London.
The Royal Society (1983) *Human Fertilization and Embryology*, Submission to the Department of Health and Social Security Committee of Inquiry, London.

Books and Articles

Bijker, W.E. and J. Law, eds (1992) *Shaping Technology/Building Society*, Massachusetts Institute of Technology Press, Cambridge, Mass. and London.
Clarke, M. (1985) 'Voluntary Authority Set Up', *Nature*, vol. 314, p. 397.
—— (1986) 'Another Bill Bites the Dust', *Nature*, vol. 319, p. 349.
Connor, S. (1985) 'Scientists Licensed to Work on "Pre-Embryos"', *New Scientist*, 21 November, p. 21.

Davies, D. (1986) *Nature*, vol. 320, p. 208 (letter to the editor).

Duden, B. (1993) 'Visualizing "Life"', *Science as Culture*, vol. 3, part 4, no. 17, pp. 562–600.

Dunn, E. (1984) 'Meddling with the Conception', *Sunday Times*, 25 November.

Edwards, J. (1993) 'Explicit Connections: Ethnographic Enquiry in North-West England', in J. Edwards et al., *Technologies of Procreation: Kinship in the Age of Assisted Conception*, Manchester University Press, Manchester and New York.

Edwards, J., S. Franklin, E. Hirsch, F. Price and M. Strathern (1993) *Technologies of Procreation: Kinship in the Age of Assisted Conception*, Manchester University Press, Manchester and New York.

Franklin, S. (1993) 'Making Representations: The Parliamentary Debate on the Human Fertilisation and Embryology Act', in J. Edwards et al., *Technologies of Procreation: Kinship in the Age of Assisted Conception*, Manchester University Press, Manchester and New York.

Haraway, D. (1989) *Primate Visions: Gender, Race and Nature in the World of Modern Science*, Routledge, New York.

Huxley, Sir Andrew (1985) 'Research and the Embryo', *New Scientist*, 11 April, p. 2.

Ironside, V. (1985) 'How to Breed Healthy Babies', *Guardian*, 18 November.

McLaren, A. (1986a) 'Why Study Early Human Development?', *New Scientist*, 24 April, pp. 49–52.

—— (1986b) *Nature*, vol. 320, p. 570 (letter to the editor).

Mulkay, M. (1994) 'Changing Minds about Embryo Research', *Public Understanding of Science*, vol. 3, p. 195–213.

Nature (1982) 'The Future of the Test-Tube Baby', vol. 299, p. 475.

—— (1987) 'IVF Remains in Legal Limbo', vol. 327, p. 87.

Pfeffer, N. and A. Quick (1988) *Infertility Services: A Desperate Case*, report for the Greater London Association of Community Health Councils, 100 Park Village East, London NW1 3SR.

Spallone, P. (1989) *Beyond Conception: The New Politics of Reproduction*, Macmillan, London; Bergin and Garvey, Massachusetts.

—— (1994) 'Reproductive Health and Reproductive Technology', in S. Wilkinson and C. Kitzinger, eds, *Women and Health: Feminist Perspectives*, Taylor and Francis, London.

✦ 13 ✦

GYNOGENESIS:

A LESBIAN APPROPRIATION OF

REPRODUCTIVE TECHNOLOGIES

Elizabeth Sourbut

The purpose of this chapter is to open up the debates around reproductive technologies in such a way as to include lesbian mothers and to help empower all women as active participants in the processes of assisted conception, pregnancy and childbirth.

I will examine the ways in which lesbian mothers transgress the accepted boundaries of motherhood. In doing so, I will focus on the theoretical possibility of women using reproductive technologies to conceive children with two genetic mothers and no genetic father. Following the lesbian feminist writer Ryn Edwards, I will call this process gynogenesis (Edwards 1990). At the moment gynogenesis is not a practical possibility. It is science fiction. But as a concept it is a way of bringing lesbians into the debates around assisted reproduction, debates which have been largely restricted to heterosexual, married couples.

On one level of analysis, lesbian mothers are women who have children, like any other mothers. They simply exhibit a different range of sexual object choice from heterosexual women. They may have conceived their child during a previous heterosexual relationship; they may have chosen to introduce the sperm using alternative insemination (either donor insemination through a registered clinic, or self-insemination at home through a private arrangement with a sperm donor); or they may have adopted. Their families take a range of forms, including single parents, lesbian couples, and families including the genetic father and/or other adult women or men, some or all of whom may live in the same home or separately (Martin 1993; Saffron 1994). This diversity of family form, it can be argued, is a private matter, and in an ideal world the law would be liberal enough to recognize such families on equal terms with the families of heterosexual couples.

Looked at in a different way, lesbian mothers become monstrous. A potent site of contested meanings, they threaten the very fabric of society. The ideological basis of modern Western society has no space for lesbian mothers.

Lesbians were defined as a category by sexologists in the late nineteenth and early twentieth centuries (for example, Havelock Ellis 1918). The sexologists argued that people could be defined by their sexual natures; 'that lesbians, say, could actually be thought of as a separate type of person' (Ruehl 1985: 166). Ellis considered lesbianism (which he called sexual inversion) to be a deviation from heterosexual, procreative sex, and so sterile and inferior (Ruehl 1985: 168). Adrienne Rich argues that lesbians have been silenced and marginalized because we challenge what she describes as the patriarchal institution of 'compulsory heterosexuality', which attempts to force women into dependence upon men (Rich 1986).

Mothers are a crucially important element in the construction of society. Rich writes that the institution of motherhood has kept women from being incorporated into power structures and has created the split between the private and public spheres of life (Rich 1977). Mothering takes place within the family, and women's family role in industrialized countries is centred around childcare and taking care of men (Chodorow 1978: 4–5). Motherhood has been glorified at many different periods in history, mothers having responsibility for passing on moral and cultural values to their children.

To conflate the deviant category of *lesbian* with the glorified (though often abused) category of *mother* is to create a monstrous hybrid creature which threatens the ideological basis upon which society is structured.

Lesbian mothers have, of course, always existed, but I suggest that their increasingly high profile as a conceptual category is a direct challenge to ideological constructions of the family, and hence to the shape of the private sphere, one of the two basic supports of liberal political theory.

Were gynogenesis to become a real possibility, it would offer lesbian couples the chance to build families with children who are genetically related to both parents. In some ways, this could be seen as colluding with the conventional image of the nuclear family and reinforcing the emphasis placed upon genetic relatedness. However, the nuclear family is very much a patriarchal institution (Pateman 1988). While two lesbian parents of biologically related children would fulfil the structural and genetic requirements of the family, the crucial ideological component requires that the two adults must be a man and a woman (Haimes 1990).

The chance to conceive children together would certainly be welcomed by some lesbians. Rose, who was interviewed by Lisa Saffron, commented: 'I suppose I could accept it [parenting] easier if I was contributing the seed. Then it would very definitely be something we were doing together' (Saffron 1994: 97). Certainly some lesbian couples already undergo a degree of technological intervention comparable to that which would be required by gynogenesis in order to share the process of motherhood as much as possible:

> There are lesbian couples in the United States where one partner is implanted with an embryo created by her lover's ovum and donor sperm. That partner, technically a surrogate, then gets to give birth to her lover's baby. (Martin 1993: 358)

As well as allowing lesbians to mingle their genes, gynogenesis would give us the ability to conceive children (who would all be daughters, since all eggs carry an X sex chromosome[1]) without any biological input from men. The daughters so conceived would have no genetic fathers, although the first generation would, of course, have grandfathers.

In the next section, I will look at possible lesbian applications of methods of assisted reproduction. I will consider the technological steps required in the process of gynogenesis and will briefly explore the reasons why, at the moment, it doesn't work. Technological innovation on its own, however, isn't enough. The possibilities opened up by gynogenesis are in tension with the ways in which reproductive technologies have been presented up until now. The medical establishment stresses their use as a cure for infertility, while many feminist texts have been concerned with the ways in which they are being used to control women's reproductive processes (for example, Arditti et al. 1984; Corea 1988; Spallone 1989).

I will look at the current discourses[2] of infertility and will then move on to explore how considerations of lesbian feminist desires might help us to change these discourses to empower women as mothers and as users of technology, rather than simply as passive recipients of medical interventions. I will consider gynogenesis both as a real possibility and as a metaphor serving similar theoretical purposes to Donna Haraway's figure of the cyborg – cybernetic organism, part-human, part-machine

– in exploring the borderlands between human, animal and machine (Haraway 1990). In particular, I ask what changes are necessary if we are to accommodate the notion of lesbians using and controlling the technology which will enable them to become mothers.

GYNOGENESIS – THE RESEARCH

Gynogenesis would require considerable surgical and (usually) hormonal interventions into the reproductive process. The steps necessary would be similar to those used for *in vitro* fertilization (conception in a test tube or petri dish), except that a second egg would be substituted for the sperm. Two ripe eggs must be removed from the ovaries of the potential mothers and their genetic material fused. This could be achieved using techniques of micro-injection, which have already been developed to achieve fertilization using non-motile sperm. The fertilized egg would then be replaced into the uterus of one of the women, where it must be persuaded to implant and develop to term.

There is a considerable body of research in mainstream genetics into the possibilities of parthenogenesis, gynogenesis and androgenesis in mammals (for example, Kaufman 1983; McGrath and Solter 1984; Solter 1988). Parthenogenesis is the attempt to create an individual from a single egg with just one, female, parent; in gynogenesis the genetic material from an egg is added to a second egg to create an individual with two female parents; and in androgenesis the genetic material from two sperm is inserted into an egg, and the egg's own genetic material is removed to create an individual with two male parents.

So far, it has proved impossible to persuade parthenogenones, gynogenones or androgenones to develop far beyond the point of implantation into the wall of the uterus. Research on mice has shown that the contributions of genes from the maternal and the paternal genome are not identical, and that both are necessary for an embryo to develop to term. Although, in theory, both maternal and paternal genomes carry all the information necessary to create a new individual, not all the genes are able to function. In a process which geneticists call imprinting, different genes are switched on and off during different stages of embryogenesis, and 'some genes are differentially expressed when contributed by the maternal or the paternal gamete' (Solter 1988).

Parthenogenetic embryos have only one parent. They may be haploid, having only half the normal number of genes, or their complement of genes may be doubled up to produce a diploid set. It is normal for mammals to have paired chromosomes – the diploid state. Each gene site therefore contains two genes which potentially perform the same function, one from the maternal genome and one from the paternal. These genes may be similar, known as homozygotic, or different, heterozygotic. The importance of heterozygosity is that it protects against many genetic diseases. Often these diseases are recessive, only expressed if the relevant gene sites are homozygotic, and both genes carry the disease. It is therefore far more likely that diploid parthenogenones, which are completely, or substantially, homozygotic, will express lethal genes. Gynogenetic embryos have two parents and are therefore substantially heterozygous. However, Solter observes that:

> Despite such a potential advantage both gynogenones and parthenogenones all die within a few days following implantation [into the lining of the uterus], apparently because of poor development of extraembryonic components. (Solter 1988: 130)

It seems that genes responsible for the full development of the placenta are only expressed if they have come from the paternal genome. Conversely, androgenones, containing two sets of paternal genes, develop a normal placenta but no foetal tissue. The genes responsible for the development of the foetus itself must come from the maternal genome.

The techniques required to create these experimental embryos are immensely delicate, requiring the removal of genetic material from within one egg and its replacement into another. Control experiments are performed using the same techniques but maintaining the pairing of one maternal set of genes with one paternal set. While many embryos created in this way fail to develop to term, about 5 per cent do develop. None of the gynogenones or the androgenones develops to term. The likelihood of this being due to chance is very low (McGrath and Solter 1984). It appears that something other than the research techniques is preventing full development. This failure to develop could be explained in terms of some nongenetic component that is essential for development, but experiments to test this idea make it seem unlikely (Solter 1988). It seems that gene imprinting is the most likely explanation.

The exact mechanism by which genes are imprinted is not yet understood. Solter suggests that 'molecular probes' for genes are needed in order to find out, and that these are not yet available (Solter 1988: 135). Several hypotheses have been proposed, however, and research continues. If the interpretation of these experiments is correct, then imprinting is the key problem for gynogenesis. If a way could be found to control or manipulate it, then the genetic material from one egg could be given a paternal pattern of imprinting before it is merged with the other. The genes are already there; they simply have to be persuaded to switch on and off at the necessary times.

Research continues into gene imprinting, not only because of interest in gyno- and androgenesis, but because of the patterns of transmission of some human diseases. Some, such as Huntington's disease (a lethal disease which appears in adulthood), are transmitted in a way that suggests parental imprinting. In the case of Huntington's disease, onset is noticeably earlier if it has been transmitted via the father than via the mother (Solter 1988: 139). Clearly, a lot of work remains to be done, and gynogenesis, if ever possible at all, is going to be a more complex process than it might at first appear. However, with the high profile of the Human Genome Project, and genetics research in general, these subtle interactions may yet come to be understood.

Lesbian feminist researchers could potentially aid the process by bringing a different emphasis. Ryn Edwards, writing in the journal *Lesbian Ethics,* uses the term 'choreography' in preference to 'imprinting':

> Scientists use the term *imprinting* rather than *choreography.* Both terms suggest a pattern, but *imprint* implies a fixed state, while *choreography* implies a more dynamic, nonstatic condition, a pattern reflective of and changing with time. For me, *choreography* holds a more feminist meaning, that of essence resulting from the interplay or interactions with others, other choreographies. (Edwards 1990: 46; italics in original)

This distinction is more than semantic and suggests an interpretation of genetics which is moving away from reductionist approaches. Edwards adds:

> From the scientific perspective, we are beginning to understand that life is more complicated, inter-relational, and situational than most of us can even now imagine. (Edwards 1990: 47)

ETHICAL DILEMMAS

There has been a lot of work in the past few years by feminists critical of the natural sciences, particularly the biological sciences. Some writers are completely against science, seeing it as an irretrievably patriarchal project with which women should not get involved (for example, Griffin 1984). Most see the issues as being far more complex than this (for example, Keller 1985; Harding 1986) but argue that science is gendered, and that we need to explore the ways in which this gendering happens.

In her article 'A Manifesto for Cyborgs', Donna Haraway exhorts us to take responsibility for the social relations of science and technology. She writes that this means:

> refusing an anti-science metaphysics, a demonology of technology, and so means embracing the skillful task of reconstructing the boundaries of daily life, in partial connection with others, in communication with all of our parts. (Haraway 1990: 223)

Earlier in the same article, she writes that movements for animal rights are a 'recognition of connection across the discredited breach of nature and culture' (Haraway 1990: 193).

The experiments described in the previous section are performed upon the bodies of mice. Thousands of mice are injected with hormones to make them superovulate, operated upon for egg recovery, made pregnant with embryos created from the gametes of mice of a different strain, and finally 'sacrificed' (McGrath and Solter 1983: 181) at various stages during pregnancy so that they can be dissected and the embryonic tissue examined in detail. Mice are useful research material because they have a short gestation period, they can be easily bred in the laboratory and, ethically, it is considered acceptable in most circles to kill them in the interests of science.

If we, as lesbian feminists, are to use and develop this research, we have to acknowledge the means by which the knowledge has been gained. We cannot simply reject all animal research out of hand, because much of what we know about hormones and about cycles of ovulation and the workings of the female reproductive system in humans has been learned partly through experiments on animals (Pfeffer 1993). Much of this knowledge has been appropriated by the women's health movement (for example, Boston Women's Health Book Collective 1989), with the aim of helping women to take control over their own fertility.

As Haraway suggests, however, we need not unquestioningly accept animal experimentation. Animals are not inanimate objects, and part of the aim of a feminist approach to science is precisely to reintegrate humanity with the rest of the organic world. We must think seriously about how to learn about ourselves and the rest of the world without using animals and other humans as though they were our possessions.

Gena Corea, a journalist who is intensely critical of reproductive technologies, writes movingly of her visit to a pioneer in the field. She asked to see the laboratory animals and found that she identified with them, rather than with the man who was showing them to her:

I entered the laboratory. Passing through three or four rooms, I saw rabbits, mice, rats, monkeys in stainless steel cages. I felt like an imposter. The biologist and the technician spoke to me as though I was one of them. But I was one of the animals. (Corea 1984: 48)

She argues that scientists, in their research into women's reproductive processes, use animals and women in a similar way, seeing us all as research materials. Other feminist writers have made similar observations. Patricia Spallone writes that, in a paper for the medical journal *The Lancet*, Robert Edwards, a pioneer of *in vitro* fertilization research, listed women's eggs in the section headed 'Materials and Methods' (Spallone 1989: 92). The arguments that women and animals are seen as part of nature to be experimented upon by white men, who are above or beyond nature, are numerous (for example, Griffin 1984; Merchant 1980). These feminist analyses point to a justifiable concern for the integrity of human and animal life in the hands of science as currently practised. They highlight the ways in which science supports patriarchal control over women.

However, the conclusion which often seems to be drawn is that women are indeed a part of nature, and that this is good. Technology, in all its forms, is bad. Haraway, with her cyborg metaphor, is moving beyond this position and suggesting that the opposition between the organic and the machine is no longer as clear cut as it was. We are both connected with nonhuman life and able to play with the possibilities offered by science and technology. The difficulty, and the skill, lies in reconstructing boundaries and deconstructing dichotomies.

This approach suggests that we must change the ideological system within which science is done and also the processes by which knowledge is accumulated, and indeed the definitions of what counts as knowledge (see, for example, Easlea 1981; Keller 1985; Harding 1986 for an expansion of these arguments). These things all go together: a science which sees itself as being at the top of a hierarchy, which aims to control the natural world, will have no qualms about using the things it studies. On the other hand, a science which seeks to break down boundaries and sees knowledge as situational and dependent upon that which it studies is likely to be more respectful.

THE DISCOURSE OF INFERTILITY

Assisted reproduction technologies are presented as cures for infertility. But they are policed in an attempt to make them available only to certain infertile people: heterosexual couples living together in stable relationships (Warnock 1984: 19). In this section, I look at Sarah Franklin's discourse analysis of infertility (Franklin 1990).

Franklin analyses popular representations of reproductive technologies and looks in detail at how such accounts act to reinforce the status of marriage and the heterosexual nuclear family. She argues that, because reproductive technologies remove procreation from the private sphere and relocate it within the scientist's laboratory, the resulting redefinitions of family ties and kinship will become subject to state and legal control (Franklin 1990: 201). The form and extent of this control will have considerable repercussions for women's reproductive rights, and she finds it worrying that this issue doesn't appear in either formal debates or popular accounts. Instead, women's interests are only mentioned in terms of the putative increase in choice and control offered by these technologies so that 'popular representations of infertility contribute to the formation and widespread acceptance of this now common myth of the benevolence of new reproductive technologies' (Franklin 1990: 201–2).

Franklin goes on to consider the narrative and discursive forms of popular, mainly newspaper, accounts of reproductive technologies. She argues that these narratives are presented as stories structured around the emergence of an obstacle, infertility, and the need to find a resolution, which is provided by reproductive technologies. By beginning with the desperate married couple, the storyline is seen to have a 'natural' progression through medical intervention to the happy ending of the 'miracle baby' and the affirmation of heterosexual married bliss. Other viewpoints, such as the single woman or the lesbian couple who desire children, are silenced by exclusion.

At a discursive level, these representations function to present a regime of medical-scientific knowledge, or 'truth', of infertility. Franklin identifies three discourses of infertility at work across a variety of representations, from newspaper accounts to the Warnock Report (the report of the British Government Committee of Inquiry set up in 1982 to look into the implications of the new reproductive technologies; for a detailed discussion of the report, see Chapter 12 in this volume) (Warnock 1984). These are: the discourse of social loss, the discourse of biological destiny, and the discourse of medical hope.

The discourse of social loss concerns the features of infertility which contain it within the institutions of marriage and the family. Infertility is conflated with childlessness; whereas, in fact, the two are only the same for people medically diagnosed as infertile who want a biologically related child. The problem is defined entirely within the parameters of the traditional nuclear family.

The discourse of biological destiny defines infertility within the terms of biological science. Heterosexuality and the nuclear family are presented as natural. Only procreation through heterosexual intercourse within marriage is seen as producing legitimate parenthood. This, of course, is profoundly disrupted by the new reproductive technologies, which not only bypass heterosexual intercourse, but often involve third-party donations of gametes. This contradiction can only be contained by rigid discursive conventions which privilege genetic inheritance over all other forms of parent–child ties.

The discourse of medical hope holds out medical science as the *only* hope for infertile couples. The important features here are a belief in scientific progress and the ability to control and manipulate nature, a clinical definition of reproduction as a biological process, and an emphasis on the importance of medical intervention to increase reproductive choice.

Taken together, Franklin argues, these discourses seek to enunciate the 'truth' about reproductive processes. But there is more to it than that. Debates around infertility are being used to defend traditional kinship beliefs and practices against the disruption caused not only by reproductive technologies but also by the rise of single-parent and lesbian and gay families. Not only the reproduction of children is at stake, but also the reproduction of traditional sexual and procreative arrangements, and, I would argue, patriarchal power relations. Franklin adds that:

> It remains, of course, an open question as to how successful either popular representations or legislation will be in containing the transgressive potential implicit in the very existence of reproductive technologies. The contradiction between the 'unnaturalness' of test-tube conception, and the supposed 'naturalness' of the institutions these techniques are meant to perpetuate can never be resolved, but only contained. (Franklin 1990: 226)

There is a further problem for the defenders of the status quo, which becomes clear if we bring in a consideration of Carole Pateman's discussion of the sexual contract (Pateman 1988). New reproductive technologies bring procreation out of the private sphere of the family and into the public sphere of the laboratory. But these two spheres are not equivalent. Marriage is a curious sort of contract, specifically requiring the participation of one woman and one man, and conferring upon them the status of wife and husband. Within this relationship, sexual difference is normalized, and, indeed, essential for the maintenance of patriarchal sex-right (Pateman 1988).

Infertility treatment takes place within the public sphere of contract and the marketplace; therefore, those entering into such a course of treatment should be free and equal individuals. No taint of status should adhere, including the status of sexual difference. The only place for the 'couple' in contract theory is in the private sphere. Only individuals can make contracts. But the dominant discourse reserves infertility treatment for couples, who must be sexually differentiated. This is where the contradictions inherent in the use of the new reproductive technologies appear most clearly. The structures of the family have been brought into the public sphere where the sophistries designed to gloss over the tensions between a universal individual and patriarchal sex-right are clearly revealed.

The only way that the status quo can be defended is by overt appeals to patriarchal sex-right. This is precisely what is happening in such documents as the Warnock Report, which states baldly that: 'We believe that as a general rule it is better for children to be born into a two-parent family, with both father and mother' (Warnock 1984: 11). No defence of this statement needs to be made, because it is an ideological given.

The three discourses identified by Sarah Franklin: of social loss, of biological destiny and of medical hope provide the ideological power behind the narratives of heroic quest, of obstacles to the natural progressions of human life overcome by the pioneering work of medical scientists. The heterosexual nuclear family, biological processes and medical science are bound together into a structure of mythic power (Franklin 1990: 214). But this structure is unstable, it does not represent the 'truth', and, as Franklin points out, the cracks do show. Those of us positioned outside the stories are not silent observers. Lesbian parents do exist; single-parent families are on the increase; and research shows that children brought up in such non-traditional families develop quite normally (for example, Tasker and Golombok 1991). These families are forcing the discourse to change.

CHANGING THE DISCOURSE

The biological definition of infertility as the inability of couples to conceive together where they wish to do so could include lesbian couples. Sometimes infertility in heterosexual couples is caused by an incompatibility between them, which means that either would be able to have children with another partner, but together they cannot (Pfeffer 1993: 60–61). A lesbian couple cannot conceive together through their sexual relationship, and to this extent, like many heterosexual couples, they are infertile. Lesbians may become just as desperate as heterosexual women to bear their own children, and technically there is no reason why reproductive technologies should not be used to furnish them too with 'miracle babies'.

As discussed above, the existing discourses of infertility are as much about reproducing social norms as they are about reproducing children. Infertility is socially constructed as an illness that afflicts only heterosexual couples. Within these discourses, gynogenesis remains an oddity, a minority research interest with possible applications to early embryonic development (Kaufman 1983) but with no conceivable medical application. It is hard to imagine a clinical situation where the fusion of two eggs is the only way in which a heterosexual couple can be given a child. There will always be some other combination of donations and techniques involving the use of sperm which can be used.[3]

There seems to be a vast unease around any connection between technology and motherhood. Scientists intervene in women's reproductive processes, but the women themselves are conceptually distinct from these scientific activities. Indeed, as Patricia Spallone has argued (1989), women as whole people do not appear in scientific literature, which talks about body parts and specific processes.

The popular narratives analysed by Sarah Franklin (1990) shift viewpoint from the desperate infertile woman who wants to be a mother, to the heroic scientists who can overcome the obstacles, and then back to the happy, fulfilled new mother at the end. The two narrative forms of adventure and romance remain distinct; motherhood remains 'natural', and science retains its status as external to and controlling natural processes.

In contrast, Haraway's cyborg (Haraway 1990) and my usage of gynogenesis as both metaphor and scientific possibility offer a blending of technology and motherhood. Lesbian mothers decouple motherhood from marriage, from heterosexuality and from patriarchal control. Lesbian mothers using gynogenesis offer a vision of women playing with technology to conceive their own children. Women fill all the roles in this narrative.

Clearly, at the moment, gynogenesis remains in the realms of speculation. But as an idea it can help to move debate on to new ground. If lesbian parents are to find general acceptance, the definitions of what we mean by natural and unnatural forms of procreation have to change. We have to separate out the cluster of ideas which conflate women's sexuality, marriage and motherhood, all contained within the isolated privacy of the heterosexual nuclear family. Such arrangements are no more natural than the many actual and potential family groupings being explored by lesbians and by heterosexual women who want to have children without long-term commitment to a man.

Reproductive technologies pose a major challenge to traditional ideas about the family. They bring the most private of concerns into the public sphere of legislation and state control. As many feminists have pointed out, used within existing contexts of medical, scientific and political power, they pose a serious threat to women's control over our own bodies, particularly our reproductive freedom.

But if we consider that reproduction has been confined within a framework of institutional compulsory heterosexuality (Rich 1986), we may be tempted to ask who, except a few middle class, white women, have ever had real reproductive choice. The concept of individual freedom rests heavily on the idea of nonintervention by the state into the private sphere. But the individual of liberal theory is masculine, and the private sphere is his domain, within which he has authority over the women and children in his family (Pateman 1988). Arguably, individual men are free within the private sphere. Women are unfree in both spheres. We need a broader vision.

Reproductive technologies offer many possibilities. Whilst remaining wary of the dominant scientific discourses within which they are embedded, I would urge women to look again at the liberating potentials offered. Donna Haraway reminds us that, as women, 'we can be responsible for machines; they do not dominate or threaten us. We are responsible for boundaries; we are they' (Haraway 1990: 222).

There is an opportunity for lesbian parents in the remaking of boundaries between science and nature, natural and unnatural. In creating new discourses of procreation, we can ensure that lesbian parents, autonomous women and technological motherhood are incorporated as legitimate and central categories. There is no certainty of success, but visions exist, and that is the most that utopias can offer. I offer gynogenesis, not as the only answer to providing lesbian parents with autonomy, but as one way of thinking beyond existing binary categories.

NOTES

1. Babies with two X chromosomes are female; babies with one X and one Y are male. About half of all sperm carry an X chromosome while the rest carry a Y; so in heterosexual conception, we get approximately half girls and half boys.

Without sperm, there are no boys.

2. Franklin defines discourse as follows: 'The logic of discourse is ... a logic of *enunciation* defining the terms upon which knowledge is produced and deployed. It is a logic of inclusion and exclusion, of enhancement of some features and diminution of others. It is a logic which defines the positions from which legitimate knowledge is produced, thus delimiting the field of knowledge by establishing the definitive concepts and categories' (Franklin 1990: 219; italics in original).

3. One possible scenario, where gynogenesis might be used within the existing medical paradigm, is contained within the separate but related area of genetic screening. A few women are carriers of genetically inherited diseases, such as haemophilia, which, if passed on, will only be expressed in sons. In this case, gynogenesis with a donated egg, which would guarantee the women a genetically related daughter, might be considered. Her husband would then be treated as the father in the same way as if semen had been donated. However, *in vitro* fertilization using the husband's or donated semen, followed by genetic screening of the embryos before implantation, would perform the same function with the same amount of intervention and would allow the possibility of unaffected sons.

REFERENCES

Arditti, R., R. Duelli Klein and S. Minden (1984) *Test-tube Women: What Future for Motherhood?*, Pandora, London.

Boston Women's Health Book Collective (1989) *The New Our Bodies, Ourselves, a Health Book by and for Women,* British edition by A. Phillips and J. Rakusen, Penguin, London.

Chodorow, N. (1978) *The Reproduction of Mothering: Psychoanalysis and the Sociology of Gender*, University of California Press, Berkeley and London.

Corea, G. (1984) 'The Egg Snatchers', in R. Arditti, R. Duelli Klein and S. Minden, *Test-tube Women: What Future for Motherhood?* Pandora, London, pp. 37–51.

——— (1988) *The Mother Machine: Reproductive Technologies from Artificial Insemination to Artificial Wombs*, Women's Press, London.

Easlea, B. (1981) *Science and Sexual Oppression: Patriarchy's Confrontation with Woman and Nature,* Weidenfeld & Nicolson, London.

Edwards, R. (1990) 'The Choreographing of Reproductive DNA', *Lesbian Ethics*, vol. 4, part 1, pp. 44–51.

Ellis, H. (1918) *Studies in the Psychology of Sex: Sexual Inversion*, vol. 2, 3rd edn, Davis, Philadelphia.

Franklin, S. (1990) 'Deconstructing "Desperateness": The Social Construction of Infertility in Popular Representations of New Reproductive Technologies', in M. McNeil, I. Varcoe and S. Yearley, eds, *The New Reproductive Technologies*, Macmillan, London, pp. 200–229.

Griffin, S. (1984) *Woman and Nature: The Roaring inside Her*, Women's Press, London.

Haimes, E. (1990) 'Recreating the Family? Policy Considerations Relating to the "New" Reproductive Technologies', in M. McNeil, I. Varcoe and S. Yearley, eds, *The New Reproductive Technologies*, Macmillan, London, pp. 154–72.

Haraway, D. (1990) 'A Manifesto for Cyborgs: Science, Technology, and Socialist Feminism in the 1980s', in L. Nicholson, ed., *Feminism/Postmodernism*, Routledge, London, pp. 190–233.

Harding, S. (1986) *The Science Question in Feminism*, Open University Press, Milton Keynes.

Kaufman, M. (1983) *Early Mammalian Development: Parthenogenetic Studies*, Cambridge University Press, Cambridge.

Keller, E. F. (1985) *Reflections on Gender and Science*, Yale University Press, London.

Martin, A. (1993) *The Guide to Lesbian and Gay Parenting*, Pandora, London.

McGrath, J. and D. Solter (1984) 'Completion of Mouse Embryogenesis Requires Both the Maternal and Paternal Genomes', *Cell*, vol. 37, pp. 179–83.

Merchant, C. (1980) *The Death of Nature: Women, Ecology, and the Scientific Revolution*, Harper & Row, San Francisco and London.

Pateman, C. (1988) *The Sexual Contract*, Polity Press, Cambridge.

Pfeffer, N. (1993) *The Stork and the Syringe: A Political History of Reproductive Medicine*, Polity Press, Cambridge.

Rich, A. (1977) *Of Woman Born: Motherhood as Experience and Institution*, Virago, London.

—— (1986) 'Compulsory Heterosexuality and Lesbian Existence', in A. Rich, *Blood, Bread, and Poetry: Selected Prose 1979–1985*, Virago, London, pp. 23–75.

Ruehl, S. (1985) 'Inverts and Experts: Radclyffe Hall and the Lesbian Identity', in J. Newton and D. Rosenfelt, *Feminist Criticism and Social Change: Sex, Class and Race in Literature and Culture*, Methuen, New York and London, pp. 165–80.

Saffron, L. (1994) *Challenging Conceptions: Pregnancy and Parenting beyond the Traditional Family*, Cassell, London.

Solter, D. (1988) 'Differential Imprinting and Expression of Maternal and Paternal Genomes', *Annual Review of Genetics*, vol. 22, pp. 127–46.

Spallone, P. (1989) *Beyond Conception: The New Politics of Reproduction*, Macmillan, London.

Tasker, F. L. and S. Golombok (1991) 'Children Raised by Lesbian Mothers: The Empirical Evidence', *Family Law*, vol. 21, pp. 184–7.

Warnock, M. (1984) *Report of the Committee of Inquiry into Human Fertilisation and Embryology*, HMSO, London.

POSTFACE

Nina Lykke and Rosi Braidotti

NON-INNOCENT NATURES AND BODIES

Feminist science and technology studies nowadays are about non-innocent 'natures' and 'bodies' which escape identification as essential, purely 'natural' entities – that is, entities unmediated by language, myth, politics, and so on. Although a reductionist constructivism which considers science as mere text or power game is criticized in this book (Chapter 5), constructivism is emphasized throughout as an important approach for feminist science and technology studies. We want to argue that constructivism liberates natures and bodies from being othered by scientific regimes, which leave them no position other than that of acting as passive objects for the disembodied gaze of the scientist seeking to reveal their universal and context-independent truths. Constructivism shifts this perspective. Seen through the lens of constructivism, no scientific object, from cosmologies (Chapter 4) to embryos/pre-embryos (Chapter 12), can any longer count as a 'pure' work of science. It is made clear that science contains elements of myth; it is embedded in narratives based on certain choices of actors and themes. The constructivist approach makes visible the monstrous web of text, myth, politics and materiality that constitutes the scientific enterprise. We consider this important for science studies which seek to include feminist as well as anti-racist perspectives.

While relying on socio-cultural constructivism, feminist science and technology studies can also be read as a kind of plea for the integration of 'nature', including bodily matter, into the extended framework of feminist cultural analysis. Feminist science and technology studies seem to tell us that it is not only gender, race, ethnicity, age, sexual preference and so on that should be included in the feminist agendas. Another slippery category, 'nature', should be taken into analytical and political account as well.

Ecological feminists have for a long time argued explicitly for the integration of 'nature' into the framework of feminist analysis. They have, for example, pointed out how the logics of violence and domination, inherent in the modern techno-scientific enterprise, make sexism, racism, ethnocentrism and classism intersect with a fifth 'ism': naturism. The term 'naturism', coined by ecofeminists in analogy to sexism and racism (Warren 1990: 132–3), refers to abusive and violent treatment of non-human nature, or 'earth others', as the Australian ecological feminist Val Plumwood has poetically named the worlds of animals, plants, minerals, and so on (Plumwood 1993: 137).

One of the points we want to stress is that feminist science and technology studies can also be read as a kind of implicit or explicit argument for the integration of 'nature' and 'bodily matter'. It is obvious that 'nature' and 'matter' are much more difficult to avoid when you move into the monstrous area of feminist studies of the natural, technical and biomedical sciences than when you remain within the 'purer', more unambiguously 'human', realms of the humanities or social sciences. As 'nature' and 'matter' are the subject areas of the natural sciences, they keep arising in science studies discussions. Even convinced constructivists in the field would agree that the performances of natures and bodies cannot be ascribed exclusively to the symbolic or imaginary orders created by the linguistic and phantasmatic activities of human beings. We believe that in some way or another natures and bodies must be considered as part of a materiality that goes beyond these symbolic and imaginary orders. The bodily pain of the woman who suffers from osteoporosis is one of the examples (see Chapter 11) that illustrates the pressure on cultural studies of science to try to articulate matter and the materiality of the body in a way that goes beyond a reductionist constructivism. Our implication in the environment is another example. 'There is nowhere we can go, nothing we can do to get away from this implication,' says Catherine Roach (Roach 1991: 53). Nature and bodily matter are, as Evelyn Fox Keller has incisively put it, 'humble reminders of our mortality' (Keller 1989: 43). Both science and science studies are confronted with this fact in a pressing manner.

The kind of feminist science and technology studies we defend here also emphasize, however, that 'nature' and 'bodily matter' are very slippery categories. This means that their integration into the framework of feminist analysis is an exercise in theoretical tightrope-walking. The message is clear: while offering strong arguments for the integration of 'nature' and 'bodily matter' into feminist analysis, science and technology studies are also giving us powerful warnings. Given that 'nature' and 'bodily matter' in the postmodern era infiltrate the feminist agendas with urgent questions about embodiment, the recognition of our embeddedness in 'nature', and our inescapable implication in the natural 'environment', they also give rise to pressing new lines of interrogation. These entail such questions as: Which 'nature'? How do we construct our knowledge about it? Who are 'we', the knowers? What roles do race and sexual difference play in the framing of these questions? This is the double message of feminist science and technology studies. The complexity must be respected, otherwise it might be difficult to avoid simply falling back into naive, essentializing and universalizing positions which authoritatively maintain what *nature is* – that is, into positions which may be compared to those of positivist science, even though they may be taken up by eco-activists and feminists too (Braidotti et al. 1994).

One aspect of complexity which confronts feminists who want to integrate 'nature' into their framework of cultural analysis stems from the fact that 'nature', unlike gender, race, age, class, sexual preference, and so forth, does not refer to actors which speak a human language. This lays 'nature' bare to interventions on the part of various kinds of 'ventriloquists' (Haraway 1992: 311) who maintain that they know what 'nature' has to say. The problem of ventriloquism, or 'speaking for nature' (see Chapter 7), concerns feminism in several ways. It is not only a question of raising feminist critiques of the authoritarian and repressive ways in which modern science seeks to voice the 'secrets of nature' in order better to exploit them. The 'master' voice of modern science has such counterparts as, for example, the women ventriloquists whom a gendered division of mental labour in modernity has called to defend 'nature' naively against its scientific colonizers.

Another aspect of the slippery complexity of the category 'nature', articulated vehemently by feminist science studies, is the question of what indeed 'may count as nature' (Haraway 1992: 295) in the cyberworld of the late twentieth century. We live in a time and space where the modern dichotomy between the 'artefactual' and the 'natural' is being quickly deconstructed, simply because the realm of the former is about to cannibalize the latter totally more rapidly than ever before.

As illustrated by Susan Leigh Star's story (see Chapter 2) about a couple of electronically untagged mountain lion cubs causing a lot of commotion in a US state park, 'wild nature' is symptomatically being redefined today as 'that which gives us no information – that which is outside the Net', and since the integrated circuit of the Net is rapidly heading towards all-inclusiveness, there are fewer and fewer 'outsiders'. 'Wild nature' is disappearing at a great rate these days. Furthermore, the notion of 'nature' is made even more slippery by the fact that the quicker 'wild nature' disappears, the more intensely it is reinvented as a multilayered icon for human desires and politics. This is clearly illustrated by the overwhelming contemporary interest in, for example, dolphins (see Chapter 3). 'Appropriate' representatives of 'wild nature' are today cast as boundary figures which are supposed to perform paradoxically as healers of the broken bonds between man and his vanishing 'wild' others.

Slippery complexity is also called effectively to the fore when bodily 'nature' is considered by feminist science and technology studies. Bodies are continuously being reinvented by biomedicine. Whether we look at the medicalization of menopause (Chapters 10 and 11), focus on the story of the invention of 'the pill' (Chapter 9), or look over the shoulders of the embryologists and geneticists (Chapters 12 and 13), it becomes clear that new theories as well as new practices of scientific investigation and intervention create new bodies in a discursive, but also in a material-practical, sense. Natural bodies are moving towards their vanishing point while reinvented nature, cyborg nature, spreads even more quickly.

Through their complex display of non-innocent natures and bodies, feminist science and technology studies perform as a kind of teratology, a science of monsters. We want to argue that monsters redefined as 'process without a stable object' (see Chapter 8), as objects of scientific inquiry which together with cyborgs, goddesses and female sexuality never let themselves be trapped into one stable identity, is precisely what feminist science studies articulate in a radical way (see Chapter 1).

Furthermore, feminist science and technology studies expose and confront the persistent epistemological haze that surrounds the key social issues at the end of this millennium. As illustrated in this volume, they account for these issues in a set of intersecting axes of questioning: about 'natures', 'bodies' and the forms of techno-scientific mediation that recombine them in a variety of unexpected ways. On this epistemological level, too, feminist science and technology studies situate

naturism

themselves *in medias res* when they combine the critique of science and technology, which play such a crucial role in contemporary society, with feminist deconstructions of the interrelated 'isms': sexism, classism, racism, ageism, naturism, and so on, which represent an important net of key social issues.

Being *in medias res* may, however, also represent an epistemological danger, the existence of which should not be forgotten. It is possible to become blind to central aspects of one's own situatedness. It is therefore important not to ignore the fact that the agenda of feminist science and technology studies has in many ways been set by US feminists. They have developed invaluable critical analyses, as discussed in the introduction to this book. Nevertheless, it should also be kept in mind that the unfolding of feminist science and technology studies in a North American context coincides with the powerful and hegemonic techno-scientific position of the USA in the world today. This book contributes to the broadening of the feminist science studies agenda by balancing the US perspective with European ones.

Nevertheless, the majority of authors are situated in the North-Western high-tech world, and it is important to discuss what this kind of situatedness means in terms of self-reflection. Thus, Julia Martin warns us that we must not forget that the cyberspace which we in the North-Western part of the world may take for granted may be a far from evident point of departure for a lot of people in the Two-Thirds' world (Chapter 6). Susan Leigh Star, moreover, reminds us that even in the contemporary high-tech USA access to cyberspace is not self-evident when you are a non-'homed' person (Chapter 2).

MONSTERS, CYBORGS AND GODDESSES IN THE EPISTEMOLOGICAL HAZE OF THE LATE TWENTIETH CENTURY

The epistemological haze of the late twentieth century is a web of increasingly complicated interrogations, the best illustration of which is the paradox of the new information technologies such as the Internet. The World Wide Web is a paradoxical mixture: it confronts us, on the one hand, with a cheerful cacophony of clashing bits and bytes of the most diverse information, and, on the other, with the threat of mono-culture and the largest concentration of military-industrial monopolies in the world. We could not think of a better image for the paradox of globalization and concentration, uniformity and fragmentation, which lies at the heart of the epistemological haze of our late postmodernity.

One way of expressing this historical condition is in terms of the trans-national economy and the decline of nation-states as a regulative economic and political principle.

In a way, this volume is a manifestation of this new global condition, in so far as it brings together feminist intellectuals from two international networks: the Gender–Nature–Culture Network coordinated by Nina Lykke and the Network of Interdisciplinary Women's Studies in Europe (NOI♀SE), which Rosi Braidotti coordinates. Had it not been for these transverse lines of connection, which take place in the contested zone of new European and global spaces, the contributors gathered in this volume would never have met. The meeting grounds for such diverse viewpoints can be described less in terms of theoretical fast-tracks than as political quicksands. We shall return to this.

Science and technology are crucial players in this framework. Post-modernity is marked by the historical decline of the devalued 'others' which constitute the specular complement of the subject of modernity: the woman, the ethnic other and nature. In a set of carefully crafted but ruthlessly implemented strategies of containment, modernity produces itself through what it excludes as much as through what it asserts as central. In modernity, women, black, oriental and colonial subjects as well as 'earth others' are constructed as non-includable and therefore as the indispensable others of a system of capitalist, white, masculine and heterosexist (re)production.

Postmodernity experiences the return of these excluded 'others' with a vengeance. The women's movement has marked an indelible scar on the symbolic tissue of phallocentric culture; emergent subjectivities from the post-colonial horizon have displaced the Euro-centred world-view; Islamic fundamentalism as well as both communist and post-communist constructions of Russian nationalism have created other powerful images of avenging others, a process which confuses the distribution of values according to self–other dichotomies even more. To top it all off, ecological disaster spells the end of the drive towards mastery of nature, while the technological revolution makes it all the more urgent to resolve issues of access to and participation in a democracy that is threatened by the informatics of domination (Haraway 1991: 161).

All this is to say that difference, in these late post-industrial times, is a set of interlocking questions that throws open centuries-old acquiescent conventions about 'human nature'. 'Human' and 'Nature': these are the two pillars on which Western humanism has erected itself, bearing as its corollary historical instances of systematically sustained exclusion, domination and extermination. The different chapters of this book highlight many facets of the crisis of these foundational values and thus both explore and deepen the crisis of value and the loss of mastery which commonly go under the name of 'postmodernism'.

On the horizon, clearly defined against the post-industrial epistemological haze, emerge new, alternative and somewhat scary figurations of our present concerns. They are hybrid, and yet 'woman-friendly': monsters, goddesses and cyborgs. They are familiar, yet idiosyncratic and slightly disconcerting; they jolt us into further questioning, short-circuiting facile answers, self-congratulatory certainties and easy-made solutions. There is no fast food for thought.

We take these images as figurations of otherness, of incommensurable difference, which nonetheless strike us as being intimately close to our daily existence in these high-tech days of disillusionment and yearning. They are also reminders of factors of resistance to and transcendence of the nihilistic components of the contemporary crisis. Figurations such as these are empowering political myths which may provide some guidance through the maze and haze of contemporary social and political feminist theories. They are also highly evocative political fictions which call for the recombination of elements that are too often separated. In this respect, monsters, goddesses and cyborgs stress the need for new theoretical and political coalitions; that is to say, for sets of alliances which go far beyond the trivial heterogeneity of male-stream interdisciplinarity. Let us spell out some of these new coalitions.

The alliance among feminist critics of science who attack rationality as one of the foundational myths of Western science and post-colonial, black and 'Eastern' feminisms is important. The meeting ground for this coalition is the shared conviction regarding the historical decline of the Western and Eurocentric model of development which was informed by the Enlightenment belief in rationality and progress.

Of special significance are the efforts aimed at bridging the gulf that has come into being between environmentalists and feminists across institutional and disciplinary boundaries. These new alliances rest on the rejection of holistic appeals to a unified idea of 'nature', as much as they resist any essentialistic notion of women's privileged relationship to nurturing and caring for 'earth others'. They emphasize instead an ironic variant of embodied materialism, manifestly opposed to psychological, social and biological essentialism. They also aim to undo classical dualistic oppositions and to replace them with living processes of transformation and a redefinition of female feminist subjectivity through respect for diversity and cross-cultural alliances.

It is our firm conviction that feminists need to integrate environmental concerns into their framework of cultural analysis. Of special urgency is the question of the complete deconstruction of the natural realm through the artifices of science and technology. What is needed is a set of contingent and shifting foundations for feminist environmentalism, as opposed to essentialistic understandings of women's relationship to 'nature'.

No Nietzschean transmutation of values may immediately follow. Yet the process of transformative repossession of knowledge to which this volume subscribes has only just begun. This being the case, it is our hope that the execrable beauty of a thousand monsters, goddesses and cyborgs may fill our collective imaginary and redirect our will-to-power towards the pursuit of hybrid coalitions and nomadic alliances. Let the impact of positive figurations of difference lead us out of the epistemological haze into the generative void of a post-human universe. Through the unknown, we plunge into the new, walking backwards into a future whose promises of solace may not match the pain or the relief of unfamiliarity.

REFERENCES

Braidotti, R., E. Charkiewicz, S. Häusler and S. Wieringa (1994) *Women, the Environment and Sustainable Development: Towards a Theoretical Synthesis*, Zed Books, London.

Haraway, D. (1991) 'A Cyborg Manifesto: Science, Technology, and Socialist-Feminism in the Late Twentieth Century', in D. Haraway, *Simians, Cyborgs, and Women. The Reinvention of Nature*, Free Association Books, London, pp. 149–83.

——— (1992) 'The Promises of Monsters: A Regenerative Politics for In-appropriate/d Others', in L. Grossberg, C. Nelson and P.A. Treichler, eds, *Cultural Studies*, Routledge, New York and London, pp. 295–337.

Keller, E.F. (1989) 'The Gender/Science System, or, Is Sex to Gender as Nature Is to Science', in N. Tuana, *Feminism and Science*, Indiana University Press, Bloomington.

Plumwood, V. (1993) *Feminism and the Mastery of Nature*, Routledge, London and New York.

Roach, C. (1991) 'Loving Your Mother: On the Woman–Nature Relation', *Hypatia*, vol. 6, no. 1, Spring, pp. 46–59.

Warren, K. (1990) 'The Power and the Promise of Ecological Feminism', *Environmental Ethics*, vol. 12, no. 2, pp. 125–46.

LIST OF CONTRIBUTORS

Sylvia Bowerbank holds a joint appointment in the Department of English and the Arts and Science Programme of McMaster University, Hamilton, Canada. Her publications include: 'Literature by Native and Metis Writers in Canada' (*Feminist Studies*, Fall 1994); 'Towards the Greening of Literary Studies' (*Canadian Review of Comparative Literature*, September 1995); and miscellaneous essays on early modern women. She is now writing a book entitled *Speaking for Nature: Ecology and Women in Early Modern England*.

Rosi Braidotti, D.Phil., is professor at the Department of Women's Studies, the Arts Faculty, University of Utrecht, the Netherlands, and director of the Netherlands Research School of Women's Studies. She is the author of *Patterns of Dissonance: A Study of Women in Contemporary Philosophy* (Cambridge 1991); *Nomadic Subjects* (New York 1994); and many articles on feminist history of ideas, feminist theory, poststructuralist thought and comparative literature. She is currently doing research for a book on monsters.

Mette Bryld is associate professor at the Department of Slavonic Studies, Odense University, Denmark. She has published numerous articles on Russian and Soviet literature and culture as well as the book *Carnival of Cybernetics* (in Danish, Odense 1992). She is currently writing a book (with Nina Lykke) on gender, science and technology where the dolphin re-enters the stage together with Pavlov's dogs, spaceships and astrologers. E-mail address: met@litcul.ou.dk.

Kirsten Gram-Hanssen is an engineer and took her M.Sc. degree in 1991. She is a research fellow at the Institute of Technology and Social Sciences at the Technical University of Denmark. Her chapter in this book is based on her Ph.D. thesis 'Views of Nature, Technology and Ethics'. She has published articles and contributed to books on gender, science and technology. She is the mother of two boys.

Renée Heller graduated in women's studies and physics at Utrecht University, the Netherlands in 1995; she is a Ph.D. student at the Department of Atomic and Interface Physics, Utrecht University. The research presented in this book was part of her master's thesis in women's studies called 'The Quantum Leap into a New World View; Narratives of Paradigm Shifts in Popular Science, New Age and Feminist Literature'. Part of this research was conducted at Odense University, Denmark.

Bettina Leysen, M.D., is a gynaecologist at the Department of Obstetrics and Gynaecology, University Hospital of Antwerp, Belgium. Her feminism made her choose to work in this (formerly) male-dominated field. She is very interested in the interaction between psyche and body. She is the editor of the book *Vruchtbaarheid, psychosomatisch bekeken* (Leuven 1990), and has published numerous articles on psychosomatic gynaecology, obstetrics, feminism and psychotherapy. She is the mother of three sons.

Nina Lykke, D.Phil., is an associate professor at the Department of Feminist Studies, Odense University, Denmark, and the coordinator of the international feminist research network Gender–Nature–Culture. She is the author of *Rotkäppchen und Ödipus* (Vienna 1993) and has contributed to many books and published articles on feminism and psychoanalysis, feminist theory, and feminist science and technology studies. She is currently writing a book together with Mette Bryld on gender, science and technology in postmodernity.

Julia Martin teaches English at the University of the Western Cape, South Africa. She is on the steering committee of an environmental NGO and is interested in the relevance of Buddhist teaching in these contexts. She has published several articles in this field and is the editor of a forthcoming collection of essays on Buddhism and Ecology for the Cultural Centre of HH the Dalai Lama. She also publishes stories and poems, is married to Michael Cope, makes ceramic sculpture and digs in the garden.

Nelly Oudshoorn is professor at the Department of Philosophy of Science and Technology, University Twente, the Netherlands, and lecturer in the Department of Science and Technology Dynamics, the University of Amsterdam. Her research interests include the social and material shaping of gender, bodies, and technologies. She is the author of *Beyond the Natural Body: An Archeology of Sex Hormones* (London 1994).

Elizabeth Sourbut graduated in 1985 from Durham University in England with a degree in physics and has completed an M.A. in Women's Studies at York University. Her dissertation title is 'Lesbian Parenting: Contemporary Experiences and Future Visions'. The chapter in this book is a shortened version of her dissertation. She also writes science fiction. Her most recent publication is a short story entitled 'The Last Phallic Symbol', published in November, 1994 in *New Worlds* 4.

Pat Spallone, Ph.D. In 1985, after working for twelve years as a biochemist in medical research in the USA, she began researching and writing about reproductive technologies and genetic engineering as a student in the MA. programme in the Centre for Women's Studies at the University of York, England. She works as a freelance writer and part-time teacher associated with the Centre. Her most recent book is *Generation Games: Genetic Engineering and the Future for Our Lives* (London and Philadelphia 1992).

Susan Leigh Star is associate Professor of Library and Information Science, and Women's Studies, at the University of Illinois, Urbana-Champaign, USA, and Affiliate Research Scientist at the Institute for Research on Learning, Palo Alto, California. She is the author of *Regions of the Mind: Brain Research and the Quest for Scientific Certainty* (Stanford 1989), and editor of *The Cultures of Computing* (London 1995) and *Ecologies of Knowledge: Work and Politics in Science and Technology* (SUNY 1995). Her current research is in the development of large-scale information infrastructures, and she writes feminist theory and poetry.

Ineke van Wingerden was trained as a biologist. Since 1988, she has held a research position in Women's Studies in Science at the Department of Science, Technology and Society, University of Utrecht, the Netherlands. Her research addresses the debate on osteoporosis, brittle bones; the title of her Ph.D. thesis is 'Bones and Gender: The Female Body in the Debate on Osteoporosis'. In 1992, she conducted a collaborative international research project funded by the EU which addressed women's views on the ethical, social and legal implications of the analysis of the human genome.

INDEX